Air America in Laos

The Flight Mechanics' Stories

by

Stephen I. Nichols

Nichols/Martin
Ledyard, CT
860-536-4581
wjmartin@snet.net

ISBN-10:0615742599
ISBN-13:978-0615742595
Library of Congress Control Number: 2012923703

Acknowledgements

A special thank you to:

Contributing authors Hal Augustine, Roger Burdwood, Frank DeVito,
Fred Frahm, Gary Gentz, Dennis Griffith, Rusty Irons, William Long,
Matthew Luca, David L. McDonald and Richard Strba
Joseph Lopes for his support and loan of documents and audio tapes
on Air America history
Fred Frahm, Peter Guinta and Agnes Hall for editing assistance
William Edwards for assistance with photographs and maps
And last my friend, Roberta "Bert" Martin, for pulling everything together

Cover photograph:
Recovery of H-30
Pilot John Fonburg and Flight Mechanic Champ Champanil
Matt Luca and Dick Conrad making the hook up
Photo taken by Steve Nichols

Air America Headquarters
Thai Royal Air Force Base, Udorn, Thailand
Photo courtesy of Roger Burdwood

"During the war in Laos, Air America was called upon to perform paramilitary tasks at great risk to the aircrews involved. Although lacking the discipline found in a military organization, the personnel of the air proprietary continued to place their lives at hazard for years. Some Air America pilots flew in Laos for more than a decade, braving enemy fire and surmounting challenging operational conditions with rare skill and determination. As pointed out by a senior Agency official [James N. Glerum] during the dedication of a plaque to Air America personnel at CIA Headquarters in May 1988: 'The aircrew, maintenance, and other professional aviation skills they applied on our behalf were extraordinary. But, above all, they brought a dedication to our mission and the highest standards of personal courage in the conduct of that mission.'

"The exploits of CAT/Air America form a unique chapter in the history of air transport, one that deserves better than a misleading, mediocre movie."

William M. Leary
E. Merton Coulter Professor of History
University of Georgia
CIA Operations in Laos, 1955-1974
Supporting the "Secret War"
www.cia.gov

This book is dedicated to the flight mechanics of Air America who gave their lives in the fight against communism in the country of Laos

1962 - 1974

Cornelio "Pappy" Pascual	August 18, 1964
Franklin D. "Jesse" Smith	October 12, 1965
Romeo B. Crisologo	April 9, 1966
Lowell Z. Pirkle	August 3, 1967
Earl E. Bruce	August 8, 1967
Robert E. Lee	May 5, 1968 (Saigon)
Bernardo L. Dychitan	December 7, 1968
Patrick F. McCarthy	December 7, 1968
Montano L. Centeno	July 17, 1969
Glenn R. Woods	August 14, 1969
Ernesto M. Cruz	January 20, 1971
Alfredo J. Alor	May 19, 1972
Feliciano C. Manalo	July 16, 1972
Valeriano P. Rosales	April 7, 1973(South Vietnam)
Manu Latloi	April 18, 1974

www.cia.gov/library/publications/cia-maps-publications/index.html

Lima Sites in Northeastern Laos

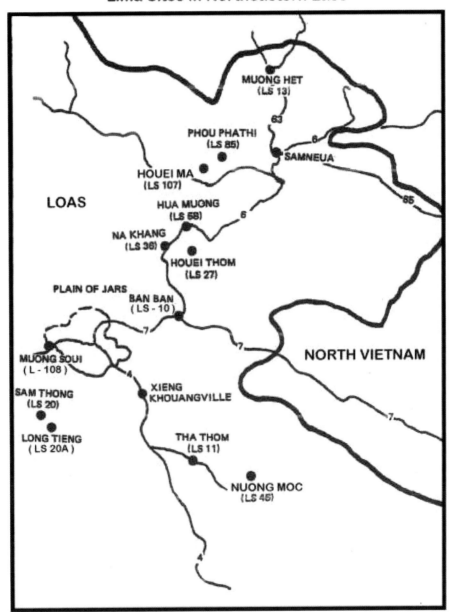

Based on an unclassified map in the National Security Archive. The War in Northern Laos, Victor B. Anthony and Richard R. Sexton, Center for Air Force History. MORI DocID1255435

"If Laos is lost to the Communists,
all of Southeast Asia could be lost"

President Dwight D. Eisenhower
1961

Contents

Prologue

Air America was a civilian airline secretly owned by the U. S. Government and operated by the CIA from 1950 to 1976 in support of covert operations in various foreign countries. At the time I arrived in Thailand in May of 1965, the CIA was heavily involved in a secret operation supporting the Royal Lao Army and Hmong guerilla soldiers under the command of General Vang Pao in the Laotian Government's fight against the communist invasion of their country. I was about to join that fight as a flight mechanic for Air America.

The company was a cost-effective, self-sufficient operation. It was well run and the employees were dedicated and professional civilians. To defray costs, the CIA also contracted us to other organizations in Southeast Asia. It is my understanding from Allen Cates' book, "Honor Denied," that when the airline was discontinued in 1975, we turned in a goodly sum to the U.S. Treasury.

We were not mercenaries. We did not knowingly carry drugs, and contrary to what some Air Force people thought, our pilots did not receive a $10,000 bounty for picking up military pilots shot down in Laos. We did what was asked, sometimes at great risk to ourselves, for a regular pay check. I do not remember a flight mechanic ever turning down a mission.

Air America was a great convenience for the U.S. Government during the CIA involvement in Laos. Our government was prohibited by the Geneva Accord of 1962 from having a military presence in Laos after 1962, but the United States needed military logistical support for their clandestine activities at that time. Hence, we became a tool of the CIA as a civilian airline doing work that the U. S. military forces were not permitted to do and probably couldn't do without prohibitive costs and losses.

The flight mechanics whose stories we are about to tell were a vital part of the helicopter crews flying out of Udorn, Thailand, upcountry into Laos. Our role when upcountry was to keep the aircraft flyable in the event of mechanical failure or damage from enemy gunfire. We loaded and unloaded food, ammunition and soldiers throughout Laos often under adverse conditions and enemy fire. More than the pilots, we interacted with the people of Laos, the injured, the terrified and the dead. We suffered the trauma of war up close and personal.

This book is only a sampling of the stories. I apologize to those flight mechanics that I missed in writing this book. There are many more stories to be told about our people and what we accomplished.

It is unfortunate that Mel Gibson's movie, "Air America," was not a truthful representation of the people and mission of this great organization. The movie was a disservice to an American icon. We hope this book contributes to preserving our legacy of humanitarian efforts on behalf of the people of Laos and our dedication to country and freedom.

These are the stories of some of the unsung heroes of the CIA secret war in Laos many of who did not make it home.

Chapter I
And There I Was

Stephen I. Nichols (SIN)

Flight Mechanic   May 1965 – December 1967
Line Chief   December 1967 – June 1968
Superintendent
Aircraft Maintenance/Helicopters
July 1968 – May 1972

Introduction

And there I was, twenty four years old, making a pass at a mountain hilltop, hanging by one hand, kicking ammunition out of an UH-34 Helicopter to Hmong rebel fighters somewhere over Laos. It was 1965, the early years of the Vietnam War and I had joined Air America, the world's most shot at airline, as a flight mechanic.

I grew up in Wequetequock, Connecticut. Wequetequock, which means land of the ducks, is a small section of a small town in Stonington located on the shoreline of southeastern Connecticut. It was there that I spent countless hours swimming with the neighborhood kids in the saltwater inlet behind my home. Little did I know that this would serve me well years later in a helicopter crash into the Mekong River in Laos.

As a kid I was a dreamer inspired by childhood classics like "Treasure Island" and Viking exploration books. I knew that someday I would "ride to the sounds of the guns" and eventually I did.

I was a terrible student in high school. I had hated school from the age of five where my mother had to literally drag me kicking and screaming from the house to attend school. My high school years were no different. I barely graduated but thought that it didn't matter much as I had been working 20 hours a week since I was 14 and thought hard work was the answer to success. Six months out of high school working two jobs, I discovered I was wrong. My plans to set the world on fire ended with my wet matches.

In 1959, six months out of high school, I did not have any good job prospects. I was delivering grain, pumping gas and staring at being drafted into the Army. I was in the best physical condition I had ever been in, before or since, as I had been hauling 100 pound bags of grain around all day for months. So I decided to join the U.S. Marines. After taking all the tests and passing the physical, I found out they would not guarantee me a school in aviation but that the Navy would. I made myself unavailable for signing into the Marines and joined the Navy instead. That didn't make the Marine recruiter very happy but I guess he got over it.

I attended boot camp at Great Lakes outside of Chicago, Illinois, from January to March 1960. It was cold as hell. I went from there to Memphis, Tennessee. I selected the longest course that was offered for my rate, which was helicopter school. After all, "To fly is human, to hover is divine."

Upon graduation I filled out my dream sheet for the next duty station. My three choices were Guantanamo Bay, Cuba; Rota, Spain or Quonset Point, Rhode Island. I figured if I could not get an exotic place, I might as well be close to home at Quonset Point and Quonset Point it was.

Initially it was crappy duty. I was assigned to the Beach Masters Crew. At the time, 1960, the Navy still had the Martin P5M flying boat long range patrol plane based out of Norfolk, Virginia. One day, a crew flew up from Norfolk to Quonset and we set about pulling their aircraft out of the water using the sea plane ramps that Quonset had.

The P5M was huge, weighing about 80,000 pounds without landing gear. To get it out of the water, we floated wheels attached to large metal floats out to the aircraft that was tied up to a buoy.

My job was to get into a World War II era MK4 exposure suit, which was like an old hard hat divers' suit without the helmet, put on a Mae West, inflate it and swim more or less out to the plane with a rope. Then I would help the crew attach these large wheels to this obsolete aircraft.

While we had completed this procedure successfully before, the Chief, on this day, wanted to try something a little different and it failed miserably.

I was in the water up to my waist looking like an ancient astronaut when the large rope tied to the main tow traction snapped straight like a bow string. The line hit the crew of three or four guys on shore, cutting into their legs and causing some injury to all of them. Ambulances were called and they were all taken to the hospital.

In the midst of this mess, the pilot of the P5M who had been standing off to the side, yelled, "Untie my aircraft. Untie my aircraft."

I did and off they went back to Norfolk. They never came back and shortly thereafter, the Navy scrapped the P5Ms.

I was left by myself at the scene to climb out of my suit and make my way back to the beach master's shack. I felt miserable sitting in the shack wondering what the hell kind of circus I had joined and what would be my next job.

But fate intervened. I didn't have to wait long.

The air station at the time was using three Piasecki H-25 HUP-2s as the station rescue planes. They had just changed the aft gear box on one of the aircraft and miss-rigged it badly. When they ran it up, the rear blades hit the fuselage right behind the pilot's head and wooden blade parts went everywhere. At the accident board it was noted that none of the crew had any helicopter maintenance training. They went looking through the personnel files for someone with helicopter training, and "there I was."

I remember I was hanging out in the beach master's shack, freezing my butt off, knowing that I was probably out of a job because of the recent Martin P5M incident when I got the phone call from the department Executive Officer.

"This is the XO. Is this Nichols?"

I think, "*Oh, crap. What now?*"

I responded, "Yes, Sir."

"How would you like to be on the station helicopter crew?"

I thought, *would I?* This was the best billet on the air station with full flight pay and zero duty status, meaning no watch standing. It was mostly flying dignitaries back and forth to the War College in Newport, Rhode Island.

I responded, "Yes, Sir. I'd like that."

I spent over three years on the helicopter crew at Quonset which entitled me to full flight pay of $80 a month. This money was later used to pay my way through Parks College's one year Aircraft and Power Plant Licensing Program. Back then when it was still a free country, we did not have free college, the G. I. Bill or unlimited unemployment when I left the military.

My time at Quonset Point was all right. Most of the crew were married men so when night flights came up, I would volunteer. Sometimes it seemed I got stuck with extra weekends, which I did not mind either, as I became a pretty decent chess player.

On one of those weekends, things were livened up a bit when we got to fly one of the station's H-19s in below minimum flight conditions. In 1963, the nuclear submarine USS Thresher went down during sea trials off the coast of New England. When they located it, they took pictures that were brought into Newport on a Sunday. The powers-to-be wanted them flown to the First Naval District in Boston, Massachusetts ASAP. I was on duty that weekend with a Navy chief as pilot. At that time, the Navy still had some enlisted pilots left over from World War II. Chief Emerson mostly flew the station's big aircraft like the DC-4 and DC-3 but he was helicopter qualified to stand duty. He was a great guy but not the best chopper pilot.

We were called into the operations building and told to fly over to Newport, pick up the pictures and fly them to Boston. The chief told the commander that the weather was too bad and we couldn't do it.

The commander stuck his finger in the chief's chest and said, "I'm giving you a direct order."

The chief turned to me and said, "Get out the chopper."

By now the station had two Sikorsky H-19s of Korean War vintage with only the barest of instruments. I pulled one out of the hangar and off we went. All the time I was thinking that it was just over an hour to drive a car from Newport to Boston.

Getting to Newport was not bad and getting to Boston wasn't either. Coming back was a different story. We got on top of solid cloud cover and headed for Quonset. A couple of times, the chief let things get away from him a little and the air speed would swing between 0 and 70 knots. As we got closer to the station, he called the tower for a ground controlled approach.

During the week, the chief's duties were in the tower and I think they had their eyes on us because they were right there and brought us in safely. It was really great to get back on the ground.

During my time at Quonset, President John Kennedy and Jackie Kennedy landed at Quonset Point once in separate aircraft in route to their

Newport summer home. Being the junior man on the station helicopter crew, I was handed a pair of large, bright orange gloves and told to direct "Marine One" which was the call sign for the Marine helicopter once the President boarded. Well, no one directs Marine One. You just stay out of the way. So that's what I did. I stayed out of the way under the nose of Air Force One.

It was a thrill that day to see Air Force One, a 707, and the Kennedy personal aircraft, *Caroline*, an R4Y, coming in. It was a beautiful sight, two great aircraft parked nose to nose about thirty feet apart. Years later I went to the Kennedy Library in Boston, Massachusetts, to see if I could get a picture of the event but they had almost nothing. They did dig up a movie tape of the trip to Newport but the only Quonset pictures were very cropped and showed very little of President Kennedy coming off the plane. I could never understand why they did not have pictures of the couple meeting and embracing between the aircraft as they did. If ever there was a Kodak moment that was it.

There were some good officers at Quonset during my tenure and there were some not so good officers. One of the best was Lt. James Brandau who saved my butt when I accidently damaged a helicopter and again when I became embroiled in a difference of opinion with a black shoe chief (surface craft chief versus an aviation chief who would wear brown shoes). Without Lieutenant Brandau's support, my career would have been dead in its tracks and I would not have had the great opportunities afforded to me later in life.

It was in the Navy where I got my first introduction to Air America, a civilian airline owned by the government and operated by the CIA in Southeast Asia. I was stationed with two pilots who had just returned from a tour with Air America and they told stories of fun and adventure that I only dreamed about. The stories fascinated me and I knew that was where I wanted to be.

Early on while serving in the Navy, I realized the class distinction between enlisted men and officers. It was a rude awakening. They were two different worlds separated primarily by education. I shall forever be indebted to the Navy not only for my aircraft maintenance experience and training but also for the wake-up call from the more experienced officers and enlisted men with whom I served.

Following my discharge from the Navy, I applied to Parks College in St. Louis for admission to their program to obtain my A&P (Airframe and Powerplant) license. This would be the first stepping stone towards Air America.

Unfortunately my poor performance in high school came back to haunt me and I was rejected by Parks College. Devastated, I turned to my father who was watching television with his back to me.

"Dad, Parks College rejected me. What do you think of that?"

My father had rarely given me advice before or since but this time he turned his head toward me and over his shoulder, he said, "Write them back and beg."

Well, that's what I did and for reasons unknown they accepted me. Upon completion of the Parks College program where I graduated second or third in my class of thirty plus, I applied to and was accepted by Air America for duty as a UH-34D flight mechanic out of Udorn, Thailand.

I left my family and friends for an unknown future in a foreign land. I could not have been more excited.

Steve Nichols
Quonset Point, RI
1962

Quonset Point Naval Air Station, Rhode Island
Aircraft is a Piasecki HUP-2 (H-25)
From Left: Steve Nichols, Lt. Small, Paul Scannell,
G. T. Oliver, A. J. Stewart

Steve Nichols, Boot Camp,
Great Lakes, Illinois, 1960

Arrival

And there I was on the 18th of May 1965, flying first class to Tokyo, compliments of Air America.   My final destination was the Udorn Royal Thai Air Force Base, Thailand, which was the Asian Headquarters for Air America Helicopter Operations in Laos. At the time, I was a twenty four year old wide eyed kid from Wequetequock, Connecticut, who had never been out of the United States before unless you count a trip to Mexico when I was five years old.

The recruiter for Air America in Washington, DC, had assured me that the job was not dangerous.   Flight mechanics flew on all missions as part of the aircraft crew. Their purpose was to load, unload, maintain and fuel the aircraft while on assignment. He told me that Air America policy prohibited carrying personal weapons.   And I thought, *"If the job isn't dangerous, why would you even think about carrying a weapon?"*

Understandably I was nervous. I came from a very close knit family and I had rarely been far from them. My sister, Sandy, had driven me to the Providence airport and sent me on my way.   It was an overnight flight to Tokyo.   My stomach was in such turmoil that I remember declining the prime rib dinner that first class offered and cannot remember eating until I arrived at the hotel in Tokyo. Some of my trepidation could be attributed to my offer of employment and the accompanying information on Udorn. I quote from the material I received from Air America, "Houses for rent can be found in all sections of the city...are all below U. S. Standards...some have hot water...Some have purchased electric hot water heaters...which produce sufficient hot water, depending on the electric power supply and water pressure, both of which are irregular...Tap water should always be boiled three to five minutes prior to drinking, but it is safe for cooking and washing dishes, if it is brought to the boiling point. The water has a high content of sand and should be filtered...voltage normally drops to approximately 160 volts between 5 p.m. and 10 p.m. and increases gradually after 10 p.m. ....Telephones to the city are not available...It is not advisable to bring TV sets as the closest television station is of considerable distance from Udorn, reception is poor and programs are in Thai only...Good cooks are rare...Hotels in Udorn can be rated as low second class or third class by American standards...no rooms have hot water...Restaurants in Udorn do not meet American standards for either quality or cleanliness...shopping for local products is generally done by the servants due to the early hour (0600) one must shop...and the language difficulty...Several good dentists can be found in Udorn City, however they are not highly recommended because they lack modern equipment...The company sponsored Club Rendezvous is the focal point of recreation for the foreign community."   I was thinking, *what the hell have I gotten myself into?*

I spent a day in Tokyo and then moved on to Taipei for paperwork and a flight physical, the details of which I will skip, and then to Tainan, Taiwan, where I was encouraged by Air America personnel to spend a few days looking around and to consider staying on to work for the Tainan office instead of going to Udorn. Every Air America station needed maintenance people at this point in the massive build up that was underway. After a few days in Tainan, I grew restless and was anxious to move to where the real action was proposed to be. After saying I wanted to continue on to Udorn, the legendary "Thelma Lou" was instructed to get me on my way.

The next stop was a layover in Hong Kong for a few hours where I first met Rosemary Cho.

Shortly thereafter, it was back on the plane and on to Bangkok where I was met by an Air America representative who brought me to my hotel. Each day I was becoming more impressed with the efficiency of Air America. I spent that night in another chintzy hotel room. The next day I boarded the overnight train from Bangkok to Udorn. The train ride took about twelve hours and was best done inebriated.

I had been traveling for six days and I was awestruck at every stop.

I arrived at the Air America complex in the early morning hours. I headed directly for the mess hall for breakfast as my nerves were settling and my appetite was returning.

I remember this morning well. I had chosen a table facing the door and was just starting to eat when in came a tall guy with a huge grin who spotted me instantly and came directly to my table. This was flight mechanic Jesse Smith, soon to be one of my closest friends. And soon to die.

"Hey, you must be Nichols, the new flight mechanic. Jesse Smith."

I nodded and extended my hand, "Steve Nichols."

What I will always remember most about Jesse was his never ending smile and laughter. He was always laughing.

"We just got back from flying a Thai general out to the hills. We heard there were insurgents there. I guess there were. We took three bullet holes in the tail. Really ticked me off. When you finish eating, I'll show you."

True to his word, when Jesse showed me the helicopter, I couldn't believe it. There were three bullet holes in the tail section of the helicopter. I had heard stories from the Navy pilots at Quonset Point about the action in Laos but it was one thing to hear it from others in the safety of the old USA and quite another to be staring at the bullet holes in the aircraft in a strange and foreign place. At that moment, I thought, *This is going to be one hell of a job."*

Udorn

My hotel room in Udorn was right out of a Humphrey Bogart movie with the slow moving ceiling fan and paint peeling from the walls. True to the recruitment material, the room was low second class and had no hot running water. However the bed linens were fresh and clean and the room did look better than the train ride accommodations of the previous night, which were noisy, crowded and uncomfortable.

Early on my first day, I had checked in with John Aspinwall, Helicopter Maintenance Superintendent at Air America. He told me to take a few days to get myself settled and then report to work. So for the first few days, I wandered around the complex talking to flight mechanics, looking at the aircraft and reminding John that I joined Air America as a flight mechanic not ground crew maintenance. The company was shorthanded everywhere. Just as they had tried to convince me to stay on in Tainan, I believed now, they wanted me to work on the ground. Not me, I was hired to fly.

Downtown Udorn was all dirt streets busy with primitive rickshaws and peddle cabs called samlors. The shops were primarily run by East Indians, most of whom spoke some English. Surprisingly I picked up bits and pieces of the language very quickly. I ate all my meals at the building on the Air America complex known as the Rendezvous Club. The food was good, drinks plentiful and it was the only recreational facility in existence unless you wanted to go to the bars downtown and I wasn't ready for that.

The only paved road in Udorn was the one leading into the base. The rest were red dirt, dusty in the dry season, muddy in the rainy season. Transportation to and from the base was provided by Air America which was fortunate as the other most common form of transportation was the Japanese made motor cycle which, as I later found after buying one, was dangerous to operate due to road conditions, lack of traffic regulations and the animals and people blocking the roads.

I quickly tired of being a tourist and began to hang around John Aspinwall's office, anxious for my first assignment. John was a big burly guy, an ex-Navy Chief from Bristol, RI, which relative to Udorn was practically my home town. I am not sure why John selected my first assignment at Air America. Maybe it was just to get me out of his way. It could have been to test my mettle or could have been to humble my cocky attitude. I don't know, but three days into the upcountry assignment, I remember thinking, "*In the future, be careful what you ask for.*"

My first bungalow, "Chi Mong Col"

Air America Club Pool
Photo courtesy of Roger Burdwood

Upcountry

Upcountry was a term for flying into Laos, where America's military presence was prohibited by The Geneva Accord of 1962. We had a lot of terms for various things, such as, "The Company" was the CIA. "The customer" was a CIA Agent. "Hard rice" was ammunition. "Spooks" were CIA people who came and went during the dark of night in the middle of the jungle.

This was my third day at Udorn.

"Steve." John Aspinwall came toward me. "I have a job for you. I need you to go upcountry with some of the Filipino mechanics to change out an engine in one of our helicopters."

I was excited. I was anxious to prove myself as a productive member of Air America and this looked like the opportunity. I asked, "What should I bring?" I knew I needed to bring clothes and food but was uncertain as to how much.

"You won't be there long. Maybe supplies for a day or two," he assured me.

I immediately went to the market in downtown Udorn to purchase food for the two day trip. I did not realize how totally unprepared I was for this job until this moment. I had asked a few people about supplies but they were vague and not very helpful. Maybe they were tired of babysitting the new guys. When I got to the market the food labels were all written in Chinese. I found that you could identify some items from the picture on the can but sometimes that picture was the product logo. I did my best and packed a few meals and a change of clothes sufficient for a two day trip.

The pilot and crew, the Filipino mechanics and I, along with a completely built up quick change 1820 engine unit, took off in a fixed wing C-123 that afternoon, heading for Muong Soui.

I have always loved flying and this time and place was no different.

The scenery in Southeast Asia is breathtaking. This was my first flight over this terrain and I was in awe. I expect because I was American and new to Air America, the pilot invited me to sit between him and the co-pilot in the fold-up jump seat to enjoy the flight. As we approached our destination, I could see what I thought to be an airstrip, a big fresh reddish brown strip ahead of us. As we got lower, I could see that they were clearly going to miss the airstrip. I said nothing. I did not want to appear nervous or stupid even if we crashed. We got lower and lower still missing the airstrip and eventually touching down in a grassy field. I never said a word as the pilots seemed perfectly content with their landing. When I got out, I realized that the airstrip was under construction and apparently landing in the grass was the norm.

Muong Soui, where we landed, was under the rule of Lao Colonel Kong Le, a Neutralist. The Neutralist political faction of Laos was sometimes friendly and sometimes not. I think they were mostly friendly because we paid, fed and armed them. Even then they sometimes popped off a round at us. Eventually it was discovered that the number of troops we paid for could not be mustered and counted and Colonel Kong Le took off for the French Riviera.

Muong Soui was situated at the edge of the Plain of Jars which was under enemy control and one of the most dangerous areas in Laos. It was hot and humid.

The job before us was straightforward and we started work right away. I found the Filipino mechanics to be industrious, knowledgeable and friendly. I was in my element doing a job I loved and living my childhood fantasy of adventure in a foreign land.

By the third day I had run out of food and my clothes were filthy from the oil, grease, grime and sweat. The Filipinos shared their food with me which was something like pickled chicken. I did not ask. It was very good.

On the fourth day, the job was done and we were waiting for a pilot to fly us and our repaired helicopter back to Udorn. By this time we had all run out of food and clean clothes and were wearing the cleanest of the dirty. We were way beyond filthy and had been without food for two days. We all decided to walk to a nearby village to see if they had a place to eat. We followed a trail through the jungle to a small village which had several commercial type thatched huts including what could loosely be called a restaurant. It had several tables with chairs and a dirt floor. The proprietor, a young Lao woman, did not appear interested in our Thai money but was persuaded to accept American dollars. It was obvious that she would have preferred gold or silver. Although I had been days without food and was literally starving, I was still somewhat leery of what type of food we would find in a remote village somewhere in Laos but felt safe with an order of soup. The soup was served in a bowl crusted over with food like an unclean dog's dish and flies were landing on the rim including one fly that had been half swatted with its guts hanging out.

I ate it all except the fly. It was the best damn soup I ever had.

Motorbikes and Cars

My first week in Udorn I bought a motorcycle. I didn't know how to drive it but I bought it anyway because that was what most Air America guys drove. I bought what was at the time the most common and biggest available, a 150 Honda.

The people at the hotel let me keep it in the lobby. I was to find as the years went by that the Thai people were the most friendly and helpful people that I would ever meet in my travels.

Driving of any kind was a challenge in Udorn. With the lack of skill, the heavy drinking that some did, roadways crowded with livestock, people, rickshaws, cars and buses and dirt roads with potholes everywhere, you have the makings of a disaster.

I sometimes drove at speeds between 50 to 60 miles per hour. Conditions did not permit you to really open up but relative to a pedal cab or rickshaw, I was flying. One day as I approached town there was an old stray dog slowly crossing the road. To expedite his trip, I beeped my horn. The dog stopped. If I had not beeped my horn, the dog would not have stopped and I would have missed him. He did stop and I hit and killed him. The impact launched me into the air as if I had gone up a ramp. I came down going in the opposite lane. Luckily for me there was no oncoming traffic. I turned and went back to where there were two Air Force military policemen sitting in a jeep with their mouths open staring at me in disbelief.

"Well," I said, "There's one that won't be yipping tonight."

They still said nothing so I turned and left.

My final experience with the motorcycle was again in town. I was with Rusty Irons, another flight mechanic, who was ahead of me on his bike. I was trying to catch him as we sped through the crowded streets. Suddenly a Chinese fellow on a motorcycle that was just slightly ahead of me turned directly into my path. Just as I was going over the bank with the guy between my wheels, I thought, *this is the part I hate.*

I thought I got up instantly, but that couldn't be so because when I stood up, a huge crowd had gathered. Several Thais were pushing my bike back up the hill laughing like it was the funniest thing they had ever seen.

Rusty returned but could not see me through the crowd.

"Nichols," he shouted, "Are you in there?"

"Yes," I shouted back, relieved that he had come back.

"Okay, catch you later." And he roared away.

Shortly the police came, and to my relief told me to go home, which I did.

I drove that motorcycle for almost two years before I smartened up. It was then that I decided to trade my bike in for a little Honda car. I paid $2,000 for the car which I bought from Willie Parker, another flight mechanic who had been badly burned in a crash of an H-34 and was not expected to return to Udorn.

The little Honda was like a windup toy and at high speeds whined like a banshee. It had a 600 cc engine with four cylinders, four carburetors, a chain drive and red lined at 12000 RPM. On trips to Bangkok which I did twice with this car, I used to come screaming out of the hills doing 85 mph at 8500 RPM. The little kids in the rice paddies herding water buffalos, some of whom had been sleeping on the backs of these gentle creatures, would hear me coming and run to the side of the road. They would wave like mad as they watched the crazy farang (foreign devil) go by.

The ride to and from Bangkok was never easy. It was a hot dusty six hour drive through flat plains and low mountains. I was in Bangkok one time when I ran into Rusty Irons at Max's Bar on Patpong Road which was an Air America hangout. He had driven his MG TD to Bangkok and was going to drive it back to Udorn and asked me to go along.

I said, "Sure, what the hell."

Well it turned out to be hell. That ride was unbelievably hot. We actually tied the doors open as wind scoops but it didn't help. That was one long trip.

I only had one accident with the little Honda car. I was returning from Bangkok along the Friendship Highway at a fairly high rate of speed. A young Thai woman had stopped her car in the middle of the road after being cut off by a bus. She just stopped there to chat with her sister. *Who does that?* There were no brake lights showing. I was cruising at about 80 mph and drove right into her at about 40 mph which is as slow as I could get the car after standing on the brakes. No one was hurt but she was righteously indignant and I had to pay for the repairs to her brother's car.

Four years after purchasing the car for $2000, I sold it for $1,750 when I left Udorn for the good old USA.

Rescue Mission

And there I was. I could see the downed airman below. I had the rescue harness in one hand, the coils in the other ready to drop from the helicopter when we suddenly came under heavy enemy fire. The bullets slammed into the aircraft and confetti exploded into the air and was sucked up into the cockpit. Mass confusion ensued.

"Nichols, what are they shooting at us?" the pilot shouted as confetti swirled through the cockpit.

This was my first solo flight as a flight mechanic. I had been checked out the previous week as a flight mechanic trainee with pilot Sam Jordan and flight mechanic Rudy Serafico. That morning I had pre-flighted the helicopter, H-33, picked up the flight log book, stored my gear and waited for my pilots, Dick Casterlin and Frank Stergar, to show up.

They arrived shortly and we took off on what should have been a routine mission but just after 20 minutes in the air, we received a call to go to Na Khang, Lima Site (LS) 36, and standby for a possible search and rescue. Upon arrival at LS-36, we joined a second helicopter crewed by captain Phil Goddard, co-pilot George Carroll and flight mechanic Mitch Drew.

After topping off the fuel on my aircraft, I walked over to the other aircraft and noticed Mitch tying down a tripoded 30 caliber machine gun with aircraft safety wire.

As I stood there watching him tie down the weapon, he was muttering, "This kind of shit is going to get us killed."

I recalled that Mitch had already been out on a few bad search and rescues. On one of them, he had accidently kicked a Thompson submachine gun out the door. The gun had been borrowed from a customer and there had been hell to pay when he got back without it. This morning I could tell that he was none too happy with the current situation.

The pilots, who were being briefed by Colonel Thong, area commander for the Hmong forces in northern Laos, returned to the aircraft in very short order and said it was a go. They had learned that a Navy F4H Phantom jet had been shot down and the two crewmen had parachuted down in enemy territory near Son La, North Vietnam. Son La is a little south of the infamous site of Dien Bien Phu.

We loaded a case of grenades onto H-33 and were joined by a Lao soldier with his arm in a sling who would serve as a guide back through North Vietnam in the event of a forced landing.

Both helicopters left for the Son La area with H-22 in the lead. I was not aware at the time that Colonel Thong had actually joined our mission and was aboard the other helicopter. His purpose in being there was to guide us to the Son La area as we had no maps or charts available and our pilots were unfamiliar with North Vietnam. Later I was to think, *what the hell was he doing there*? A man of his importance and influence should never have put himself at this much risk. But that was the kind of officer he was, the very best.

Colonel Thong was a highly respected leader committed to driving the communists from his country. He was held in very high regard by his men and thought to be indestructible because of all the Buddhas he carried. His men had let their hair grow long and were not going to cut it until they had driven the communists from their mountains. They were always in proper uniform and had little white cloths stuck in the end of their rifle barrels to keep the dirt out.

We headed toward Son La which was some sixty miles inside North Vietnam. The weather was good and we flew at about 10,000 feet. H-22 was in the lead taking direction from Colonel Thong and an Air America C-123. The C-123 controlled communications and operations and two USAF phantom jets were providing cover fire for the pickup.

Shortly after arriving at the anticipated pick up area, we were told there were two airmen down versus the one we had been briefed on. This lack of knowledge completely changed the SAR format. As planned, our aircraft was supposed to be the primary SAR ship. Upon learning two men were in the weeds and none had been identified as per SAR standard operating procedure, we proceeded with the mission but confusion ensued. H-22 who had arrived ahead of us began searching the area and shortly one of the downed crew members was sighted by Phil Goddard from H-22. They dropped down and were flying at about 80 feet over the trees at a low speed when apparently they were hit by automatic gunfire and started returning fire from the cargo area with the mounted 30 caliber. Within minutes, H-22 came up directly beside us and radioed they had a serious injury on board and were abandoning the mission. I could see fuel pouring from the aircraft. I could not see the co-pilot and assumed he had gone below into the cabin area to assist the injured who I thought at the time was Mitch.

It had all happened quickly and to add to the bedlam, the Phantoms making passes over the area were oblivious to the small arms fire and were yelling over the radio about the delay and asking why weren't we picking up their man. As I remember, the jet pilots were getting downright testy about it. My pilot, Casterlin, who had now spotted the downed airman decided to make another try at pick up in spite of the warnings of H-22 that the area was too hot to effect a rescue.

When Casterlin called down that we were going to attempt the rescue, I was seated by the cargo door. I had been going through the aircraft log book which was a tablet of multicolored forms with carbons between the sheets slipped inside a cover made of aircraft aluminum. I had always put my toolbox under my seat, sat on my flak vest and had the engine at my back. I used to stack the overnight gear of suitcases along my right side which came up about three feet off the floor. When my pilot said we were going in for the rescue, I swiveled to my right and slipped the log book under the top suitcase, a place I had never put it before. I grabbed the rescue harness with as many coils as possible to toss out to the airman as soon as the pilot began to hover. Like our pilot, I could now see the airman in the underbrush. At that moment, we started taking small arms fire and the cracking sound of bullets started hitting the aircraft.

As we climbed back out, turning away from the ground fire, one of the pilots yelled, "Nichols, what are they shooting at us?" as masses of shredded multicolored confetti were drafted up into the cockpit right in front of the pilots' faces and out the side windows.

I heard Casterlin transmit that we were hit badly and we had no engine control as the throttle control was locked. He told H-22 to be prepared to pick us up, as he was considering landing on a sand bar in the Black River. H-22 responded that he could not land as he had seriously wounded on board and was losing fuel. He was heading for Laos.

I had only been with Air America for two months. Things were not looking good, and I knew for sure that I did not want to land in North Vietnam. We were flying in a Sikorsky UH-34. They were my specialty. I knew these helicopters inside and out and the engine sounded good to me. I ripped open the clutch compartment door and looked in. Everything looked intact and the engine was not missing a beat. Next, I dropped to the floor, hung my head over the side and looked for leaking fuel under the helicopter but saw none.

"Dick," I yelled up to the pilot, "Everything looks good here. I think we should keep going."

Casterlin continued on not knowing the extent of our damage. The cylinder head temperature gage was at the red line and there were few, if any, decent forced landing areas along the mountainous track. We followed H-22 which was headed toward LS-107, Houei Ma, the nearest friendly field. Our return to LS-107 was slow and tense. H-22 was in the lead and we followed keeping in touch by radio. Both aircraft were badly shot up. H-22 was losing fuel and our helicopter had problems with the throttle control and I thought the engine might quit at any moment, dumping us in the jungle of North Vietnam with only a Lao with his arm in a sling to guide us back. That is if we survived the crash.

We landed at LS-107 shortly after H-22 where I learned for the first time that Colonel Thong had been aboard manning the machine gun. Apparently he had sustained serious wounds and there was a Helio Courier waiting for us at LS-107 to transport him to the US Army hospital in Korat, Thailand.

Once we were safely on the ground we could assess the damage to our aircraft. H-22 had taken about 40 to 50 rounds in the fuselage but was determined to be flyable. Operations at Udorn requested the crew to fly thehelicopter back to Udorn for repair. In H-33, I was to discover a bullet had come into the aircraft about six inches off the floor of the left side and struck the log book which was about two and one half feet off the floor on my right side, shredding one corner of it. If not for the log book, I expect that the bullet would have hit me. The confetti had been sucked up into the cockpit in front of the pilots. The bullet was deflected up through the transmission deck where it laid until I picked it up much later. I still have it today. We had also taken a round through the throttle box assembly on the engine and some BIM indicators popped, indicating blade spar damage. This damage made the aircraft un-flyable. *Was this the helicopter I just flew out of North Vietnam in?* Our crew was instructed by Udorn operations to remain overnight at LS-107. Two other helicopters and crew would be dispatched from Udorn to continue the rescue.

Staying over after spending all day in the air, nearly dying and barely making it home, meant you got to sleep in the helicopter which, when it rains, leaks, and rain it did, all night, dripping on me like a Chinese water torture. My pilot was none too happy but at least he was armed. He had been doing SAR work for over a year and self admittedly was a basket of nerves. He really did not need this overnight mission. There were two Lao soldiers guarding the aircraft all night. They touched the helicopter throughout the night which made a noise like being inside a tin can and between that and the rain there was very little sleep.

Early the next morning two replacement crews and helicopters arrived at LS-107 to make another attempt at picking up the airmen from Son La. One pilot was Bobby Nunez and the other Robby Robertson. Both mechanics were Filipinos from the Udorn shop and not regular flight mechanics. They were justifiably uncomfortable with the mission.

As one of them put it to me, "Steve, if we get captured, they take the Americans prisoners. Me, they just shoot."

I expect he was correct.

At the briefing of the new crews, they decided that Captain Bobby Nunez would lead with Dick Casterlin as co-captain to provide direction as he had done the route the previous day. For reasons I cannot explain, I volunteered to replace the Filipino mechanic in trade for his starting repair on my helicopter. I may have thought that Americans should rescue Americans or I may have thought that his anxiety might affect the outcome or maybe, at 24, I was too foolish to know better.

As I tossed my toolbox onto the helicopter and jumped in, Nunez looked down at me and expecting the Filipino mechanic, said, "What are you doing?"

"I'm going with you."

He just shook his head, "Are you crazy?" He started the engine.

Captain Robby Robertson, Frank Stergar as co-pilot and the other Filipino mechanic were the back-up crew.

We left mid morning with support from the C-123 and escort by two A-1E Skyraiders. The Skyraiders ability to carry an immense amount of weapons and stay over the battlefield for extended periods of time made it a powerful weapon. This aircraft was used to provide close air support to protect helicopters rescuing airmen downed in enemy territory. Considered to be somewhat of a relic from the Korean War, it proved well suited for fighting against the guerrilla-style war waged by communists in Southeast Asia. The Phantom jets were out there somewhere but I did not see them.

My mood was somber. I had almost died yesterday. The area had been hot then and now they had a full 24 hours to further infiltrate the area. We were all civilians, I was unarmed, and this was dangerous crap.

When we arrived at Son La, we were guided to the downed airman by the C-123 who had made radio contact with him. Again I readied myself with the harness and coils already extended for an instantaneous drop rather than lowering it with the winch which takes time. The winch has one speed, slow. It does not get any better than that. You cannot speed it up either way as much as you might want to. Something the soon to be rescued airman obviously did not understand.

We spotted the airman below, I tossed the coil, the airman snatched the harness, strapped himself in and I hit the up button. It must have seemed like an eternity to the airman as he was pulled up. I reached out and pulled him into the helicopter.

His first words were, "Why'd you leave me hanging out there?"

I was shocked as most rescued pilots were beyond grateful. I pushed him into a seat and threw my canteen at him. I had just risked my life for this guy twice and he wanted to berate me for what he perceived as a deliberate attempt to "hang him out there."

The radio came alive with, "We're getting air burst. Stand off," from the Skyraiders.

As our helicopter departed the area, Robertson and Stergar, our back up helicopter, made a pass over the area dropping fragmentary hand grenades to discourage ground fire. It was later learned that the Phantom jets leveled the Son La army barracks as well.

The rescued airman had been the navigator on the downed F4H. There was no sighting of the pilot, Capt. Paul Kari, or his parachute. It was later learned that he had been captured and held prisoner until February 1973, almost eight years, before he was released under a prisoner exchange program.

Colonel Thong was recovering in the Air Force Hospital in Thailand when he suffered a blood clot and died within a week of the incident. This was a major loss to the Lao Army and its efforts to drive the communists from their mountains. His Buddhist cremation was held in Sam Thong and was attended by diplomats, USAID people, CIA and Air America personnel including me.

Colonel Thong was presented with the U. S. Silver Star, speeches were made and I joined the procession of mourners carrying lighted candles to the pyre.

The Lao had lost a truly great leader.

An Oasis in a Foreign Land

Chiang Khong, Thailand, was located on the border of Laos on the Mekong River opposite Ban Houei Sai, Laos. It was the northernmost border crossing between Laos and Thailand.

The Air America pilots knew of a guest house in Chiang Khong that was incredibly beautiful with one of the amenities of first class lodging, hot water. After roughing it upcountry for months, sleeping in helicopters, shacks and tents, this place was a little piece of paradise. The site was close to LS-118A, the CIA training camp directed by Agent Louis Ojibway, and was, I expect, a respite for CIA personnel. It was located on a small spot right on the edge of the Mekong. It had a dirt landing pad big enough for just one H-34. A deck with a table extended out over the Mekong and I could look across the river to the ruins of a small French fort called Fort Carnot. Built in the early 1900s right out of Gunga Din, it had two large watchtowers, two large garrison buildings, and external guardhouses. It was pretty much deserted but rumored to be used by Lao drug runners.

Down river to the right, you could see the small town of Ban Houei Sai where the Tom Dooley Hospital operated. The hospital was built by Thomas Dooley III, an American ex-Navy officer who founded the Medical International Cooperation Organization (MEDICO). He then built hospitals at Nam Tha, Moung Sing and Ban Houei Sai. He was considered for canonization by the Catholic Church for his years of humanitarian work, cited by Jack Kennedy when establishing the Peace Corps, received a Congressional Gold Medal posthumously and is alleged to have worked for the CIA as an informant during our activities in Laos. He authored three books about his activities in Viet Nam and Laos. The work that he started continues today around the world helping orphans and at-risk children in Vietnam, Mexico, Colombia, Indonesia and Afghanistan under Helping And Loving Orphans founded by Betty Tisdale.

I had the opportunity to stay at the guest house in Chiang Khong twice during my time with Air America. After landing there the first time, I discovered a bad nick in a tail rotor blade. We had been flying all day and I had no idea when the damage occurred. We stayed overnight and I changed out the blade the next day.

The inn was operated by an older Chinese man. The food was fabulous and abundant and I had the first hot shower since my arrival in Thailand. Sitting on the deck at sunset surrounded by gorgeous landscape and panoramic views, I thought I had gone back in time to a more peaceful world.

My second trip there was for two nights with pilots Bobby Nunez and Dick Lieberth with H-23. We were working out of LS-118A for Louis Ojibway, a senior CIA agent who ran LS-118A, moving whatever wherever he wanted it.

There were three of us for dinner and the Chinese guy put enough food on the table for ten people. As the three of us relaxed after dinner on the deck overlooking the Mekong and the French fort, I said, "I bet I could swim across this river."

I didn't know then that, in three days time, I would be doing just that.

The Man Who Swam the Mekong

It was August 20, 1965. I had been with Air America for three months. Pilot Bobby Nunez and I were moving troops and supplies in the area around LS-118 and 118A. Our co-pilot Dick Lieberth had been recalled.

After working the area for most of the day, we were headed back to Udorn with plenty of daylight and decent weather. We had been dodging bad weather all day and knew the storms would be closing in on us shortly, so we were anxious to get home.

We were in the air for about a half an hour when Bobby got a call to go back to LS-118, Ban Nam Thouei, to pick up fixed wing pilot Calhoun who had ground looped his Helio Courier earlier in the day and needed a ride back to LS-8, Vientiane. Bobby expressed concern about the lateness of the day and the oncoming storms but turned back to pick up Calhoun.

After picking him up at LS-118, we needed to fuel up in order to reach Vientiane so we flew over to LS-118A and shut the aircraft down to refuel. It was about 4:15 p.m. While there, Louis Ojibway, the CIA agent in charge of the site, asked if he and one of his agents and two other passengers could hitch a ride to LS-20A or any point south.

Bobby agreed and we lifted off at about 4:30 p.m. with pilot Nunez, Calhoun in the co-pilot's seat and four passengers and me in the cargo compartment. After about 30 minutes in the air, Bobby asked me to ask the customer if it was important that they get to LS-20A today. The customer responded, no, that he would go all the way to Vientiane with us.

The weather held off until about 6:30 p.m. when we started going around storms and losing time and using up fuel. At about 7 p.m., we picked up the Mekong and started to follow it. The weather at this point was really bad and the light was starting to fade but the river and both banks were still visible. Bobby was flying about 50 feet over the river in heavy rain.

We were about 15 minutes out of Vientiane when the low fuel signal came on. If everything went well, we would make Vientiane. Bobby was talking on his headset to a pilot in the Vientiane area who said the weather had cleared there and he would continue to circle until we landed. I was sitting in the flight mechanic's seat facing aft. The customers and passengers appeared to be sleeping. I knew when we arrived at Vientiane I would have to refuel, so in anticipation, I turned to get my flashlight from my equipment bag. I knew that I would need it for refueling. I dug for my flashlight and as I turned back in my seat, looked out the door, which was open about six inches and saw we were about to hit the water. I reached for the intercom to alert Bobby but it was too late. We hit the water.

As it hit the helicopter rolled over to the right and continued to roll until it was totally upside down. The door was open about six inches but I couldn't open it any further. I tried to pull the door release but I couldn't get my hand around it because the plastic breakaway shield was being held in place by a metal strip riveted over it. I let go of the door and was being swept toward the back of the aircraft.

I remember very clearly thinking, *Well this is it. There's no getting out of this one.*

A real calmness came over me. I remember thinking that my girlfriend of many years would never know where I was. Never once did I panic. I was completely at peace, a really strange feeling.

I didn't know which way was up or down and it was so black I could see nothing. As the water carried me towards the back, I thought, *I'd better grab on to something or I'll end up in the tail cone.* As my hand brushed along the side of the helicopter, I felt an opening where a small plastic window should have been. The window may have been pushed open by water pressure. When I think of it today, none of it makes any sense. I was able to squeeze through the small opening and popped up to the surface like a cork.

The aircraft was upside down with only the fuel cells and part of the tail cone and pylon above water. I was hanging on to an aerial wire and the two pilots were somewhere nearby.

"Are we the only ones out?" Nunez called out.

"I think so," I replied.

I was in the middle of the Mekong at night and the helicopter was sinking. Due to the rainy season, the river was swollen way beyond its usual size and the water was raging at about eight knots. Still grasping part of the helicopter, I struggled to remove my combat boots before I lost my grip on the aerial wire but couldn't do it.

There was a short discussion among us as to what side of the river was closest and in a blink of an eye, Nunez and Calhoun were gone presumably towards the Thai side of the river. I thought the Lao side was closer and yelled to them that I was heading for Laos. They were already gone. It was every man for himself.

I was a strong swimmer and in great physical condition. I set off with confidence, swimming across the current toward the tree line on the Laos shore. Eventually one boot came off but not the other. I made slow progress, going over rapids formed by submerged islands, losing direction and possibly swimming in circles. Twice exhaustion overcame me and I sank maybe 30 feet below water. Not being able to breathe is a strong motivator and I kicked my way back to the surface. I am an atheist but for a while I thought about praying but made a conscious decision not to do so. If you don't pray in the good times, you don't pray in the bad. Eventually, I rolled over on my back and floated. This worked great. Why don't they tell you that in survival school? I found if I tipped my head way back, I could see the tree line on shore and using the back stroke, made very slow progress across the rapid current toward shore.

Finally after hours, I reached the shore line but could not get out of the water because of the heavy vines, brush and undergrowth so I went about another 100 feet downstream where I found a clearing.

Grabbing vines, I pulled myself out, laughing to myself. *You didn't get me this time,* I thought in exhilaration. I had been two hours or more swimming the Mekong. It was about 10 p.m. I was cold, wet and miserable and had swallowed gallons of the muddy river.

I never felt more alone in my life. It was pitch black jungle. My only friend was my wrist watch which was still working along with its illuminated dial. I spent the night talking to my watch.

About midnight, I startled some kind of an animal in the underbrush. I'm not sure who was more spooked, me or the beast. As I had visions of tigers, it was back into the river for me as I thought my chances would be better. If the critter decided to attack, we'd both be in the water.

I spent the remainder of the night kneeling in the water with a beehive of mosquitoes over my head. As the night dragged on I began to formulate an escape plan for the next day. I did not know where I was in Laos. The Pathet Lao could have been anywhere. Plan A was to be rescued by a helicopter at first light. Plan B was to steal a canoe. I knew I couldn't walk through the jungle so I decided I would walk down river, steal a canoe from the first village I came to and then float it all the way to Vientiane. The plan gave me some comfort and I actually think I dozed off a couple of times.

At daybreak, I knew I had to find a clearing nearby in order to be spotted by the rescue crew that I knew would be coming at first light. I was fortunate in quickly locating a small clearing, maybe a banana grove. It was 6:15 a.m. when I arrived in the clearing and barely light. I could already hear an airplane making circular loops down the river and coming closer with each loop. Shortly I spotted a Caribou plane. I was waving frantically. They spotted me and dipped their wings in acknowledgement. Within minutes, I could hear the flap, flap, flap of the helicopter approaching. There is no sweeter sound. I did not wait for the helicopter, which I think was H-15, to land. It was still about five feet off the ground when I made a running leap for it and was pulled in by my flight mechanic friend, Veera Champanil. The pilot was Marius Burke.

"Anyone else with you?" he asked.

"No." We were off, headed for Vientiane, food and a warm bed.

When we landed at Vientiane, the central post for the search, I was questioned by a few people and examined by a doctor. I remember being famished. So following the questioning, I limped to the cafeteria, one boot on and one boot off. Fellow flight mechanic Jesse Smith met me at the door. He couldn't contain his laughter. "Gee," he said, "Am I glad to see you. Timens had you dead on the flight line this morning and said it was too bad as you were a nice guy." Timens was the Udorn line chief at the time.

After eating, I was given a place to sleep and then flown back to Udorn. I went back to my lodging, showered and was back at work in the afternoon.

The co-pilot Calhoun was picked up by a Thai fisherman some three miles downriver and pilot Bobby Nunez, a non-swimmer, managed to hang onto a tree limb and floated some 60 miles downriver. CIA Agents Louis Ojibway and E. Johnson, Lao Special Guerilla Unit Officer T. Syborravang and Royal Thai Army Officer R. Ramut did not survive. The aircraft was never recovered.

Malaria

After about two months on the ground following my swim in the Mekong, I was back to flying.

I was upcountry somewhere. I was so sick I don't even remember where it was. We were loading and unloading cargo and I was feeling desperately ill with freezing chills, nausea and weakness. I had not been feeling that well for about a month, but this day, I was in trouble. They had sent for a relief for me but I continued to load as I waited for him to arrive.

When my relief arrived, I was sent back to Udorn to their infirmary. I was shaking out of control and it seemed like everyone was looking at me with quizzical stares. I think I may have been hallucinating at that point. From the infirmary, I was sent by air to the Bangkok Christian Hospital where they diagnosed malaria. I lost two days in the hospital before I regained consciousness. I was in the hospital for several weeks.

On the flight in to the hospital, there was a young fixed wing Air America pilot with the same problem as me. We were receiving identical treatment each day at the same time, which was a two hour drip of some type of green medication that looked to be about a gallon. Each day the young pilot would come in to talk within ten minutes of the medication injection.

One day I asked him, "How come you can get up so fast? My drip is still working."

"Oh, that's easy." He walked toward my drip paraphernalia. "See this clamp," and he reached up for it.

"No, no," I yelled, "Don't touch it." Apparently as soon as the nurse left, he just opened the clamp and let the medication flow into his vein. I didn't think that was a very good idea so I left it alone. He was great company while I was hospitalized but I never met him again after our stint at Bangkok Christian.

The Recovery of H-30

Pilot John Fonburg, a Dumas, Texas, guy, and flight mechanic "Champ" Champanil flew a team of mechanics to an area near Luang Prabang, the site of the crash of H-30. The pilot of H-30 had, for whatever reason, come in short of the landing pad and hit the trees. Flight mechanic Bob Bedell broke his arm in the crash.

The recovery team consisted of Dick Conrad, Matt Luca and me. We were not happy campers because when the company pulled you from your flight mechanic schedule and sent you as a mechanic on a recovery mission, you did not get flight pay, hence a reduction in pay. I remember Matt Luca was particularly down during that trip and as the lead flight mechanic, I tried to boost his moral but he continued to mutter as we worked to tear down the helicopter, readying it for transport back to Udorn.

I give the company great credit. They never walked away from an aircraft regardless of the severity of the damage. Unlike Humpty Dumpty, they put them all back together again or at least retrieved every part they could. H-30 would fly again as good as ever or maybe even better.

As I was getting the main transmission ready to lift off, I noticed a young Hmong boy about six or seven watching me from about two feet away. I was about to disconnect a hydraulic line which I knew would run red like blood, so I signaled to the boy that I was about to cut the throat of the helicopter by making a cutting motion at my throat. As I disconnected the line, red fluid ran out. I looked at the boy but there was no reaction what so ever to what I had done. He just stared at me stoically as he had been right along. I was disappointed. He took all the fun out of it.

After one failed attempt the day earlier, we readied what remained of the helicopter for transport and I signaled the pilot to come in for the hook up.

Dick made the hook up and then jumped to safety. As he did so, he tripped and fell onto a tree spike that punched into his chest. It knocked the wind out of him. He managed to get clear and then collapsed. For the second time, the load was too much for the helicopter so H-30 was dropped again. The pilot landed and Champ jumped out with the first aid kit from the helicopter to tend to Dick. He was lying there seemingly unconscious. Champ revived him with smelling salts which really impressed me, as previous to this, I would have said the first aid kit was the most useless piece of equipment on the helicopter. It didn't have much to offer when you consider the seriousness of most crashes.

Dick had no serious injury other than having the wind knocked out of him, bruising his ribs and scaring the crap out of the rest of us. He was sent back to Udorn and Cris Crisologo was sent as his replacement.

We went back to the business of getting the remains of H-30 back to Luang Prabang.

H-30 lived to fly until the fall of Saigon in 1975. There were numerous incident reports and repairs from 1966 to 1975. In 1975, the helicopter escaped from Laos to Ubol, Thailand, where it remained for many years. Rumor has it that H-30 is the anonymous UH-34 that is now preserved at a temple in Pathum Thani, northeast of Bangkok.

H-30 Rebuilt at Udorn 1966

Guns and Air America

There were two big falsehoods told to me at my interview for Air America in Washington, DC. One was "the job was not dangerous." The other was "Air America personnel are not permitted to carry personal weapons." The job was dangerous as hell and most people carried personal weapons. They just carried them where you couldn't see them.

In the early days of Air America, before they instituted the no personal weapons policy, most personnel did carry guns, some of whom looked like villistas from the Mexican Revolution. Apparently after a night of heavy drinking, a gun fight ensued and shortly thereafter, on paper, personal weapons were banned.

Air America would issue you a weapon for any assignment warranting a weapon but it had to be checked out and returned after each assignment. That was not very practical as every trip upcountry had the potential for coming under attack, and most air rescues and prisoner transports were assigned on short notice and usually while already upcountry.

Initially I did not have a personal weapon but after the airman rescue and my night in the jungle, I was rethinking the wisdom of that. So I started looking for a gun to buy. I learned one of the wives who had just returned from a visit to the States was looking to sell a nine shot 22 revolver. No one else wanted it because they usually went for more powerful weapons. But I didn't care. I didn't want to be in a shootout. I just wanted to kill a small animal for food in the event I was stranded on the ground in a remote area. The 22 revolver was my first gun.

After a few more trips upcountry, I moved up to an AK-47 that I got from a Lao Army officer after a firefight at LS-107. He got onto my helicopter carrying three or four of them. I hand signaled to him that I wanted one. He jotted down the serial number and handed it to me.

The reason for the no personal weapons policy was made clearer to me following an incident that resulted in some good people going back from whence they came.

There were three of them doing some heavy drinking in the privacy of their bungalow. After getting fired up on an undetermined amount of liquor, they took it upon themselves to go out into the darkness of the yard and started firing an AK-47 and other weapons. They fired at a pile of bricks until they ran out of ammunition.

Unfortunately they were on the edge of the Udorn Royal Air Force Base and the base thought they were under attack and went on some form of alert.

The following day the incident was investigated by the Air Force. When the Air Force APs knocked on the door of their bungalow the next morning, one mechanic was cleaning his self-modified, cut down folding stock M2 Carbine. He let them into the house and when they saw the gun, they said, "Well, that's why we're here. We'll have to take that."

The mechanic said, "Well, you can't. I need it in my work. Let me get you another one." So they took both.

When the APs asked what the shooting was all about, he said, "We held off an attack by commies, but as usual, they carried off their dead and wounded."

The pulverized brick pile and yard full of shell casings told a different story. Air America would probably have overlooked the whole incident except that the Air Force was really ticked off. So to appease the Air Force, three good men, two of whom were flight mechanics, went home.

When I stopped flying and took the line chief job on the ground at Udorn, I sold my 22 revolver and my AK-47 to Glenn Woods. I had paid $150 for the revolver and the AK-47 was given to me free. I sold them to Glenn for $100. Glenn later used the AK-47 to shoot down a Russian Colt over LS-85 in the infamous attack on the site on January 12, 1968.

Father Bouchard

I was staring at the passenger seat in the cargo department of my helicopter. It had just been vacated by the leper and I was wondering if there were any precautions I should be taking.

This story begins with Father Lucien (Luke) Bouchard, an American Catholic priest, known to most of Air America as "The Walking Priest of Laos." He lived in Laos from the mid 1950s to the mid 1970s, until he was forced to escape to Thailand to avoid capture by communist forces. He was a beloved man who walked around Laos ministering both medically and spiritually to the Hmong people. He was about thirty-five years old, affable and fit enough to hike the mountainous terrain of Northern Laos on a daily basis dressed in jeans and sneakers carrying nothing but a knapsack. He lived, ate and slept with the Hmong people. Although very little has been written about him in histories of the secret war in Laos, he spent nearly two decades there and was incidental in staving off a massive cholera outbreak, worked with the lepers at a colony located near Padong and administered medical treatment to the Lao people.

The word at Air America was, if Father Bouchard needed a favor, find a way. And so we did that morning when he approached us at LS-20 and asked if we could pick up a leper at a remote spot and transport him to the leper village near Padong. I was not aware lepers existed anywhere in the world but apparently they still did in Laos. The pilots agreed, we hopped aboard and were off towards a hillside on the edge of the Plain of Jars.

The Plain of Jars was an area of Laos considered to be very dangerous as it was occupied by the communist Pathet Lao. The area was also very unusual as there were hundreds of stone jars ranging from three to eight feet high to about three feet wide spread across the area. No one could give an explanation as to where the jars came from or what they were used for. Great numbers were destroyed by the bombing of the communists during the war. Today this area has become a tourist attraction in Laos.

At the time I was there, anywhere near the Plain of Jars was reason for concern because the place was crawling with Chinese and Pathet Lao. Father Bouchard who knew the area better than any CIA agent had assured us that this area was friendly but we knew what was friendly yesterday was not necessarily friendly today. However, the enemy was not what bothered me this morning as we flew towards our destination. What bothered me was sharing my helicopter with a leper.

We followed the directions given by Father Bouchard and cautiously dropped down to land near a shack on a grassy side of a hill. Two Laotians ran toward us carrying a bedraggled old man by his under arms. He was in typical black trousers and shirt and his extremities were wrapped in filthy rags. He was in a crouched position when they loaded him. I don't know whether he could even get out of the crouched position. The Laotians placed him in the passenger seat, still sitting on his haunches, with a shit ass grin on his face.

We were up and out of there in seconds in route to Padong. The leper never stopped grinning at me the whole trip. *What makes these people living under such dire circumstances so happy?* I was thinking. Maybe it's not happiness, but abject fear that keeps them smiling, as if they can placate powerful forces around them with their humorous expressions.

We landed at the leper village and two other lepers came and lifted our passenger from the helicopter. Mission accomplished.

We returned to LS-20 later that day and I was starting my routine maintenance checks thinking about the leper. I knew that my chances of getting leprosy were next to nil because the disease was only mildly contagious, but when Father Bouchard happened to walk by, I called out, looking for some sort of reassurance from him.

"Say, Father Bouchard. Are there any precautions I should be taking about the leper?"

"No," he said as he passed. I was relieved. He went about six feet, stopped and turned. "You might want to wash the seat down."

Now I was worried. But in the middle of nowhere, there was nothing to wash the seat down with. For the rest of that trip I was very careful not to touch the passenger seat.

Father Lucien (Luke) Bouchard (OMI) in one of his two leper villages in Northern Laos. He is a member of the religious congregation of the Oblates of Mary Immaculate (OMI). The photograph was taken by Dr. Charles Weldon and made available to us courtesy of Father Bouchard

Jan. 15, 2013

Dear Bert,

    This photo was taken of me with a group of lepers in one of my two leper villages that I had helped set up during my missionary work in Northern Laos. I am a member of the religious congregation of the Oblates of Mary Immaculate (O.M.I.). This photo was taken by my close friend Dr. Charles Weldon who had come to visit the lepers. When some communist rebels were getting too close to their area, I decided to transfer them to Fr. Jean-Marie Ollivier's leper village at Vang Vieng which was about 120 miles away. It took four helicopters a full day of rotations to make that transfer to Vang Vieng. I remember I left on the last rotation of the remaining helicopter. I'm sure your flight engineer friends remember this also.

        Sincerely,

        Fr. Lucien Bouchard, OMI

Nam Bac - Operation Cleveland

Nam Bac was a beautiful valley in the lowlands of Laos. It was a pleasant place with an old French runway. Off to one side of the runway was an old wrecked aircraft that I always wanted to check out but never got the opportunity. The old French sites always interested me and peaked my curiosity about the history and what might have happened there in the past.

Nam Bac, LS-203, changed hands several times during the war and in 1966 was under the control of the communist Pathet Lao.

At some point in 1966, the Lao Royalist army decided with CIA support to take back Nam Bac from the Pathet Lao. Nam Bac was located about 150 miles northeast of Luang Prabang, L-54. The mission, called Operation Cleveland, was launched from Luang Prabang. I have to say it was fun. We got most of our aircraft operational all at one time, which in itself wasn't any great feat as we always had 80 percent or better availability. While it was an impressive show of about fifteen Air America helicopters providing logistical support, the taking of the site was more or less uneventful. It was probably the only lowland victory by the Lao Army.

However to hold the site, you had to hold the surrounding hills. A short time later, the Pathet Lao moved in and took back a site close to Nam Bac which we were unaware of on this particular day and which resulted in one of the more tragic incidents of my time in Laos.

On November 8, 1966, pilot Larry Wilderom and flight mechanic Dennis Griffith flew H-41 into the site which was no longer friendly. They had on board two young sons of an area customer who were just along for the ride. They landed and were taxiing to the end of the short runway when the concealed enemy opened up with automatic weapons.

According to Larry, he had to pick it up into a hover and depart. The aircraft took over 140 hits. Everything that could be hit but still fly was hit, rotor blades, fuel cells, hydraulic lines, tires, struts, rudder pedal, etc.

Larry had the heel of his boot shot off and Dennis took shrapnel in his leg. One brother was killed the other seriously injured.

As they returned to Nam Bac, communications were not possible between the pilot and flight mechanic due to the damage. Larry later told me that he was stamping his feet on the floor to let Dennis know he was okay. I couldn't help thinking that if I had been Dennis, I would have thought the stamping of feet meant the pilot was in the throes of death and at any moment we would crash to the ground. The terror and tragedy for everyone on board remains indescribable.

They limped back to Nam Bac and set down just as the engine quit. The damage was unbelievable. It took us a week just to get the aircraft fit to ferry back to Udorn. Once back at Udorn, Maintenance circled all the bullet holes with chalk and the helicopter started to turn white.

Dennis Griffith tells his story on page 159.

Like most of the positions we took from the Pathet Lao they would rebound and counter attack, retaking the position. They did retake Nam Bac.

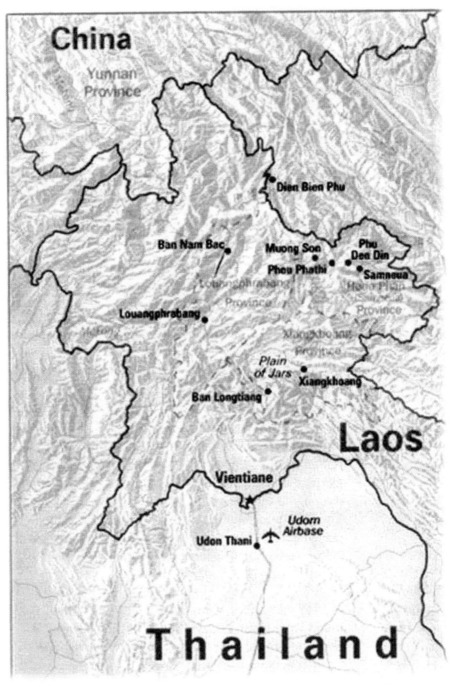

www.cia.gov/library/publications/cia-maps-publications/index.html

Tony Poe

Tony Poe was the most infamous CIA Agent of the U.S. Secret War in Laos. There has been much written about him, some of which I believe is exaggerated. The funny thing is that Tony's tactics, mannerisms and accomplishments did not need embellishment. He clearly was one of the most bizarre characters I have ever met.

Tony operated in the hills of Laos helping to arm and train Gen. Vang Pao's Hmong tribesmen in their struggle against the Pathet Lao.

In January 1965, communist forces were moving westward toward Phou Pha Thi. In the field, Tony became frustrated with the Hmong's inaccuracy when shooting at the enemy. Ignoring CIA regulations to stay out of combat, he began firing an M-1 carbine at the enemy. As the story goes, he killed about twenty of them before being hit and badly wounded. He kept fighting by lobbing grenades until the firing stopped. Then he walked about five miles until he could go no more and his Hmong fighters carried him to an area where he was picked up by an Air America helicopter piloted by Bobby Nunez and flown to a hospital in Korat. He later read in the North Vietnamese newspaper that he had been killed by the Pathet Lao. To some, his actions were heroic but his CIA boss, Bill Lair, was none too pleased.

There were a lot of people who did not like Tony. Perhaps they thought him too powerful, arrogant and out of the box. I liked him. I thought he was a very funny guy. He got the job done and I had great respect for his knowledge and experience. When he sent you on a mission, he provided details on enemy locations and possible trouble spots. His knowledge of the enemy could be relied on more so than any other customer and we rarely got into trouble on any of his assignments.

My first encounter with Tony was one evening at LS-36, a site constantly under attack. Four helicopters had landed at the site and were parked where we serviced the helicopters and then the pilots and crew all walked over to a thatched hut which was the command post. It was dark and gunfire was flying over the trees and tents. Tony was sitting at the end of a long table eating his dinner and Lao soldiers were frantically running in and out of the hut conversing with Tony. He greeted us affably and invited us to sit down. He appeared to be somewhat intoxicated but, as I eventually learned with Tony, you never knew if it was real or an act. The gunfire and activity continued and Tony, a big burly guy, calmly ate his dinner while the rest of us tried to make ourselves comfortable while the bullets continued to fly over head.

Finally one of the pilots stood and said, "Tony, would you be offended if we take the helicopters and get out of here?" The pilot seemed hesitant to offend Tony as most people were. His reputation made him a formidable character and it seemed like people thought he might pull out a revolver and shoot them.

Tony barely looked up, "No, go ahead. No problem." He waved a hand in dismissal and kept right on eating. "But when you fire up those engines and the exhaust stacks light up, what do you think they will be shooting at?"

The pilot sat back down.

"Don't worry," he said, "My people have it all under control. They're just fighting in the rice paddy over there." It was maybe 300 feet away.

He pointed towards a huge pile of every kind of weapon imaginable in the corner of the hut. "If you're really worried, grab one of those guns over there."

Nobody moved for the guns, but, like me, I bet they thought about it.

Eventually the activity ceased and the night quieted down. We all spent the night at LS- 36 in primitive shacks that were made from empty 55 gallon fuel drums, cut open, flattened out and used for walls and roofing.

Tony used the superstitions of the tribes' people to our advantage. He was having trouble with local tribes helping the communists. He told them repeatedly that the Buddha would be angry if they helped the communists. Several times, to convince them that Buddha was angry, he had a PC-6 Porter aircraft load 1500 pounds of small stones, fly high enough so as not to be seen or heard and then drop the load from the Porter drop door, which was like a bomb bay, onto the villagers. It would be hard to make a more persuasive argument.

Upon the loss of Native American paramilitary officer, Lewis Ojibway, who died along with four others in the crash into the Mekong, Bill Lair sent Tony to replace Ojibway in northwest Laos at LS-118A, a relatively quiet area on the Chinese/Burma border.

Everyone knew that Tony collected human ears from dead victims. He nailed the ears to the rafters of his little two room hut located at LS-118A. The small hut, inherited from Ojibway, was built on stilts with open air half walls with a rough cut table in the middle of the room. The back end where he slept was sealed off by a curtain.

There were many evenings I spent at Site 118A on Tony's porch silently enjoying the evening. Occasionally a Hmong patrol leader would report to Tony. Obviously in awe of Tony and nervous in his presence, the young man would climb up the steps in oversized boots which would invariably cause him to stumble. He would stand at attention and salute as he reported in from patrol.

"Mr. Tony, we have firefight. We kill beaucoup enemy," a young Hmong reported.

"Really? Do you have any ears for me?"

"No, Mr. Tony."

"Maybe you're just bull shitting me," Tony would respond. He had a gravelly voice that was intimidating in the darkness.

"No. No. I kill beaucoup enemy."

Tony would stand up and say, "Oh, all right. Come here." And Tony, who was a giant of a man compared to the Hmong, would give the tribesman a bear hug and then he would hand him a jug of Mekong whiskey. The young fighter would go off into the darkness of the jungle.

On another occasion, another young man came out of the darkness and stumbled nervously up the steps again in the boots too big for him. I noticed he carried a plastic bag.

"Mr. Tony, I kill beaucoup enemy."

"Really? Do you have any ears for me?"

"Yes, Mr. Tony. Here." He handed the package to Tony who looked inside.

"Good job. Come here." He gave him a huge hug which I thought might crush the younger man and then Tony disappeared behind the curtain. He returned shortly with a bottle of whiskey and a chrome plated 38 revolver and presented them to the Hmong tribesman who smiled in pure delight. Face is everything to the Thai/Lao people. Tony had given him more than money. He had given him status among his people.

One day Tony asked us to take him and four or five of his troops on patrol to a place only known to the pilots and Tony. I think it may have been very near China.

They all boarded the aircraft and strapped in. The helicopter lifted off, vibrating heavily as it usually does. Tony was up front directly across from me. He pulled out his Buddha bag which was tied around his neck. He looked around furtively as if to see if anyone was looking at him, which of course everyone was, but he pretended they were not. He started to go through his bag, pulling out little trinkets one at a time and putting them back until he pulled out this shriveled up piece resembling a human ear. He looked around again and then takes a huge bite out of the ear like it's the greatest. Then he acted like he was suddenly aware that his soldiers were watching him so he leaned toward them and offered them a bite. Thinking it was a real ear, the soldiers couldn't get far enough away from the proffered ear. I thought they would jump out of the aircraft. It was one of the funniest things I ever saw. I knew it was not an ear because of all the things told and written about Tony, the good, the bad and the ugly, no one ever called him a cannibal.

One time at LS-118A when I walked into Tony's place, he had Walt Disney's annual stock reports strung out all over the place, on the floor, on the chair, on the table, just everywhere. There were four or five pilots and I, and Tony was vehemently telling us to buy Disney stock. Walt Disney had just passed away and Tony was beside himself insisting the stock was going through the roof. Well, I didn't buy any. I was too busy buying American Motors and Pan Am. Disney did go through the roof and didn't stop for the next twenty years.

There was the time that pilot Phil Goddard and I were working out of LS-118A for Tony. Tony for all his nefarious actions was really an efficient guy. If he asked you to deliver something somewhere, he would figure out something for you to bring back on the return trip. This day we delivered supplies near Ban Houei Sai. He asked us to swing by Ban Houei Sai on the return trip to pick up fuel from a dirt runway there and bring it back to LS-118A.

Air America dispersed fuel barrels at airstrips throughout Laos for general use, emergency or other purposes. While many strips were no longer in use, the locals never touched the fuel even though we knew they used the fuel when they could get it for their cigarette lighters and other strange things. In fact the local Lao people would put an empty tin can to good use for years if the opportunity presented itself. Many times while fueling upcountry, you had to keep an industrious Lao from catching the drips of fuel into their lighters. The stuff was highly flammable and lighters were known to explode in their pockets.

We landed on the dirt runway at Ban Houei Sai and Phil said, "Let's see how many of these barrels we can get in this thing."

With the aid of the rescue hoist, we loaded nine 55 gallon fuel barrels into the H-34. As there was no more room left in the cargo compartment, at least I was not going to try for more, I had to fly shotgun in the co-pilot's seat. Just before we departed a Lao soldier asked for a ride to LS-118A. Phil said he could ride on top of the barrels. We had to make a running take off at max power and flew at five hundred feet over the trees at maximum continuous power for the twenty minute trip.

When we landed back at LS-118A, we taxied the length of the runway. I kicked a barrel out of the aircraft every twenty feet or so just to make a statement.

Tony was impressed.

Shortly thereafter, a twin engine fixed wing Caribou landed.

"Tony, we have a couple of barrels of fuel for you," one of the pilots said.

"What," Tony responded. "Two barrels. That's nothing. These guys just brought nine." He sputtered a few more disparaging remarks directed their way.

I could tell from the pilots' voices that they didn't expect his reaction. No one wanted to get on the wrong side of Tony. I knew he didn't mean anything by it. It was just Tony being Tony.

Another memorable moment for me was the night in the Rendezvous Club in Udorn when a visiting dignitary came in. I was seated in the dining room and Tony was seated in the back corner of the same room eating a huge steak with his hands. Politicians, diplomats and others were always coming through Udorn and most of us ceased to notice them anymore. The latest dignitary was being escorted by the club manager who spotted Tony in the back and immediately brought the visitor around to Tony's table to make the introduction. Tony put down the steak he had been gnawing on, wiped his greasy hands down his shirt and shook the visitor's hand. This was the Tony we all knew and respected.

The last time I saw Tony he was walking across the ramp at Udorn. We spoke briefly. He had lost several fingers on one hand. I heard it was a munitions accident. He had been transferred out of Laos to a training camp in Thailand, because, as rumor had it, he threatened to kill the French ambassador.

Of all the characters from the secret war in Laos, Tony was the most colorful and infamous. He survived the war and retired to California. He never abandoned the Hmong people of Laos. In his retirement years, he financed Laotians in need and petitioned Washington for aid to Laotian veterans. He died on March 16, 2010, at the age of eighty-five. In the eyes of many Air America personnel, he was the best ever.

Rainy Season and Mud, Mud, Mud

One day while flying with Bobby Nunez as pilot and a new first officer whom I can't remember, we landed at this position on the edge of a very muddy sloping hillside. It was maybe 800 to 1000 feet to the bottom. It had been raining for days and the ground was a mess. We loaded about fifteen women and kids with baggage.

Bobby was in the co-pilot's seat which in the H-34 did not have brake pedals on that side. The new guy was in the captain's seat. As he started to pull up on the collective stick, the aircraft got light on the wheels and started to slide over the edge.

I heard Bobby yelling, "Brakes, brakes, brakes," but it looked like we were going over.

Very quickly I decided someone should remain behind if this happens so I nimbly stepped out onto the V part of the landing gear preparing to jump just in case. Meanwhile the passengers were just looking at me with great interest.

Someone in the cockpit dropped the collective putting weight back onto the tires and the aircraft stopped sliding about one-half foot from the drop off. At this point Bobby took over the controls, I jumped back in and we departed in the normal fashion.

I used to feel badly for the new pilots because they had to learn by scaring the shit out of themselves. Unfortunately, we flight mechanics were along for the ride.

Meanwhile, when incidents like this were happening, the Lao people always seemed to accept it as normal, just sitting there looking forward to the trip.

Rudy Serafico

Rudy Serafico was Filipino as were a large percentage of the mechanics at Air America. The company hired numerous third country nationals and provided training in various career fields. They were great people and did one hell of a job.

On this day, Rudy and I were in a rice paddy with our arms up to our elbows in aviation fuel, trying to stop the leak in the fuel tank by tearing up shammy skins and shoving the little pieces of cloth into the bullet holes. Time was of the essence. His helicopter had just been shot up and we needed to repair it and get out of there before the enemy found our position.

We had been flying to a friendly area over a ridgeline into the valley. There were two or three helicopters all carrying Hmong troops. There were three of us on my helicopter, a pilot, a trainee flight mechanic and I. We landed without incident, unloaded the passengers and took off in formation with pilot Jim Williams and Rudy directly in front of us. As we passed back over the ridge line, Rudy's aircraft took several rounds up through the belly, one passing through the vacant co-pilot's seat and out the roof window. A couple of other bullets passed through one of the fuel tanks. Williams opted to land at the first opportunity to assess the damage and chose to put it down in a dry rice paddy.

Because we had a flight mechanic trainee on board to cover for me, I called to my pilot to put me down with them. "Let me see if I can help them out."

My pilot dropped me off and split. I found Rudy tearing up a shammy skin to stuff into the bullet holes, which you could only find by opening up the tank and sticking your arms into the aviation fuel to feel for the holes. Where automobile fuel is 87/93 octane, the aviation fuel we used was 115/145. The smallest spark would have blown us and the helicopter to smithereens. One gunshot and we would have been toast. Miraculously, we effected the repair and got out before the enemy knew we were there.

You might wonder why we had been shot at if the area was friendly. It could have been that the area was no longer friendly as things changed quickly in Laos or it could have been for any number of reasons you might come up with. There was an incident once at LS-36 where one of the friendly soldiers at an outpost surrounding the site took a shot at an Air America H-34 flying by. The pilots complained to Col. Vang Pao who sent soldiers out to investigate. When questioned as to why he shot at the American plane, he said because he wanted to die. They brought him back to the landing strip and shot him dead on the runway.

Rudy's time with Air America while I was there was without a serious crash or enemy attack that I can remember. He did however have one of the better stories to tell. In the early years of CIA involvement in Laos there was a lot of confusion. He told me that on one flight to deliver weapons to the troops, they landed at a communist Pathet Lao enemy camp by mistake. Flew right in and put it on the ground. They were surrounded by the enemy but all our helicopters were unmarked and everybody had them including the Russians. The minute the helicopter hit the ground Rudy and the pilot knew they had made a mistake. Rudy jumped out and started handing out the guns and in his broken Lao dialect explained they would return with more guns. Once they were unloaded, he jumped back in and they took off, not one bullet being fired.

Rudy was there when I arrived in Laos and had already been there for some time. He was a personable, reasonable guy. I only had one issue develop with Rudy and that was when I was superintendent for helicopter maintenance. A new American mechanic had arrived at Udorn and for some unexplainable reason, Rudy and the new guy, an ex-marine, developed an intense dislike for each other. Rudy was a family man who lived locally in Udorn and did not hang out at the bars so I knew the problem did not stem from there.

The antagonism between them did not go unnoticed by the rest of the workforce and it was escalating. I would call Rudy in and ask him what the problem was and he would take off on a tirade finishing with, "I'm going to kill that son of a bitch."

I would call the new guy in and ask him what the problem was and he would take off on a tirade finishing with, "I'm going to kill that son of a bitch." I explained to him that Rudi had years with Air America, was highly respected and if they could not work it out, he, as the new guy, was the one likely to get sent packing.

They didn't work it out and the problem escalated so the new guy was sent back home. I never did find out the reason behind their animosity, but it was intense.

Rudy stayed in Udorn with Air America until 1974 when U.S. activity ceased in Laos. I do not know where Rudy is today but I sure would like to talk to him again.

The Major

I was looking down from the helicopter at the U. S. Army artillery major that I had just decked. He was now lying flat on the ground in a heap of 60 mm mortar rounds with incoming enemy mortar rounds pounding the area all around him. *There goes my job for sure,* I thought.

Pilot Frank Stergar and I were transporting ammunition from LS-36 to a forward position and taking refugees back out. We were carrying 1,500 pounds of loose 60 mm mortar rounds which started out as a big mound but with the vibration of the helicopter turned into a floor cover of about a foot thick. When we landed, the plan was to unload the rounds and then let the passengers board. But the area suddenly came under enemy mortar fire and chaos ensued. I was on my hands and knees with my back to the door scooping out the loose mortar rounds and people were trying to board.

My pilot is yelling, "No more than seven, Steve. No more than seven," referring to the number of passengers to allow on board.

I am trying to scoop the ammunition out and count boarding people at the same time and one more than seven got by me so without turning around the next person who tried to board got my elbow straight to his gut with all the force I could muster. I yelled to the pilot to take off still scooping out the rounds of ammunition as he attempted to lift off. He kept losing RPM and we did three hops across the ground before we became airborne at which time I looked down and saw the major lying on the ground. *There goes my job.*

We landed back at LS-36 and within minutes a customer approached the aircraft asking where the major was.

"We had to leave him at the site," Frank responded.

"What?" The customer was furious. "You need to go back and get him, right now."

Frank looked at him. He was an older, seasoned veteran of World War II. "You have a little problem with mortar fire over there. When you take care of that, we'll go back."

I don't recall the exact words but the customer said something that implied Frank was chicken. Frank who was still in the pilot's seat, started to rip off his harness and I thought he was going to leap out and teach the customer some manners but he caught himself and let the guy walk away.

Frank and I worked another site for the rest of the day and returned to LS-36 to fuel up towards the end of the day. As we were fueling, I spotted the major across the dirt runway up at the Headquarters bunker.

"Frank, excuse me a minute. I have to go apologize to this guy. If I don't, I'll probably get fired." I ran across a dirt runway and up the hill to Headquarters.

"Excuse me, sir," I said. "I am really sorry about what happened back there. We were already over the number of passengers and I couldn't let anyone else board."

He looked at me and laughed good naturedly. "No problem," he said. "The only thing that bothered me was I had to run a hundred yards under fire to get to the helicopter. Then I had to run another hundred yards under fire to get back to the dugout."

Just one more exciting day at LS-36.

Flight Mechanic Johnny Sibal and Pilot Frank Stergar

The Guillotine

It was March and the weather was good as the rainy season had not yet begun. The rainy season generally ran from May to November. During the good weather beginning in November, communist forces would attack and take over Lao territory. From May to November during the rainy season, the Lao forces would take it back with air mobility support of Air America. In the early part of the war, very little territory actually changed hands.

Communist forces had overrun LS-48A at Moung Hiem and our mission that day, along with several other helicopters, was locating and picking up pockets of Lao soldiers in the area of LS-48A and transporting them to a safe location.

The area we were flying in was heavily overgrown and difficult to work. A day or so earlier a band of soldiers and camp followers had been spotted in a high altitude boxed canyon. An H-34 piloted by a seasoned crew attempted the pickup but found themselves instead at full available power looking up at the ridge line in the boxed canyon. With nowhere to go, they peddled it around sharply. When you do this in a helicopter, your air speed drops and you lose altitude. They dropped down into the top of the trees. With the co-pilot pushing on the windscreen to keep the tree from coming through, they regained air speed and came out the other side. The aircraft was still flying but had a profound vertical vibration. After landing safely, new blades were sent up from Udorn to replace the damaged ones which were so badly bent they wouldn't fit into the blade racks back at Udorn.

On this day, my pilot was Charlie Davis. Charlie was a good pilot and a determined one. When he had something to do, he got it done. Charlie tells this story in his book, "Across the Mekong." However there are differences between his story and mine which is understandable as he was in the cockpit and couldn't see me and I was below in the cargo compartment not always fully understanding what the hell was going on in the cockpit.

As we scanned the area, we spotted a small group of soldiers in a heavily overgrown area. The vegetation made landing to effect the pickup impossible. That made lifting them out with the rescue harness the next option, except for the fact that the guillotine was not working. The guillotine was the device used to cut the cable if, for some reason, the harness cable became snagged or inoperable. I had told Charlie the guillotine was not working earlier in the day but we decided to try the pickup anyway.

Knowing that fleeing Lao troops were easily panicked and did not understand English well, I had some reservation about dropping the harness without benefit of the guillotine to get us out of trouble but did so anyway.

As I expected, four soldiers grabbed onto the harness and would not let go. As I attempted to raise the harness, the helicopter, which was hovering at maximum power, began to sink. I immediately increased the slack on the cable and the helicopter recovered.

Charlie and I were shouting back and forth.

"What's going on?"

"Too many people."

"Get them off."

"I'm trying." I was leaning out of the door trying to hand signal to them to get off.

"Only one." I yelled, holding one finger out. Even if they understood English, they could not hear me over the roar of the helicopter. I continued signaling to no avail, knowing that we could not continue to hover for very long at max power.

"Cut the cable," Charlie shouted.

"Right," I muttered to myself.

Just then, the soldiers got it and two let go of the harness and we were able to pull the other two up into the helicopter. Once on board, Charlie swung the helicopter back around and said we would try to pick up the others.

"Charlie, I don't think that's a good idea."

But he told me to drop the harness, so I did it again.

Again three or four grabbed the harness and we went through the drill again. Finally it seemed we were down to one or two guys on the lift when the helicopter commenced to leave the area.

"Charlie," I yelled, "The guy is still hanging on to the ring."

The helicopter moved forward and we gained speed. I could see a soldier still hanging by his hands, streaming out behind us as we dragged him through a bamboo grove. He came out the other side still hanging on with a vine wrapped around his neck. The helicopter continued on and there was no place to land. I kept hoisting the soldier up until I was able to reach out and drag him into the helicopter. He didn't say a word. He just plopped down on a seat and smiled.

The Lao people never ceased to amaze me. I'll never forget the sight of him hanging there a hundred feet below the helicopter and two hundred feet above the ground, holding on to a six inch ring on a cable with his bare hands.

Stranded Pilots

We had been upcountry for several days, wearing our cleanest of the dirty, unwashed and unshaven. Our helicopter had an impeller seal leak which streaked the side of the aircraft with oil and made it smoke like a son of a gun. It was running great so I just kept pouring in the oil.

We parked at Pakse and had just shut down for the night. It was already dark when the customer approached and asked, "Would you guys mind picking up a couple of airmen at a small strip close by? They had a mechanical problem and I don't want them spending the night in a hostile area."

In fact, the pilots had been flying a Douglas A1E single engine attack bomber of Korean War vintage. While flying, a metal chip detector light had come on which meant the engine might quit at any moment. Rather than risk crashing, they put the plane down at a CIA landing strip close to a contested area.

Flying at night into a hostile area was not my idea of fun but our pilot, Lloyd Higgins, said, "Sure, we'll go." So Roger Burdwood, flight mechanic trainee, and I climbed back into the belly of the beast. We were tired, sweaty and filthy and Roger added to the picture with his always unlaced combat boots.

We flew out with no lights in this nasty dirty aircraft, unmarked and smoking. We located the air strip, dropped down for the pickup and Roger and I jumped out. A Jeep with the two pilots and the customer waited for us in the darkness.

"Who are you?" a nervous voice called from the blackness of the night.

The pilots did not have a clue who we were.

Starting to see the humor of the situation, I responded, "Never mind, who we are. Just get in."

Encouraged by the American voice, the pilots approached cautiously from out of the darkness but still kept their distance, clearly hesitant about boarding the aircraft. They were probably thinking it would be safer to fly their disabled plane than to get into this helicopter which was puffing like a dragon.

They looked back at the customer who had apparently been silent up to this point.

"Go ahead, hop in. These guys are Air America," he assured them.

The two airmen looked at each other in silence, put their parachutes on and climbed aboard.

I laughed to myself. *Good luck with the parachutes.*

A Really Bad Day

We had been upcountry for almost a week. LS-36 had been overrun by the communist Pathet Lao, and Gen. Vang Pao was attempting to retake it. We were transporting his troops and supplies to an area close to LS-48.

The weather had been good for most of the week and my pilot Larry Wilderom was familiar with the landscape and route in and out. So when bad weather rolled in, we were still able to locate the drop area with minimal problem. Not so for the other pilots who joined our effort that day.

The weather had turned very bad. The rainy season could be brutal. Visibility could get so bad that pilots were forced to fly within 75 feet of the tree line at speeds as slow as 20 knots making us sitting ducks to sniper fire. Their other choice was to go up over the weather and rely solely on instruments but you'd better know where you were going and how long and at what speed to get there. If not, you could come down and fly into a mountain as many invariably did.

There was a flight of about five or six helicopters. We had made several runs early that morning. On the third trip, the first helicopter to the drop site over shot the site and came under heavy gunfire, took several bullets but pulled away in time to avoid a catastrophe. The pilot attempted to radio other helicopters that the area was hot but got no response. The next helicopter coming into the site was piloted by Bill Wilmont with flight mechanic Matt Luca. They came under the same enemy fire, the pilot was hit and the helicopter crashed, exploded and burned. We presumed that the pilot, flight mechanic and the Hmong troops had all been killed.

Following the crash, all the helicopters, five in all, collected at LS-48. It was a grim group of about fifteen to twenty Air America guys milling about until a Skyraider radioed that he had just made a pass over the crash site and saw movement.

"I think you have survivors," he radioed.

Without a minute of hesitation, one of our pilots, Steve Stevens, turned to his flight mechanic, Rusty Irons, and said, "Come on, Rusty. Let's go get them."

As they started toward their helicopter, someone in our group said, "Hold up, Steve, we need to check with Udorn first. We need permission to go back in there."

Stevens responded, "We don't have time for that bullshit." He and Rusty walked toward the aircraft. A customer stepped up with several Hmong soldiers. They boarded the aircraft and manned the windows with weapons in anticipation of a firefight at the accident scene.

While I had great admiration for Stevens at the time, I felt it was really looking for trouble. I was glad it was not my pilot who decided to play John Wayne. Stevens even looked the part of a Wild West hero with his handlebar mustache curled up at each end.

When they landed at the crash site, there was no resistance. They found pilot Bill Wilmont dead along with the Lao fighters who had died from bullets, the crash or the explosion and fire. Rusty was loading a Hmong soldier badly burned but still alive onto the helicopter when Matt Luca, severely injured, crawled out of a ditch and came up behind him nearly scaring Rusty to death. Matt was badly burned on his arm and had taken a bullet wound to his leg. Rusty helped him into the helicopter. They were up and out of there in minutes. They returned the injured to LS-48 and transferred them to a fixed wing plane which then flew them to the hospital in Thailand.

While the rest of the aircraft spent the remainder of the day transporting troops and supplies, fighting the weather and trying not to hit each other as they went back and forth, our aircraft was dispatched to LS-49 at Lak Sao. I loaded two barrels of fuel as we did not know what would be available at LS-49 and took off up through a hole in the clouds and proceeded towards Lak Sao flying above the clouds. We had flown about an hour to where LS-49 should have been but the area was totally socked in and we could not find a break in the clouds to descend. The risk of smashing into the side of a mountain was just too great so my pilot decided to return to LS-48. After about an hour of flying time on the return trip, we looked for a hole in the clouds to descend through to get our bearings. Larry spotted one and corkscrewed the helicopter down through the hole and back onto the ground at LS-48.

Finally at dusk, we all departed for Sam Thong, LS-20, for the night, as the area we were in was too close to the enemy. Larry and I were transporting a Hmong soldier sick with what was believed to be malaria to LS-20 for medical treatment. The helicopters departed at the same time trying to stay under the weather but not in formation as the weather was worsening. We never made it to Sam Thong as visibility and darkness forced us all to land on the dirt air strip at Muong Soui which was under Neutralist control and supposedly friendly to the Americans. The Neutralists had changed loyalty several times during the conflict so you were never quite certain when they might switch to unfriendly again. All five of our helicopters and crews arrived safely at Muong Soui and under other circumstances we might have celebrated but everyone was feeling the stress of the day and the loss of Bill Wilmont.

While the pilots left to relax and eat dinner, the flight mechanics serviced their helicopters and readied them for the next day. It was then I noticed the sick soldier who had been babbling and wandering around had slipped away. He had been destined for LS-20 for medical treatment but we could not get there and there were no medical facilities at Muong Soui. I looked everywhere but he was gone. I had caught malaria within six months of arriving in Thailand. I knew how badly he felt. To this day, it bothers me that I could not have done more for him.

Our senior pilot, Marius Burke, had negotiated a place for us to sleep which was a decent tent with sufficient cots for all of us. After a dinner of my usual fare of beanie weenies from a can, I picked a cot and lay down. As the rain poured down on the tent, I lay there sleepless thinking of the events of the day, the ugly weather, the sick soldier, the loss of Wilmont and the fate of my friend, Matt Luca.

Matt never returned to flying. After recovery, Air America gave him a mechanic's job on fixed wing aircraft. After a few months, he returned to the U.S. He remains a good friend today.

Rusty Irons and Matt tell their stories of that day on pages 171 and 208, respectively.

Pilot Bill Wilmont in the cockpit. Gary Sizelove and Steve Nichols.

Wilmont was originally a flight mechanic with Air America. He returned to the US and got his helicopter pilot rating. He then returned to Air America as a pilot. He was a damned good pilot and would shoot full auto-rotations just because he enjoyed it. He died from enemy fire on May 19, 1966.

"Anything, Anytime, Anywhere, Professionally."

The Air America motto was "Anything, Anytime, Anywhere, Professionally." And we did just that. We picked up and delivered all kinds of cargo. We carried refugees, livestock, prisoners, food, supplies, dead bodies and ammunition all over Laos.

We carried some interesting cargo over the years. When carrying refugees, we invariably carried their livestock, usually pigs in burlap bags, cows and chickens.

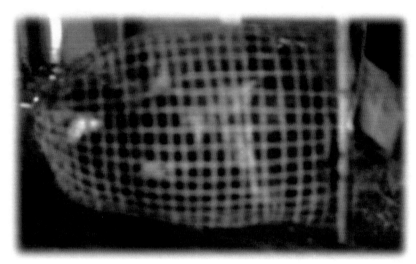

Lao chicken going to market by helicopter.
Chickens sold for $3.00
Photo courtesy of Rick Strba

Unfortunately as the helicopter goes up, the air pressure decreases and the livestock especially the cows crap all over the place. It can make for a very unpleasant trip, especially if the trip upcountry lasted a week and you had to sleep in the helicopter.

Most of the refugees, some of them pretty primitive people, had never ridden on or in anything before. For their first trip ever, we loaded them onto vibrating, bouncing helicopters. They would climb on scared to death, almost tearing my shirt sleeve at times as they grabbed on in terror. Some would run into the tail cone. I would have to go and bring them back out so that their weight did not affect the aircraft center of gravity. Most would sit on the floor as they did not know what the seats were for. One particular family, a couple with one child, stands out in my mind. They boarded at a remote site, climbed up onto the seat, huddled into a bunch sitting on their haunches and pulled a huge black cloth over their heads. They barely took up the space of one person. They remained that way until we landed again. I often wished I could alleviate their terror because to me flying was a thrill to be enjoyed, especially by the children. The children broke my heart and one of my few regrets about Laos is that I did not hand out much of anything to the kids.

Sometimes, trips could get boring so I would do little things to amuse myself. One time we were carrying just pigs in burlap bags. It was the second trip of pig cargo when I decided to set the pigs up in the seats so they couldn't escape from the bags and run into the tail cone. I placed each one on its butt on a seat and strapped it in. When we arrived, I opened the cargo door and there were all the pigs sitting in their seats. The Lao people were highly amused.

Then there was the dried fish trip from Ban Houei Sai to LS-118A. Oh, my goodness. We were carrying baskets of little dried fish about three inches long. The baskets were about four feet across and four inches deep and stacked one on top of each other. We took off and as helicopters do, it started to vibrate as it traveled to our destination. Shortly, I noticed that the floor of the helicopter was turning white. I looked closer and discovered there were freaking maggots shaking loose from the baskets. Millions of maggots were spreading across the floor from the dried fish. I said things a lot worse than, "Oh, crap." I raised my feet as high as I could off the floor for the rest of the trip. I decided to eat my own food that night.

One day I had this mischievous Lao soldier on board carrying about five jars of fish in some kind of red smelly sauce. The jars were cylinder shape, about two feet deep and ten inches wide. We were delivering them to five separate sites. As we traveled the kid opened a jar and dug his arm in almost up to his shoulder and removed the fish, leaving just the sauce. He put the fish into the fifth jar which he had set back from the others. He continued to do this with each jar.

The pilot called down, "Steve, what is that stink?"

"You wouldn't believe it," I answered back.

At each drop site, the kid handed off the jars of sauce, holding back the last one filled with the fish until he reached his stop and jumped off with his bounty. The grin on his face told the story. That night he was the winner.

Transporting prisoners was the most uncomfortable for me. I could not get used to having people five feet from me who wanted to kill me. Their hands were bound but that was it. The only thing between them and me was my AK-47 and believe me, I would have used it in a heartbeat. Another flight mechanic had a prisoner get loose and had to subdue him. The little Lao soldier who was supposed to be the guard climbed on top of the parts cabinet in the back. Fortunately the mechanic was big and burly and came out on top.

The most common cargo was a variety of supplies including rice and hard rice. I had a system of stacking the 105 howitzer rounds so that by removing the one cargo strap and using the rounds as a tread mill, I could unload 30 rounds real quick.

Sometimes I ate the rice. Living quarters at some of the sites like LS-36 were awful and food nonexistent. While upcountry, I lived on cold cans of beanie weenies, which as the week went by became almost unpalatable. Many mornings the first flight of the day from LS-36 was taking sacks of fresh steamy sticky rice out to the hilltop positions. A quick job with my trusty Randall knife and breakfast was served, and it was still warm.

On one occasion, we were delivering supplies to a variety of drop sites. In many cases, we could not land but would have to go low and slow to drop the supplies on a designated area. This day my pilot told me he was in a hurry and to drop the supplies as soon as we passed over. Well, he came in too high and too fast.

As soon as he passed the location, he called down, "Did you drop it?"

"No," I yelled back. "You were too high and too fast. Try lower and slower."

He was ticked. I think he had a hot date in Udorn that night. But there were people on the ground and I didn't want to kill anyone.

So he came around again, a little lower but not much, and I kicked the load out and watched below as the people at the drop site scrambled for cover. We repeated this exercise at the remainder of the sites. At each site, the people below were dodging and diving off the drop site platforms in fear for their lives. I don't think we killed anyone because Udorn did not receive any complaints from the customer.

Another time with a different pilot, we were finishing up after a long day upcountry and took off from LS-49 to drop off one bag of rice at a site marked with the letter I. The pilot was looking all over for the letter I marker but could not spot it.

"Steve, I can't find it," he said in frustration. We were both tired and ready to head home.

Shortly, I hear, "What the crap? I see it. It's about a hundred yards from where we took off."

I looked down. They could have carried it across a small brook in far less time and cost. My pilot was ripped.

"They want it in their tent. I'll give it to them. Steve, I want you to drop it right in the middle of that damn tent."

Now I was good at dropping rice. I had dropped tons of it and I knew I could hit the tent.

"I don't think that's a good idea," I responded. "There might be people in that tent."

"Drop it in the middle of the tent," was his firm reply.

Well, I just couldn't do it. I kicked it early and barely missed. They probably thought we were really good.

As I have said, we delivered a lot of goods throughout Laos during the war. In "CIA Air Operations in Laos 1955-1974" by William M. Leary, he states that during 1970 alone, Air America delivered an estimated 46 million pounds of food to the Lao people. Over the course of the war, we transported tens of thousands of troops and refugees and rescued downed airmen throughout Laos and North Vietnam.

We did one hell of a good job and I loved almost every minute of my involvement in it.

Steve Nichols, March 1966, H-33
Sleeping somewhere over Laos

The Laotian People

The Laotian people are kind, gentle souls. At the time they lived in primitive conditions and were highly superstitious. I recall landing in an area so remote that the tribe lived and dressed more like the ancient Papua New Guinea natives than Lao. We were chasing down a rumor that there was a downed pilot in the area. We landed very near the village but didn't shut down. The pilot kept the aircraft running near take off power while the customer went to talk with the local village chief.

As we waited, I noticed two warriors creeping up through the foot tall grass toward the tail of the aircraft. They looked like jungle cats as they slithered forward on their bellies, each holding a small crossbow.

"You see these guys, Steve?" my pilot asked quietly through the headset.

"Yeah, I'm watching them," I replied just as quietly with my AK-47 in my lap.

As they came near the underbelly of the aircraft which was kind of bouncing on the tail wheel, they would reach up to touch it. Each time they would pull back fearful of what I can only imagine. After three or four attempts they finally worked up the nerve to touch the fuselage.

The customer returned and we left as promptly as we had arrived and never returned. I expect the two warriors were glad to see us go as they could not figure out what or who we were. I was pretty happy to get out of there myself.

There was another incident indicative of the primitive thought process of the Lao natives that was told to me second hand. The communists were brutal people who, when overtaking an area, would behead the village chief and display his head on a spike for all to see. They would enslave the people as coolie labor and commit other unspeakable acts against the village population, facts never reported by Walter Cronkite.

This incident happened during a refugee evacuation of hundreds of Lao following a communist takeover of an area. The landing zone was extremely noisy as helicopters landed, loaded and took off. Amidst this bedlam and terror, there was a village leader gathering and talking to the people as they waited for their turn to board the running aircraft. The customer was impressed with his ability to keep order in utter chaos so he sent an interpreter over to the man to find out what he was telling the people.

It turns out he was explaining what he thought should be obvious to everyone. Once the aircraft was loaded and ready to go, the pilot, sitting up there in plain sight all by himself in an environment so noisy no one could possibly hear him, could be seen talking to someone. His lips were moving but there was no one there. Instantly as if by magic because the people on the ground couldn't see the left hand pull up on the collective stick, the aircraft would lift off and depart. The pilot was obviously asking Buddha to take them to a safe place. This was what he was telling the people and apparently they believed him.

Not only were the Lao people beautiful in their simplicity but the whole country was beautiful and teaming with history. Flying over it sometimes was just unbelievable. In one little valley that we flew over frequently, there was an old rusty tank, small, maybe French or Japanese. I know that it most likely had a great story behind it but we will never know what it was.

One memorable evening at Site 36 that I often think about occurred early on before the site was lost the first time. We had finished flying for the day. It was clear, no rain and the sun was still up. I was on top of the helicopter looking everything over and greasing everything that moved. The Lao people were playing their musical instruments and the sounds were everywhere. Amongst this incredible setting, the soldiers were firing off a 105 Howitzer sending the rounds directly over the top of the helicopter. I could hear the actual rounds as they hummed over head. It was really a rare and beautiful evening at LS-36.

On one great flying day, I was with pilot Mike Jarina and trainee flight mechanic Jim Agnew. We were loading out of LS-49 at Lak Sao at an old French landing strip with remnants of old cement or stone buildings. The roofs were gone but one had a date inscribed on it, something like 1917. Can you imagine being there in 1917?

We were transporting miscellaneous supplies to LS-85 which had an elevation of 5500 feet. Mike wanted to lighten the load in order to carry more cargo. We knew Agnew was doing fine so I stayed behind at LS-49 while they continued to transport the supplies. The landing strip was deserted except for a few Lao troops in the area. There was a small brook about 30 feet wide passing by so I found a shady spot on the bank and was lying there enjoying the peace and quiet.

I found myself watching a stream of small white butterflies landing in the mud. Apparently this mud-puddling phenomenon is common to some species of butterflies in Asia and according to Wikipedia is primarily restricted to the male butterfly. Nutrients such as salt are drawn from the mud and are provided as nuptial gifts for the females during mating.

As the minutes ticked by, the white clump of butterflies grew bigger and bigger. It grew to be about 15 to 20 inches across when I noticed a small Hmong boy, maybe seven or eight, skipping along the bank. Suddenly he spotted the butterflies and stopped in his tracks. He never saw me but I was watching him and I could almost read his mind. He sneaked up a few more steps and then leaped into the pile of butterflies. For a second or two, you could only see a cloud of white butterflies. That picture stays in my mind to this day. I only wish I could have captured it on camera.

Many of the places we went into seemed to have an abundance of kids running around. Even in the rain, you would land and here they would come, barefoot, unkempt, water dripping from their smiling faces - just happy kids. When you took off, they would jump in the air and let the rotor wash blow them back. Then we were gone. The biggest group of kids was always at the soccer field in Luang Prabang, L-54.

The Thai New Year begins mid-April at the beginning of the rainy season. For three to five days as part of the celebration, the Thai people throw water on each other in fun. The New Year is celebrated in Laos and Cambodia at roughly the same time. Most of us foreigners (farangs) found it hard to endure, especially when on a motorcycle. One day coming in to land at L-54, we noticed a group of young women washing clothes on the river bank. They were in the water up to their ankles. We circled around, dropped down very low and came in behind them. When they saw us, they scattered, jumping into the river. Payback is hell.

About the same time period, working out of L-54, we noticed a Thai T-28 pilot putting on his own little air show of various low flying escapades. When we came back in, we noticed a pile of debris on the runway. On closer examination, it appeared to be a T-28, or what was left of it. Apparently the Thai pilot had pulled up, straight up, stalled and couldn't recover. He hit straight down as everything was in a nice round debris field.

We gave him a ride back to Udorn. I rode upstairs.

As much as I loved the country, I have never gone back to visit Laos. In 2004, the book, "Sunsets, Bulldozers and Elephants: Twelve Years in Laos, The Stories I Never Told," was published by Howard Lewin. In his book, he tells of the helicopter accident in the Mekong which took the life of CIA Agent Louis Ojibway. He stated in the book that there were no survivors of the crash to which I took immediate exception, as I was a survivor of that crash. I contacted him and we talked at length about Laos. Not long after that he called me back to tell me he had just returned from Laos and that I would not believe the changes. The Country had been rebuilt and modernized. There were now numerous bridges crossing back and forth across the Mekong. The population had doubled but the average age was under 35 and no one even remembered the war. The people were just happy the American tourists were visiting their country and spending money. I am glad that I never went back. I left too many friends and memories there. It would be too hard.

My Thai house girl Aeed

Dick Conrad being greeted by the Lao children on the soccer field, Luang Prabang

To Fly or Not to Fly

I was in the Rendezvous Club having just lost back to back at 21 Aces. What are the odds of that? I had just wrecked my motorcycle that week. Was my luck running out? I had lost a lot of friends. What are the odds of flying for over two years as a flight mechanic, sometimes flying 200 hours a month, and not buying the farm?

I had just been offered the position of line chief on the ground at Udorn and I was debating with myself as to whether or not I wanted to stay on the ground. I loved flying. I loved the adventure. The irony in all of this was I had actually come here to earn money sufficient to buy a farm in Connecticut. I had that money now so did I really want to continue to risk it all for nothing but the thrill of flying? Air America was averaging one casualty a month at this point in the war. Life was becoming more precious to me.

Two flight mechanics had died recently and I was particularly bothered by them.

The first was Lowell Z. Pirkle, a family guy who didn't hang out at the bars much. He was ex-Army and therefore biased toward the performance and capability of the Huey. As the Sikorsky H-34 was my baby, he and I joked back and forth about Hueys versus H-34s. Ironically he died in an H-34.

Lowell was flying with pilot Charlie Weitz near Luang Prabang in August 1967. They were flying in supplies and transporting wounded troops out at a site on the side of a mountain. The area was under attack, and upon landing, the helicopter was struck by enemy fire and Lowell was hit and fell back into the helicopter. Weitz tried to lift off but the aircraft was too severely damaged so he abandoned his efforts and escaped from the aircraft with his co-pilot just before it was hit again and burst into flames. Lowell died from his injuries and the ensuing fire. The pilots and friendly troops escaped. The enemy overran the area and Lowell's remains were not recovered until 1995. On August 3, 1998, Lowell Zinn Pirkle was buried with honors at Arlington National Cemetery thirty one years, to the day, from the date of his death. Through his family's perseverance, he was buried at Arlington based on his two Purple Hearts while serving in the Army in Vietnam.

Earl Bruce was the second flight mechanic to die that August. His pilot chose to fly in particularly bad weather when most other pilots elected not to fly. Pilots could make these choices while flight mechanics did what they were asked. Their cargo that day, if I remember correctly, was 105 Howitzer rounds. The aircraft flew into the mountain and everyone died.

Earl had been with Air America for less than a year. He was a quiet kid who no one really got to know. It was his second crash in the short period he was with us. The first incident was an engine failure where the aircraft crashed and burned. Both he and the pilot survived although Earl suffered a broken arm. Like my own experiences, most serious incidents seem to have happened in the first six months. After that you learn that the pilot can't always take care of you. You need to look out for yourself.

At the end of December 1967, after much consideration and thought and after two and a half years of an awesome life, I opted to accept the position of line chief on the ground at Udorn.

Six months into the line chief job, I was called into the superintendent's office. John Aspinwall, the current superintendent, and Marius Burke, senior pilot for Air America, were there comfortably seated on an old weathered couch. I stood facing them wondering what the problem was.

"Steve," John addressed me, "We want you to take over the superintendent's job when I leave." He was taking a job with the company in Tachikawa, Japan.

My mind raced. This was a huge responsibility. John had been there for years. My present job required me to oversee the morning flight schedule and resolve problems that came up. If I couldn't resolve the problem, I bumped it up to the superintendent just as everyone else did. Now I would be the one fielding the multiple problems. The buck stopped there. Was I ready for this?

They took my hesitation as uncertainty, and John said, "We want you to do it."

What the hell, I thought. *If I don't like it, I'll quit and go back to flying.*

"Sure," I responded, "I'll do it." I felt confident knowing that I would have great people behind me including both the office staff and the maintenance people on the line and in the hangars. They were the best in the world.

I left the office that day feeling pretty proud of myself. There I was, twenty-six years old and Superintendent of Aircraft Maintenance/ Helicopters for Air America in Laos. Damn, it felt good.

From right: Flight mechanics Orville Mock and Johnny Sibal and Rico, an Air
America machinist/welder who was exceptional at his trade.
Photo courtesy of Orville Mock

Photo was taken in 1966 on a trip upcountry to recover several
crashed helicopters that were abandoned years earlier by the company.
Later they decided to recover the hulks and return them to Udorn.

There was an H-34 standing by to sling load the wrecks out after we
got the jungle cleared away. The area was more than likely not secure as
there was a helicopter nearby to pick us up if we had to leave in a hurry.

Chapter II
The Flight Mechanics' Stories

Flight Mechanic Tom Cournoyer

Flight Mechanic
Harold H. "Hal" Augustine

Dang and Hal Augustine
Udorn, Thailand

April 1966 to May 1974

My Time with Air America

I was stationed at Naval Air Station Los Alamitos, California, and nearing the end of my enlistment when I spotted an advertisement for helicopter flight mechanics for Southeast Asia in the Los Angeles Times. I showed it to a couple of the Marine Corps gunnery sergeants who were also stationed there. They had just returned from a tour of duty in Vietnam and they immediately knew that it was Air America.

I responded to the ad and received a telegram stating that if I were still interested in a position, I should call them. I called and Red Dawson hired me over the telephone pending a background check. I was an ideal candidate since I had been working on the Sikorsky H-34 helicopters for several years. After passing the background check, he called and asked if I could leave for Southeast Asia the day I got out of the Navy. He agreed to give me a couple of weeks to return to my hometown in Wisconsin and prepare for my departure.

Hal Augustine
1965 Green Bay, Wisconsin

I started my travel to Taipei on Easter Sunday, April 10, 1966. I was told that someone would meet me in Taipei, Tainan, Bangkok and Udorn. As it turned out, I was not met at any of those destinations. I arrived in Tainan and met with George Stubbs. The plan was to spend about a week there doing some sort of orientation. After about three days there, I was given my ticket to Bangkok.

I arrived in Bangkok with no one there to meet me. I started walking down the ramp with my suitcase and toolbox when a Volkswagen bus stopped to ask me where I was going. As it turned out this was an Air America crew bus. They took me to the office on Patpong Road. I was given a train ticket to Udorn the next day. I arrived in Udorn the following morning. There were no taxis at the train station. I ended up taking a samlor to the Air America gate where a guard got someone to come and pick me up.

I didn't spend much time in ground maintenance orientation since I had already been working on the same aircraft that I would be assigned to as a flight mechanic. My first flight upcountry was with Larry Wilderom and Dennis Griffith. This was to L-39, Savannakhet.

After approximately three years of flying, my new wife convinced me to request a ground position. A couple of her friends had lost their husband/boyfriends upcountry. I was initially given a maintenance crew chief position working for Steve Nichols and ultimately Jack Forney, two great guys to work for.

There was a decision made a short time later to start a flight mechanic training program primarily for Thais as well as a few Filipinos. It would also grow to include training for flight mechanics of all nationalities on new equipment introduced into the fleet. This included the Chinook CH-47C, Hughes 500 and the Sikorsky S-58T helicopters. I reported to John Rigel, a crusty retired Army/Air Force enlisted man who had served in WW2 as well as the Korean War. He was a highly decorated Army veteran who was at the battle of Anzio and was later wounded in the Korean War. It was at that time he was transferred to the U.S. Air Force. He was very unassuming and a no nonsense, no excuse guy.

I believe that the training of Thai flight mechanics became a priority for both economic as well as political capital with the Thai government. It also coincided with the hiring of Thai helicopter pilots. This did not particularly set well with some of the Filipino flight mechanic hopefuls. It also basically ended the hiring of American flight mechanics. The Filipino candidates enjoyed an edge over most of the Thais due to their English comprehension. Thais that failed the course would be sent back to their mechanic positions, whereas Filipinos would be sent home which indeed did happen on occasion. As I recall there was only one Thai flight mechanic prior to this program being started. One of the first students to complete the course was Manu Latloi, who was an excellent student. I had the impression that he wasn't overly thrilled about flying, however. He was convinced by someone to do it. He would later be killed in an upcountry accident with one of the Thai pilots who survived the crash. Overall I believe the program was successful and met its objectives. I do not recall how many personnel we trained. I know it was substantial. Several of the Thais that we trained went on to have very good careers after Air America ceased to exist. One of them is a Bell Technical Representative in Bangkok. Another is a helicopter engineer with EXXON in southern Thailand and another, a director of maintenance for a helicopter company in the U.S.

I was also sent to a base in Taiwan on a special project assignment to provide a maintenance course to Taiwanese military personnel on the Hughes 500. The only person to speak English was an officer who acted as an interpreter for the rest of the students. It proved to be quite frustrating. Upon completion of that course, I went to Tainan to give the same maintenance course to Air Asia maintenance personnel.

After approximately two years, I was transferred back to the flight mechanic department in the capacity of assistant chief flight mechanic. The duties involved proficiency check rides for flight mechanics, filling in for the chief flight mechanic, as well as routine scheduled flights.

Flight Mechanic Training Program Class, 1968
Standing: Hal Augustine
From left: Boonying Kongkeaw, Nopporn Pola-one,
Phichet Empremsin, Samran.

A Swim in the Mekong River Tributary

As I recall Steve Nichols and I were the only two ex-U.S. Navy flight mechanics when I arrived in Udorn. It is ironic that both of us were involved in a crash into the water. Steve's was much more serious than the one I was involved in.

In September 1967, John Ford and I were flying out of Savannakhet in H-47 in support of a USAID contract. The weather was particularly bad so we were flying at approximately 500 feet above the river using it as a point of reference. We had a load of 100-kilo bags of rice on board stacked in the doorway.

The engine suddenly backfired and went dead. John immediately executed an autorotation into the river. I remember kicking the first bag out which hit the water about the same time that we did. When the rotor blades contacted the water the aircraft ended up rolling to the left and sinking fast. Navy training had emphasized that you wait until the cabin fills up before attempting to exit the aircraft. This was to prevent you from being swept into the tail cone of the aircraft. I was prepared to do this until the aircraft momentarily hung up on something. I immediately exited the aircraft since the rotor blades were no longer turning. John exited about the same time. The aircraft then sank completely below the waterline. The only thing we retrieved from the aircraft was the Very pistol, a flare gun, which came floating out of the aircraft.

Neither one of us were wearing our survival vests, consequently no survival radio. We swam to shore and immediately went into an evading mode scurrying into a wooded area. This was because this particular area of Laos was no man's land. There were Royal Lao, Neutralists and Pathet Lao in the area.

We were due to transmit an ops normal report about the time of the crash. John did not have time to radio a mayday due to the rapidly changing events, probably the last thing on his mind at the time considering our altitude.

I don't remember how long we stayed undercover. Our hopes were that Air America would start a physical search for us since we had already missed our 30 minutes ops normal check in time. The Air America policy was that after one hour of non-reporting, a search and rescue situation would be initiated. Our location gave us a good view of the river. I don't recall how long we were in hiding.

We suddenly spotted a long boat coming down the river with uniformed military personnel on board. One of the soldiers standing up had an officer's rank. We decided to get their attention by firing a round from the Very pistol across their bow. It definitely succeeded. They started yelling and pulled over to the shore. As it turned out, they belonged to the Neutralist army. They took us back upriver to their encampment area where their first order of business was to run down a chicken, kill it and put it in the pot.

I don't recall how long we were there. They started talking about moving us to another location, which neither of us was too keen on doing.

I suddenly heard a fixed wing aircraft in our vicinity. It turned out that it was Lee Mullins in a Helio Courier. I grabbed the Very pistol and fired a shot in front of the aircraft. I think that it startled him as he made a hard bank away from our location. A short time later H-58 flown by pilot Vern Clarkson with flight mechanic Jim Petersen (aka brand X) swooped in to pick us up.

An attempt was made to recover the helicopter some time later after the river had subsided. Ironically, it was John Ford and I who slung the engine out. A U.S. Army CH-47A was dispatched from Vietnam to recover the airframe. It was rigged by Air America personnel. The helicopter was much heavier than anticipated due to the amount of silt that had washed into the airframe. The Chinook made several attempts to lift it out. It finally succeeded. It traveled a few kilometers at which time the sling failed and slapped up against the Chinook causing considerable damage. H-47 spiraled to the ground and was destroyed. It could have been disastrous had the sling contacted the Chinook rotors.

Inspection of the engine revealed a magneto shaft failure. There was a prior service bulletin published to prevent such occurrences. The U.S. Navy incorporated the bulletin, however the Army chose not to. The magneto's last shop visit was to an Army maintenance depot.

Can Chickens Fly?

I spent considerable time flying out of LS-118A where the infamous Tony Poe was assigned. I enjoyed working with him because he wouldn't send you to any place that he was not willing to go. The only downside was the dank, rat infested quarters that he provided as well as his drinking in the evening. I didn't mind his drinking. However he insisted that all participate. It was very rare that I drank while upcountry. I would try to sneak off after dinner to my bed. He would later throw on the lights and roust me out. His drink of choice was scotch, which I was not a fan of. He would pass the bottle and insist that we drink. I learned to blow back into the bottle causing bubbles that he mistook for swigging.

One afternoon after flying, Tony got into it with the pilot I was flying with. The pilot's name escapes me. The subject was 'can chickens fly?' Tony insisted they could while the pilot insisted they couldn't. A bet was made and it was decided that we would take a chicken up in the helicopter and toss him out approximately a thousand feet above the runway. I grabbed a big rooster and we spiraled up above the runway.

Upon reaching our assigned altitude, I threw the rooster out. He initially started frantically flapping his wings. His feathers were open with the air going through them. After a few seconds of that, he tucked his wings in and went into a death spiral. Tony lost the bet. I often wondered how much that experiment cost the U.S. Taxpayer.

A Dangerous Lapse of Judgment

In all organizations with a number of employees there are good and not so good maintenance, flight mechanics and pilots. The not-so-good pilots either knew their limitations, quit or were killed along with the crew and passengers. Overall, I believe that a large majority of the flight crews were above average and some excelled to the ranks of the likes of Scratch Kanach.

We were flying out of L-54, Luang Prabang and were instructed by the customer to fly to a landing zone (LZ) near Pakbang as I recall. We were briefed that it was a hot LZ and not to spend any time there. The load consisted of ammunition and one soldier.

I stacked the ammunition in the doorway of the helicopter in anticipation of a fast touchdown, kick the load and get out. We landed, ammo dumped and soldier kicked off. I suddenly heard the main rotor winding down. I looked and observed the pilot doing some paperwork.

The first recoilless round landed on the sloping side of the LZ throwing debris everywhere and killing the soldier that we had delivered. The main rotor speed was below takeoff RPM. It seemed like an eternity before we were able to lift off. The next round landed where we had been sitting. It blew holes in the main rotor blades and fuselage. We managed to limp off to a secure LZ a couple of kilometers away where the aircraft was grounded for rotor blade replacement prior to returning to Udorn for further battle damage repairs.

In Conclusion

After eight years and a bit more from that Easter Sunday in 1966 and more than 5,000 hours of flying time, it sadly ended. Air America was the greatest experience of my lifetime.

In early 1974, it became obvious that Air America's role in Laos was about over. The company allowed Bell Helicopter personnel to come to Udorn and interview employees for positions in Iran. I was offered a position of senior mechanic in Esfahan. I accepted knowing that Air America would be furloughing people within a few months, which indeed is what happened. My time with Air America was the most enjoyable and rewarding in my working career.

I went on to work for four other companies finally retiring from Rolls-Royce North America as a product support manager. They were all good companies but nothing compared to the camaraderie of Air America.

Dang and Hal Augustine

Flight Mechanic
Roger K. Burdwood

The only flight mechanic to shoot up his own helicopter, smack
Col. Vang Pao around and get puked on by a leper.

Roger Burdwood with his 1953
Austin Station Wagon
Udorn, Thailand
1966

Introduction

This is a collection of incidents I was involved in as a flight mechanic for Air America from the fall of 1965 to late summer 1967. I lived in Udorn, Thailand, and worked primarily upcountry in Laos. My job was to do routine maintenance and minor repair to the aircraft while upcountry, and I was also responsible for loading aircraft as per pilot's orders. Sometimes we had to mentally and quickly calculate the estimated weight of stuff as it was loaded. The aircraft involved was the Sikorsky UH-34D, generally considered the best piston powered helicopter ever built. It was a rugged and reliable machine and got the aircrews out of hundreds of tough situations.

Flight Mechanic in Training

As flight mechanics in training, we would go on several trips with an experienced man who would show us the ropes. My first trip to upcountry Laos was with Dennis Griffith on Christmas Eve 1965. Dennis was a conscientious guy from Minnesota. We spent the first night at Lima Site (LS)-20, a relatively safe area with decent living conditions. Lima Site was the method of identifying the many different places in Laos where we would work. This site served as a distribution point for whatever had to be distributed.

The second night we spent at LS-36, a site famous for problems with the bad guys. The living conditions here were horrendous. The "customer," the code name for CIA guys, and his USAID friend were drunk on their ass and did not inspire much confidence. One was Tony Poe the other, Pop Buell. These guys pretty much ran the show upcountry and were generally competent guys. In fact over time they both became legends in the war in Laos. But this day they were celebrating the Christmas holiday.

Dennis and I serviced the machine and had something to eat. I do not remember what. As it started to get dark, I heard machine gunfire and saw some flares in the not-so-far distance. This alarmed me to a considerable degree so I bugged the customers for some sort of firearm. They got me a beat up carbine. We all slept with our boots on and I slept with the carbine beside me. As I later found, that type of activity was pretty much routine for LS-36. Not long after that trip, we lost that site to the communists but got it back at a later date.

The rest of my first trip upcountry was routine, almost fun.

My second training trip was with a Filipino flight mechanic Joe Gaculias. I won't name the pilot, but he was a jerk. Things were going okay and I was sitting in the flight mechanic's seat. We were going to an area that apparently was not popular with the Lao soldiers. The landing area was particularly rough and out of the way. Upon landing, the pilot told me to load on just so many men. I opened the door and was immediately overwhelmed with guys who wanted to get the hell out of there. The pilot chewed me out, and Joe and I managed to unload a few against their will. The pilot wrote me up for this, which I thought was unfair due to my lack of experience and the panic these guys were experiencing.

Master Pilot

Herb Baker was one of the finest pilots at Air America but kind of a pain in the neck at times.

Like new flight mechanics, new pilots had to undergo training flights with senior pilots before flying on their own. This day Herb was training another new pilot also named Baker.

The new pilot was flying and apparently got into some kind of canyon.

Herb said, "Well, what are you going to do now?"

The guy answered, "Uh, well, I'm going to go there. No, maybe this way."

Herb said, "We're all dead. You have no idea what to do." He took the stick and got us out of whatever situation we were in.

Made me think some.

On the same trip, we were working out of LS- 203, Nam Bac. We took something to this small outpost with a "T" signal laid out. A "T" signal is a predetermined color coded signal set up between the customer and the pilot that tells a pilot that the area has not been overrun and it is safe to land. There had been some action there recently as we could see fresh mortar holes and several small fires.

We landed okay but we had to turn 180 degrees to get out. However, due to extreme heat and turbulence set up by some nearby small hills, we had little lift. Herb would pull in power, get a foot or so off the ground, and kick the pedal. The tail would move about six or eight feet. He did this several times before we were headed in the right direction.

Then he tried repeatedly to get off the ground far enough to nose over the hill and fly out. He would pull out all the stops, everything that old 1820 engine had, but could not quite make it.

I thought I would lighten the situation a bit and told him I knew how to get rid of 165 pounds.

He asked me how, and I said, "I'll get out of this son of a bitch and walk."

He said, "Shut the fuck up. I'll get us out of here." And he finally did, out through bushes and small trees, but we were flying and I was breathing again.

I don't believe that the majority of pilots could have pulled it off. Herb was a master.

Another Write Up

Pilot Larry Wilderom and I were taking a really big ball of rags to Vientiane in H-43, a brand new UH-34. Larry was a good pilot and a generally nice guy.

Halfway there I saw the rags were smoking. I grabbed the brand new fire extinguisher and applied it to the smoking area. It gave one very short phizit and died. We then made an emergency landing on the banks of the Mekong River. We looked things over and decided to make a run for Wattay air field. Larry called ahead to alert fire crews to the problem.

We landed on the side of the runway and I heard the sirens screaming as three or four fire type vehicles sped right by us to the end of the runway. Then they figured out where we were and came screaming back. One Chinese fireman with a respirator on jumped into the cabin with a big fire fighting device.

He looked at me and said, "Get out. This stuff is poisonous."

I said, "Right," and bailed out.

The whole thing was kind of a comedy act. The phrase, "As fucked up as a disorganized fire drill," came to mind.

Anyway, the problem started because the auxiliary power unit, which is a small gas engine powered generator in the back of the aircraft, did not have a shield on its muffler. This caused the rags to burn from the hot exhaust.

I got written up because I did not notice the missing shield. Never mind the defective fire extinguisher.

Another Nam Bac Tale

On this day, I was working with Hal Jowers, a competent pilot and nice guy but a bit of a risk taker. We landed at Nam Bac and Hal was taxiing way too fast, maybe 35 mph. Out of the blue, I heard what I thought was heavy automatic weapons fire, really close. I looked out the door and the air was full of pieces of aluminum.

I thought, *my God, we're being cut to pieces.*

In a tenth of a second, I saw that our rotor blades had cut into the nose of a Lao C-47 that was sitting perpendicular to the runway.

Wow, I've got to change four rotor blades, but I'm going to live.

As I started to breathe again, the customer, I think a USAID guy, came running up and screamed to get the hell out of there. The Lao air crew was way past being upset. They were threatening death and the customer said he could not control them.

I immediately got on the horn (intercom), and told Hal to lift off and leave. He said he couldn't because of the damage to the rotor blades. I told him it would probably at least fly, and it was better than getting shot. He said he didn't think things were that serious and shut down. Then the Lao pilots showed up, backed up by a couple dozen Lao soldiers. One guy ran up to Hal's window with his 45 drawn, cocked it, pointed it at Hal's head and pulled the trigger. There was no noise. He had neglected to jack a round into the chamber. He then threw some type of fruit at Hal and hit him in the helmet. About now Hal got the message that he had a problem. He asked me if I had a weapon with me. I said yes, I had a carbine with a 15 round clip and there were at least 30 soldiers out there. I asked with some sarcasm what he thought I should do. I was scared and really pissed that he had not taken off when we had a chance. So I said to hell with it and slid the door closed. By this time, the customer was getting things cooled off and they all went to look at the damage to the C-47. We waited for the rotor blades.

Shortly after installing the new rotor blades, either that day or the next, we started out very late in the day for a destination I cannot remember. It was really too late to go anywhere but Hal started out anyway. We flew cross country in absolute darkness for 25 or 30 minutes. You just don't do that in Laos. We had no navigational aids at all, nothing but dead reckoning. This means you keep track of airspeed, direction and time and hope you know what you're doing. I was in the co-pilot seat, really too tired to care. It had been a long day.

In the dark my eyes began playing tricks on me and I thought I could see tracer rounds coming at us. I finally decided it was sparks from the engine exhaust, which I'm sure was normal, but since I had never flown in pitch black before, it could have been anything. This was too much for the hierarchy in Udorn and Hal was canned for the combination of screw ups.

But yes, we got to where we were going with no problem.   His navigating was right on. As I said, he was a competent pilot but a bit of a risk taker.

Damaged C-47 at Nam Bac
Photo courtesy of MacAlan Thompson

One More Nam Bac Yarn

Nam Bac was under attack and it looked like the communists were winning. We were hauling all kinds of stuff out of there to L-54 at Luang Prabang.

In one load there was a wooden box about twenty inches square and six inches high with no cover. In the box there were about fifteen crude homemade hand grenades, probably made right in the jungle somewhere. They consisted of a cast iron ball about the size of a tennis ball with a hand carved wooden handle. I picked one up and looked for a pin or something that would activate it. I saw nothing at all. Some of them were wrapped with leaves in such a way as to form a protective layer over the ball. Some were not wrapped at all.

I pondered this for a short time. Then, aha! I got it.

These things were designed to be thrown and to go off when they hit something, thus the protective vegetation. But most of them were bare. I thought about the quality control that went into the manufacture of these things and didn't like what I came up with. Some of these might be a great deal more sensitive than others and I hate surprises. So I asked the pilot if I could just throw them out the door, carefully.

He said, "No, the customer might want to see what the other side was using." However, after landing and looking them over, he agreed, they should have gone overboard.

All's well that ends well.

Photo courtesy of MacAlan Thompson

Father Bouchard

Much has been written about Father Bouchard, the "walking priest" of Laos. Just a young man, his work to relieve the suffering of the Lao people was so highly regarded that the other side, the bad guys, reportedly had a price on his head.

Working out of Sam Thong, LS-20, he was in charge of relocating a leper colony. He asked us to take these people out to a spot of raw jungle and let them carve out a life for themselves with our help. So we made trip after trip carrying people and supplies to this designated spot.

They were very appreciative of our efforts. One old guy who had lost his fingers to the disease smiled at me on one trip and gave me the Buddhist symbol of hands together in front of his chest.

On another trip a young girl carrying a baby got on and sat opposite me. She was terrified. I smiled at her but that did nothing to ease her fears. A few minutes into the flight she barfed all over herself, the baby and me. She was upset of course, but I did not indicate to her that I was upset at all. Actually, I wasn't. It was just part of the job. The rice dried and I wiped it off.

After three or four days our job was done.

Father Bouchard came up to me after we shut down and said, "I suppose I could have told you when we started that there is no danger in being close to these people."

I said, "Yes, you could have told me that."

What the hell, the money was good.

"Someone Down There Doesn't Like Me"

Part of this job was going places where there were enemies like the Pathet Lao, the Lao communist forces. Some guys ran into North Vietnamese army people on occasion. I may have once.

My first experience with ground fire from enemy forces took place while working out of Luang Prabang, L-54. It wasn't very dramatic and I can't remember all the details.

We were fairly high up, maybe 2000 feet and were circling this one place. For whatever reason, the pilot did not elect to land and we went back to L-54. We did not know that we were being shot at, but when I checked the aircraft after landing, I found one rotor blade had two bullets still stuck in it about two feet apart. I figured the weapon's rate of fire was in sync with the rotor RPM which is why we did not hear it. Anyway, the helicopter, H-43, was a new machine, the same one we had the rag fire in a few weeks earlier. A blade was sent up from Udorn and because everything was new, the repair job didn't require tracking, a procedure which gets all the blades flying on the same level and was not my favorite job.

Tracking blades at that time meant standing just at the circle that the rotor blades travel, and holding this fixture so it would just barely hit the ends of the blades. The fixture called a tracking flag had a tough piece of fabric attached to it in such a way as to allow it to barely hit the blades. The blades had previously been marked with crayons on the end, a different color for each blade. this color would in turn mark the fabric and let you know if the blades were all on the same level. It took a delicate touch on the fixture. I wasn't too bad at it but still did not enjoy it.

So that was my first experience being shot up. It might have been more exciting if I had known we were being shot up at the time but fortunately I did not know about it until I was safely on the ground.

The second incident occurred when I was with John Tarn, a good pilot and a nice guy. I can't remember where we were but we were flying down through a valley, not far from trees close on either side. There were a half dozen Lao soldiers on board who all of a sudden started acting nervous and agitated, looking around all over the place. I had been hearing little popping noises in my earphones. Then, aha! I remembered someone saying that gunshots would sound like that.

Just then, John says, "The chip detector light is on." This is a sign of potential engine problems.

I said to him, "I have some more good news. They're shooting at us."

We got to where we were going shortly. Upon inspection of the helicopter, I found that a round had hit the lower pylon area, on my side, and at about the height of where I was sitting. If the shooter had been a teeny bit earlier on the trigger pull, I might have had another button hole.

The chip detector problem was not a problem. A small piece of metal had made the light come on which was normal wear on the engine, I think.

Those guys in the cabin with me must have thought I was a pretty brave guy. Little did they know.

Getting out of the valley was an interesting challenge as well. It was a steep climb, and the sides of the canyon were so close together that John had to fly thru a "tunnel" created by the trees growing on each side and growing into each other. I was looking ahead out the door and it was pretty thrilling.

The third time that I was aware of being a target was with pilot Mort Shearer. We were east of Savannakhet looking for wounded soldiers. I was sitting in the co-pilot seat as there was a trainee flight mechanic downstairs. Mort was not familiar with the area and got somewhat too far east. We came to a big valley quite flat on the bottom that had literally thousands of bomb craters. I couldn't believe it. Obviously something had been going on there that we wanted nothing to do with so we quickly turned back.

We came over another area that from our altitude looked like a pastoral farm scene with little white cottages and crops growing. All of a sudden there was this incredible noise, a kind of loud rattling noise. I thought the rotor head was coming apart until I caught a short, strong smell of cordite, gunpowder, and knew that someone was trying to do us serious damage. Mort pushed the stick ahead to gain some speed and we got the hell out of there.

As we fled the area unscathed, the flight mechanic downstairs said he had his carbine ready.

Mort replied, "Good, let's go back and get those bastards."

That lightened the situation and we had a good chuckle. Mort did say that he had seen an orange ball fly up just outside the rotor blades which was probably either 20 or 40 mm stuff. A solid hit from that stuff would have brought us down in flames.

We had a couple more shoot-um-ups at Nam Bac. We were loading some soldiers and ammunition. One guy passed in a dismounted 30 caliber machine gun. The guys all settled down in their seats with the gun between two of them. The butt was on the floor with the barrel up, resting on the top tube of the troop seat that held the flimsy seat fabric. The gun was within my reach, and just before we took off, I casually reached over and pushed the trigger. I have no idea why I did that, because unfortunately, there was a round in the chamber. The gun fired and hit the tube which in turn splintered and caused a hole about two inches in diameter in the outer skin of the aircraft. The pilot started pulling pitch, but I told him to relax. Unlike the fire incident, I had sense enough to lie thru my teeth this time, blaming it all on the soldiers. Of course all weapons were supposed to be cleared before coming aboard, which was impossible for the flight mechanic to check. Anyway, I cleared that one.

At another time with pilot Larry Wilderom, we were at a pretty active spot. We had just landed, and there was a guy in a trench five feet from me, shooting at something with a Browning automatic rifle. When I looked out, he looked at me as if I were awful brave or awful stupid. There was some outgoing mortar fire and I deduced the place was under attack. I passed that idea on to Larry. He agreed, and we left right away. I told Larry he was headed in the same direction the guy in the trench was shooting so he veered off. I don't think we unloaded whatever cargo we had that day.

Blood and Guts

The main idea of war is to hurt people and of course that is the result. We were not exposed to slaughter such as occurred in the Civil War, the Pacific Islands, and many, many other places. But we did see some horror and suffering as a routine part of the job.

My first introduction to the horrors to come was a young girl who had been wounded in several places by a hand grenade. Some of her people were "fishing" with grenades. Apparently the water was not deep enough and she was seriously injured. In spite of the severity of her wounds, she laid on the floor of our helicopter without complaint as we transported her to another site for medical treatment. I never found out if she survived.

Then there was the day we picked up a dead guy at LS-20A. He was wrapped in a shelter half and had been lying in the sun for a few days. Our job was to take him home, if we could find it. Boy this guy smelled bad, as bad as it gets. There is no smell worse than a decomposing human body. There he was, two feet from me. It was unbearable. I stuck my head out the door in the airstream and still it was bad. We flew around for an hour or less and couldn't find where he was supposed to go. So we brought him back to where we picked him up. I suppose they buried him around there.

Another time we were upcountry and got an urgent message from a porter pilot. He was on the verge of panic. He had landed on a very narrow strip on top of a ridge and unloaded his cargo. He needed to turn around to take off, and it was tricky due to lack of room. Some soldiers were trying to be helpful and were pushing the plane around. He was afraid they would push him over the side and was trying to deal with that. He said later he saw a guy run past the cabin window from rear to front. The next instant the windshield and most everything else was red. Even at idle, a turboprop turns at almost full RPM. He was afraid the dead guy's friends would blame him and do him harm. In the end, they didn't. They took the pieces of the unfortunate fellow down the side of the hill and buried them. I always wondered about the guys who had to come up and change the engines and clean the windshield good enough to see out. I saw the mess from a distance and that was close enough for me.

Another time we were called out to take a team to investigate an incident not far from Vientiane. Pogo Hunter was flying. We landed in a small clearing that looked like a logging road. The team walked up the road out of sight. We had shut down, and as I became bored, I went up the road to see what was going on. After a bit, I heard a loud buzzing. *What the hell was that?* As I came around the corner, a scene from Dante's Inferno came into view.

A large bulldozer had run over an extremely powerful landmine. It tore up the blade like a paper napkin, and the front top of the tractor, radiator, hood and everything was gone. The driver was still in his seat, head bent forward. The concussion had blown his eyes out, and there were two streams of gore from the sockets to his lap. In a tree there was an arm with a wristwatch on it, and other unidentifiable body parts were in the bushes. One guy was spread eagle on the ground. There were so many flies buzzing around that awful scene that they could be heard 75 or a 100 feet away.

There were a total of four or five people spread around, but they had never felt a thing. One of the team felt it was a strike from an aircraft, but it obviously was not.

When we got ready to leave, the helicopter engine wouldn't start because the electric fuel boost pump failed. I knew if we could get the engine started the mechanical pump would take over. The procedure to get it started was to pour a bit of gas into the carburetor inlet. I got some sort of small container, put a few ounces of fuel from the tank drains in it, got something to stand on, poured the fuel in the inlet and we started up with no problem. That was the first time I had ever done that procedure, and the whole time I was afraid the engine might backfire and blow flaming gas all over me. It could happen.

One time at Luang Prabang, we went to fire off the faithful 1820 engine but it would not turn over. A simple test showed the starter to be at fault. What to do? Waste a day's pay sitting around waiting for a new starter to be sent up? Or -- there were T-28s stationed there, and they used the same basic engine. The T-28 was a fighter type trainer that adapted well to brushfire wars and was flown largely by Lao pilots. There were also Air Force guys there to maintain them. I put my scrounging talents to work and talked a guy into trading a good starter for my bad one. There was a slight difference in the part that engaged the engine, but I swapped that out and started to remove the ailing unit.

About then a jeep drove up with a wounded Lao soldier draped over the back. Apparently he had stepped on a land mine and one of his calves was split from knee to ankle, a gash two inches deep in places. Two customers were arguing about how to treat him. One said that he had a better chance of living if doctor so and so cut his leg off. The other guy said, no, that his guy could save the leg. Then they left for a while.

As I looked at this guy, he seemed to be in shock, but was looking back at me. I thought of offering him a cigarette, but didn't. I felt guilty that I was okay and he wasn't and at any point I knew it could be me. I was very uncomfortable. In one direction, I had a routine mechanical job to do, and a few feet away, a young man was dying. I have no idea what happened to him ultimately, but I sincerely wished him well.

Not long before I left Air America, I was working with Danny Carson. I had not flown with him before and he was okay as far as I knew. In the late morning, we went to a hot spot, I cannot remember where. We picked up three or four recently killed soldiers. They were still bleeding. Fresh blood in quantity has a sickeningly sweet odor about it. I put my feet up on the flight mechanic seat to keep them clean. I made a sick comment to Danny that there must be a sharpshooter on the other side. Two of these guys were shot directly through the right eye. It was my attempt to lighten the mood that went over like a turd in a punch bowl.

We must have been working out of LS-20 because I was able to get a sandwich for lunch. Nowhere else that I can remember were we able to get lunch. It wasn't great, but it was food, and it was time to eat. But how could I eat with these guys lying at my feet? I thought it over a while and decided that I needed to eat. They did not. So I ate the sandwich.

After lunch we took off with the dead soldiers, taking them back to their village. When we arrived, Danny set the helicopter down on the side of a hill. The machine was off the ground on the door side, so we were about half flying, and the engine was roaring. One of the guys' mother was waiting there and wailing so loudly that I could hear her plainly over the noise of the engine.

All I could think was, "Here's your boy, lady. We don't need him anymore."

Some guys outside pulled the dead off the helicopter. One guy's arm caught on the edge of the door and they had to struggle a bit to get him out. We took off with me feeling guilty again because I was okay and they were not.

Most of us had come to Air America for the money. We quickly got caught up in the adventure, ladies and camaraderie. Towards the end, however, it became apparent to me that this was no joke. The work was hazardous and people were getting hurt. I usually eased my misgivings with large quantities of beer.

"Running Out of Airspeed, Altitude and Ideas"

Aircraft crashes were certainly not a rare thing at Air America. I was involved in one and witnessed several close calls of other unfortunates.

I was working with JJ McCauley, a good guy and very competent pilot. We were flying in H-43, the same helicopter that I had the rag fire in and two weeks later, was shot up in near Luang Prabang.

This day we were east of Luang Prabang, the more or less capitol of Laos. We were pretty light, carrying only a 75 recoilless rifle. Coming up a draw with hills on both sides, I again heard the old 1820 engine being asked for that which it did not have. Apparently a headwind was blowing down the draw and we did not have enough power to overcome it. There was no room or time to turn 180 degrees, so it was the oft repeated slogan, "Running out of airspeed, altitude and ideas, all at the same time."

It was not a violent crash and there were no injuries. The aircraft of course was beat up somewhat but looked repairable.

After assessing the damage to us and the machine, we decided to climb a hill to improve our chances of rescue. The elephant grass was eight feet high and very thick. You could be two feet from someone and never know he was there if he didn't move. I was exhausting myself trying to get through it until one of the Lao guys with me showed me how to get through it. Just stick a foot out ahead and flatten it a bit, step ahead a little, and keep repeating. It was slow progress, but we made it fifty yards or so to the top where it was, luckily, flat and clear. After twenty or thirty minutes, we heard a helicopter headed for us. Pilot Tom Pitkin was worried because he had not heard from us so he came back looking for us.

I got on the little emergency radio and directed him to our location and all ended well, except of course for H-43. It flew again after a few months, only to crash and be totaled later, I believe, at LS-110.

JJ gave me a good write up for this episode which I appreciated.

I went back the following day with pilot Tom Pitkin, a little guy and good pilot, and I was able to retrieve my toolbox. That wasn't the reason for going back however. I expect it had something to do with retrieving the recoilless rifle. It was a tricky place to land. In struggling up the hill with my toolbox, I almost put my head into the tail rotor blades.

The following day a helicopter was sent out to retrieve H-43. They crashed at the site. As I said, it was a tricky place to land.

Crashes and Near Misses

Pilot Steve Stevens, some Laos and I were required to remain over night at LS-50. This place was at the end of the world. There was a small shack with a rough plank bench to sleep on, no food or water at all, and it was getting chilly.

I could not face sleeping inside on those planks, so I elected to sleep in the machine. The troop seats had a brace every foot and a half, which was awfully uncomfortable. There happened to be an old parachute aboard, so I wrapped that around me and did the best I could. It was a very long night.

Sometime after getting up, a continental Porter made a landing approach. All there was to land on was a short uphill mud patch. He put it in reverse pitch about ten feet off the ground, against regulations. He hit the ground and didn't roll thirty feet. He was a hot pilot, but the next day he was dead.

He was buzzing somewhere around Long Tieng, LS-20A, and hit a guy-wire taking three or four feet off one wing. He went into a slow roll for a couple of miles, out of control. I figured he had about forty seconds to realize he was all done.

One day I was sitting perpendicular to the runway in the helicopter pilot's seat, changing an instrument, at Luang Prabang, L-54. A C-47 with oriental pilots touched down right in front of me on one wheel, then up on the other wheel and back again. I thought he had lost it for sure. He was headed off the runway where there was a group of forty or fifty people gathered. It looked like it was going to be a bloody mess, but he got a handle on it and straightened it out. Everyone gets lucky once in a while.

The next incident occurred when we were at site 48 on some operation which involved eight or ten helicopters but as I recall did not amount to much but it was fun.

This Air Force L-19, which looked brand new or freshly overhauled, landed for whatever reason, just to communicate, I suppose. But in landing he broke off his tail wheel. This still left a piece of spring steel to act as a skid and shouldn't have been that much of a problem. They got him manually turned around and headed in the right direction. The little airplane had a powerful engine and low pitched prop, like using low gear in your car. It should have been pretty routine, but it wasn't. He firewalled it and started his takeoff run, but he pulled back on the stick before he had flying speed. This lifted his front landing gear off the ground with the tail still firmly connected to the ground. Even then he could have saved the situation by reducing power and getting back to start another run. Instead he kept the power on and was coming down the field at 30-35 knots with the powerful engine keeping the wheels two or three feet off the ground. He drifted off to the right where there was a line of tents occupied by Lao soldiers. The soldiers scattered like chickens, and the tents were flying all over. I had a perfect view of the whole fiasco. He came to the end of the clearing, went down over a bank and out of sight. Air America personnel quickly followed. I handed a fire extinguisher to another flight mechanic and he left for the crash site. Nobody was hurt but the airplane was presumably destroyed as I never saw it again. However there must have been a badly bruised ego to pull a stunt like that in front of several dozen aviation people.

I can't remember where but there was another L-19 trying to leave a small grassy area. There was a storm front very close behind him, maybe 1/2 mile or so. He panicked and tried a downwind takeoff. He never made it. The last I saw of him he was off the end of the strip plowing through stumps and bushes. There must have been someone else there to pick him up as we just left.

I had not been working too long at Air America, and one month I was kind of short of flight hours. I went to complain to Marius Burke who was sitting in as chief pilot helicopter. He said okay, he'd fix me up and send me to LS-118A as there was always plenty of work there. So the next day, a pilot I will not name and I set out for the very northern part of Laos. It was a long flight, as I recall, over three hours. So we flew and flew while I snoozed downstairs. Then he called on the intercom and asked if I would recognize 118 if I saw it. I said no, I had never been there. He got to acting nervous and anxious, and I was getting pretty alert myself.

Shortly he said, "Oh, there it is. I think I see it." We headed for this dirt strip in the jungle and were less than a mile from it when he got on the radio to check things out. He was talking with another Air America pilot in the same general area. He described the place we were headed for to the other guy, and the guy started hollering.

"Don't land there! Don't go there. The place is in enemy hands."

I listened to this with intense interest, and was thinking, what the hell have I gotten into.

The other guy told us how to get to LS-118A, and we were there shortly.

After landing and walking to the living quarters, such as they were, the first person I met was the renowned Tony Poe. I won't elaborate on Tony. I expect others have. There is just too much to tell about that guy. Anyway, he waved this plastic baggie at me with what looked like pork rinds inside it.

He said, "Lookit this. Whaddaya think of these?"

I said, "What are they?"

He said, "Them's ears, Boy."

Seemed he paid a bounty on enemy ears to his local fighters. He complained he had to put a stop to it because they were taking ears where ever they could find them for the bounty. That was day one at LS-118A.

Day two was a normal, long workday lugging stuff and people around. Then it got late. It was dusk with less than 1/2 hour to total darkness when the pilot announced we were lost. Even as an inexperienced crew member, I knew this was not good. You don't fly helicopters in the dark in northern Laos or anywhere else in Laos. There is no way to tell where you are. So we went here and there, until he recognized something and got us back to 118A to my great relief.

Day three was a normal workday until we attempted to put some stuff on this mountain top outpost. It was like an upside down ice cream cone with the top flattened out to make a spot less than 40 feet in diameter with trenches around the perimeter. We would fly over about 50 feet above the outpost, and I would push out two or three boxes of ammunition. We were going too fast, and I had no practice doing this. The boxes would hit the top as the soldiers on the ground desperately tried to avoid getting hit. When the boxes hit, they bounced way the hell down the side of the steep slope. My pilot didn't want to slow down and did not trust his skill to land at this difficult place. So after a couple of tries, I decided that if I pushed the cargo out early, it would hit the side of the slope and bounce to the top. This worked with about one out of three boxes. When we were almost empty, he decided to land there. I guess he figured we were light enough by now.

He got the main landing gear on the pad, but the tail wheel was way out in space. He started to settle down and drop the tail wheel, which would have sent us rolling down the side of the hill to certain death. So I screamed not to do that, and we just took off.

I did get the rest of the load out of the ship. I do not remember any other adventures on this trip, but I had had enough already.

Odds and Ends

While the flight mechanics would stay upcountry for six or seven days, the pilots got relieved after three or four days. I was working with the first pilot on this particular trip delivering rice to this small village. It was a small circle of huts with straw roofs. These bags of rice weighed 44 kilos, or 88 pounds. I had little practice air dropping stuff, and there was not room enough to land. Soooo, I was a bit late pushing a bag out. It went right through the straw roof of one of the huts. Fast forward to the next day, to the same little village, with a new pilot.

There were certain well known tricks to staying alive in upcountry Laos. One of them was to avoid going near a spot where the native people were scattering rapidly when we approached. This could mean there were bad guys there waiting for us.

So the pilot says, "Oh oh, this doesn't look good. Those people are all running to beat hell."

I said, "Relax. They are just worried about my aiming skills."

I got the bag in between the huts this time and I have always hoped that no one got hurt the first time.

+++++++++++++++++++

I was flying with John Fonburg, a big quiet guy and good pilot. Up in the co-pilot seat with him was a training pilot. He was, of course, supposed to be learning all he could, but apparently he got bored and fell asleep.

I heard John ask, "Am I boring you?"

This guy was checked out shortly but he shouldn't have been. He killed himself and his young flight mechanic, a real nice kid, through some very poor judgment, flying in poor weather when more seasoned pilots were sitting it out. There was not much left of either of them. Someone asked our stoic Chinese Doctor Lee how he was going to separate the few remaining bones. He replied, three pounds in one bag, three pounds in another, very practical.

I should mention here that the H-34 was built largely of magnesium, which really, really burns, almost like a flare. On the first day of a tour to Luang Prabang, the bad guys had snuck in and rocketed two T-28's and one H-34, poor old H-F, the last lettered H-34 we had. Afterwards, there was mostly grayish-white ash lying where it had been, with a big lump where the engine had been, and another lump where the main transmission and rotor head remains were located. The rotor blades were lying on the ground where they had fallen, but the pylon, rear of the machine was still intact, lying on the ground. It was made of aluminum. I think Air America must have had a surplus of pylons, which is the rear upward sloping part of the machine that holds the tail rotor.

+++++++++++++++++++

The Bolovens Plateau in south central Laos was a magical place. It was surrounded on three sides by a steep high slope. I do not know now how big it was. Before the war the French used to grow coffee there. There were elephants, tigers, Sambar deer and other big game wandering around. We flew over a herd of 17 elephants. We were only a few hundred feet in the air. There were all sizes, big ones down to babies. We kind of panicked them so we didn't stay long. There were tigers there but I never saw one. However some of the other flight mechanics told of carrying fresh hides back to base camps from outposts. There were some big old circles in one place, not man-made. They may have been made by volcanoes or meteors. Who knows? There were many, at least five or six, high waterfalls which were spectacular. One is pictured on the Lao 600 kip note.

I was in the co-pilot seat taking movies of one of the waterfalls.

My pilot, Mort Shearer, said, "I'll give you some good views."

This one waterfall fell into a narrow canyon, where the other end was too narrow to fly through. In other words, once down in there, there was only one way out, straight up. I didn't like it. I quickly took some footage, and said, "Okay, let's get out of here."

Turns out, it was too dark in there and the movies didn't come out.

Lao 600 kip note depicting one of the Bolovens Plateau's Waterfalls

++++++++++

I was sitting in the door of the aircraft at Attapeu watching some native guys pump fuel into tanks. The fuel was in 55 gallon drums and we usually took three or four drums, which is a lot of pumping. They generally helped us with the pumping, except at site 110, which was neutralist territory. They did not help us there. We were lucky if they didn't shoot us. Neutralist didn't always mean neutral. Anyway, there were three or four guys taking turns pumping and all of a sudden they all jumped five feet in the air, stayed there for six or eight seconds, and landed. Well, not really, but they did do some fancy stepping. I indicated an interest in what had happened, and one of them took a stick and drew a squiggly line in the dirt indicating a snake had gone through. I never saw it, but they did and it was clear he was a bad snake. I didn't see a lot of snakes in Southeast Asia, and that was fine with me.

Going back to the "Neuts," George Carroll and I were at Site 110 fueling up in the rain one day with a bunch of neutralist soldiers under cover nearby watching us. George and I took turns pumping in the rain.

All of a sudden George started screaming at them. Something to the effect, "If you assholes think I'm here to be of any help to you, you're full of shit. I'm just here for the money." George continued in that vein, screaming at the top of his voice for a couple of minutes.

Then he calmed down and said, "There, they didn't understand a word, but I feel better."

++++++++++

This one day I was at Vientiane waiting to hitch a ride to LS-118 to replace a flight mechanic who was sick or hurt. I stood around the office at Vientiane until someone finally said, "Go hop on that C-47. He's going to 118. So I climbed aboard this old beat up World War II relic. It had a paratrooper's seat built in, and I couldn't help wondering what stories this old girl could tell.

There were two Chinese pilots, right out of "Terry and the Pirates." We didn't have much of a load, whatever it was. The pilots were pretty blasé. There was no greeting or welcome aboard. They were just doing their job. They likely couldn't speak English anyway.

As we approached 113, I could look ahead out the windshield and the dirt strip looked pretty small for this airplane. Amazingly they greased it in and I left them.

I also flew out of LS-20 on a C-123 and on a Caribou. You fly down the hill that was the runway for LS-20, off the end of the runway and make a tight climbing left turn. You're never more than 100 feet off the ground until you've made a 180 degree turn. It was thrilling to say the least. I knew one pilot on the C-123 and asked him about how tight this takeoff would be.

He said, "No problem as long as the fans keep turning."

++++++++++

I was working flood relief in Vientiane with Pappy Wright, bored and pissed because we were not making the big money. For whatever reason Pappy got our H-34 into a race with a Huey. We were low, wheels dragging thru the tree tops. The passengers were looking around and wondering what was going on. I put on my everything is normal face.

The Huey won, of course.

Later Pappy made a max performance climb, full bore down the runway, ten feet off the ground. He then pulled in all the pitch it would handle and we climbed like an elevator. The people on the ground were staring. I loved it.

++++++++++

John Burkholder and I were working the same flood relief on another day in Vientiane. We got off early one afternoon and went to the White Rose, a well known watering spot. This place was really, really well known and not in a good way. I have heard and read stories that make me blush. We were the only guys there that day with three or four really nice looking girls dressed in bras and panties. Nature took its course.

++++++++++

I once narrowly averted being in a crash in Attapeu when a certain pilot with a phony English accent went to impress some people on the ground with a fast low pass. There was a cable strung in our way. We just missed it with the machine standing on its tail.

++++++++++

We were returning from upcountry and got a radio message to stop in Vientiane to pick up a VIP.

We were in a dirty filthy helicopter with a dirty filthy flight mechanic in the cargo compartment which was pretty normal for several days upcountry. The dust and mud blew all over you every time you took off and landed and stuck to your uniform which was covered with oil and grease from maintaining the aircraft.

We landed at Vientiane and picked him up. It was the ambassador to Laos, William Sullivan. He was involved in war stuff and something was going on that required him to be in Udorn. So for the short flight he just sat there, and I was getting the log book caught up.

We landed and taxied to our parking space. He stood up and went to leave. I tried to slide the cargo door open. It opened about eight inches and would go no more. I pushed and shoved and said bad things. This was really embarrassing. So I lost it and gave the door a mighty boot, and open it did. It fell right on to the ground. Ambassador Sullivan was not abashed a bit. He just climbed off and walked away without saying a word. He was a real diplomat. Anyway, he was the only ambassador I ever saw.

+++++++++

We were assigned out of Pakse. We were sent to remain overnight at a place down in the southwest corner of Laos run by a customer called Doug. There were about five or six machines, as I recall, for a special mission. We were to take some troops and mortars up on some cliffs, where they would climb down rope ladders to the ledges and proceed to do their thing.

Doug had carefully planned this operation and was clearly thrilled by the idea of his guys climbing down the rope ladders. The flight crews were not. It puts a lot of strain on the engine and nerves to hover with no real ground effect.

That night we all slept in really close quarters in this small building - very close together. I happened to end up next to this big guy who farted and snored a lot. But we did have pancakes for breakfast, and that was really good.

We loaded up and off we went. We got to the assigned area, and my pilot, and I suppose all the others, found they could put one main wheel on the ledge, about a 45 degree slope, and support a lot of the weight that way, much safer and more stable. However I think Doug was really broken up because we didn't use his rope ladders.

Mission completed we returned to Pakse.

We found out later that they had spent all day mortaring a village that had been abandoned for two years. Your tax dollars at work. I think this was the same trip where Ed Reid set new standards of debauchery at a dismal little club in Pakse.

I Had a Good Run

We landed at LS-20A one day to pick up some people. A few of them were dressed in clean khakis. I figured they were a bunch of bureaucrats on tour.

Now the H-34 helicopter flies better with the weight, or load, as far forward as it is practical to get it. As most passengers did not speak English nor I Lao, I got in the habit of forcefully slapping people on the leg to get them to slide forward, which I did in this case. The armed guards did not like this and gave me some looks.

At this point, the pilot called down and said, "That's Vang Pao you got down there."

I instantly recognized the name. He was the most powerful man in free Laos. And I was smacking him around. I gave everyone a big toothy smile and things calmed down. Likely, I am the only flight mechanic to slap General Vang Pao around and get puked on by a leper.

Towards the end of my tour, we started putting native troops into the area of southeast Laos near the so called Sihanouk Trail to slow up enemy traffic on the road. It could have been touchy so the powers that be figured it was worth a little extra money for this duty. The flight mechanics got $50 each time we sat down, and the pilots got $100. I always wondered if that was because the pilots could get deader than we could.

My last day of flying was with Mick Prulhiere, a quiet guy and good pilot. We were pissed because they kept sending us from one place to another and we were not making so called "P" time which was $10 an hour extra for riskier areas. Anyway, we approached a mountain side pad on a pretty steep hill, and Mick was a bit low. We just barely made it on to the pad, even dented the ADF antenna housing on the bottom of the ship. No big deal except if we had been a foot or so lower, we would not have made it onto the pad and would have rolled end over end down the hill.

That night a good friend, who had been through a harrowing episode a short time earlier, and I got really drunk and we did something really stupid involving sub-machine guns and got sent home.

Drinking was a very popular activity there and I did more than my share of it. The Princess Bar was a favorite watering hole and shooting the Baht gun, a favorite activity. We were young and indestructible. There were pretty girls in abundance, lots of money and cheap booze. What more could a guy want?

The stories could go on I guess, but I have reached a point of diminishing returns. A few quick mentions is it for me.

There was the trip with pilot Ed Rudolfs and me where we were invited to the Royal Palace in Luang Prabang for a cold soda. During the same trip, Ed and I went across the Mekong with some Thai officials in a long skinny boat, to visit a grotto right on the river. The grotto was filled with hundreds of Buddhas. What a magical place.

At the end of the trip, Ed and I were in Vientiane on our way home. There was a bad thunderstorm in our way and Ed wanted to spend the night where we were. However, I had a new girlfriend in Udorn and really wanted to get back. Seven days in the wilds of Laos will do that to you.

I talked him into going, and we made it all right.

Air America was a unique experience for all of us. Lots of guys got hurt. Matt Luca had a close one, as did Willie Parker. Bob Bedell and Dennis Griffith were hurt and a lot of flight mechanics were killed. The best guys I ever worked with were there, and I will never forget them.

What is the truth? I would do it all again if I had the chance.

Roger Burdwood and friend Milly
with
1931 Model A Ford Roadster

Flight Mechanic
Khun Veera Champanil

"Champ"

Champ's Story

Champ was a flight mechanic at Udorn when I arrived in 1965 and he flew until 1971. He was the only Thai flight mechanic at Udorn until late in the war when more were selected and trained.

Champ hauled me into the helicopter the day of my rescue from the jungle following the crash into the Mekong river. I'll never forget the smile on his face as he pulled me up and into H-15. It was like being pulled from the jowls of death.

We worked together on several helicopter recoveries. Air America could not have had a more dedicated and professional employee.

I would guess that by the end of his career with Air America, he must have accumulated 15,000 hours of flight time. Talk about defying the odds. I thought I was lucky to have made 3000.

He gave me a terrible scare when I was superintendent of helicopter maintenance. I was in my office at Udorn looking out the window watching the work being performed on the second or third helicopter parked under my window. Champ was standing on the transmission service platform and inadvertently stepped backward and fell off, about ten feet to the ground. He hit the pavement and just laid there. I ran downstairs and found him out like a light. I sent for the doctor and when he arrived, he quickly revived Champ with smelling salts. After coming to, he seemed fine. I don't remember but I hope I gave him the rest of the day off.

The odds caught up with Champ on 17 February 1971. The following story by Fred Frahm appeared in the Air America Log, Volume 25-3, July, August, September 2008 Issue.

Air America Log

Khun Veera Champanil passed way Thursday, July 24, 2008, in Bangkok. Champ was a helicopter flight mechanic until he was badly injured when shot down with Bob Caron and Fred Frahm. Hal Miller, Ivor Graham and Ted Cash, along with several others, managed the rescue. Please see Fred's article dedicated to "Champ," because 17 February 71 was the day that changed his life forever. Editor

H71 February 1971 by Fred Frahm

This story began on the morning of 15 February 1971 with Bob Caron, Veera Champanil and me flying Hotel-71 from Udorn, Thailand, due north past Vientiane, Laos to the former Laotian capital of Luang Prabang. Except for the lousy weather the three hour trip was routine and uneventful - a complete contrast to what was to follow.

As we strode across the parking ramp at LP we saw Bill Johnson coming toward us headed for the C-123 that would soon take him back to Udorn. As he approached I could see his eyes were cocked up and to the left and his jaw rotated in the opposite direction - an expression of his I'd seen before that implied he didn't have very good news for us. As we drew together he spoke out of the corner of his mouth saying, "They're waiting for you inside for a briefing, but you'd better watch out for this one, they're putting a real shit sandwich together in there."

I had a lot of respect for Bill's judgment in these matters and didn't like what I'd just heard. Inside, the CIA customer was talking with Calvin Walker, the Continental Air Service's Baron pilot who was ready to take Bob on a recon to look for a couple of landing zones. They'd been waiting for us to arrive so Bob, who was now the senior helicopter pilot on site, could look over a few alternatives for a job that was coming up in the very near future - but I don't recall them mentioning anything that sounded like something I couldn't swallow, and it didn't seem appropriate to ask about it at the time. They were in a hurry to get going with the recon and I knew that as soon as Bob returned all would be revealed.

Because of the weather the recon was only a partial success and they returned without accomplishing their primary objective. Later that morning Bob told me what the objective had been and gave me a vivid description of the "shit sandwich" to which Bill had earlier referred.

Every day the Baron went out on the dawn patrol. On this particular morning Calvin spotted four guys in army fatigues waving their arms like crazy, obviously trying to get his attention. He returned to LP and reported to the customer what he'd seen and learned that a recon team of about a dozen Lao soldiers had been deposited in that area a week or two earlier. They'd been discovered by the Pathet Lao soon afterwards and had been on the run since then. It was now reasonable to think that those four men may be members of that team. What Bob and Calvin were attempting to ascertain that morning was whether that was indeed the case. Calvin was replaced that day or the next by a younger pilot, whose name I can't recall. The following morning (February 16th), due to the inclemency of the weather, another unsuccessful attempt was made to locate the four. But by the morning of the 17th the weather had greatly improved and they were able to locate their position once again. However, because the men had neither radio nor signal they could not be positively identified as the lost team members.

When these recon teams went walk-about they always had a radio and a few strips of red, orange, yellow or white cloth panels that could be displayed in a pre-arranged alphabetical signal that would identify them to the pilots who were either to resupply, or collect them. It was assumed that if these guys were split off from the rest of the team they were separated from the radio and signal as well. The only thing to do was to airmail a radio to them and check the results. They made another trip in the Baron with the radio, and took a Thai interpreter named Amnaj along to have a friendly chat with the boys on the ground - who, it turned out, spoke the right language, and favorably impressed the interpreter.

However, when they returned to LP Bob voiced his misgivings concerning the whole situation. Although Amnaj was confident that the men were who they claimed to be, and volunteered to go on the lead helicopter, it just looked, sounded and smelled a bit too fishy to be genuine. Bob noted that they were located on top of a horse shoe shaped ridgeline, and that their position was only about a mile and a half away from a village designated as LS (Lima Site) 188.

There was a well-worn path leading all along the ridge, and the entire area (approximately 25 miles in a direct line south of Dienbienphu, North Vietnam) was hostile to the government. In addition, the man they spoke with sounded just a bit too casual considering where he was, and the "deep shit" in which we presumed he would have been standing. But, after all things were considered, we caved in when the team's case officer (a customer rep) presented us with the ultimate guilt trip. If these guys actually were genuine, and we abandoned them after revealing their position, we were condemning them to certain death. Now what do you say after that except, "Saddle up."

There were three helicopters in the flight, and we started engines at 1410. Hotel-71 was leading, with H-73 in the number two slot, and H-64 designated as search and rescue. Since the LZ was covered with an estimated 7' to 8' tall elephant grass we intended to hoist two men into each of the first two helicopters while the SAR crew was on hand if needed. The Baron driver and an interpreter would provide a communication link between us and the guys on the ground, and three Lao piloted T-28s with the call-sign Mustang Blue, armed with guns and bombs for cover.

At 1505 we rendezvoused in the vicinity of the LZ and then spent 15 minutes trying to locate it. When we did the Baron made radio contact, one of the Tangos made a low, slow pass over it, and H-71 started a very slow, right-hand descent from 7500' directly over the zone.

In the early 1950s a schoolmate showed me a photo she'd taken of a road sign taken during the spring thaw somewhere on the Alaska-Canadian highway. The road that stretched through the pine forest was wet, muddy and deeply rutted, and the sign that stood beside it said, "Chose your rut carefully, you may be in it for the next 20 miles." As of 17 Feb 1971 I'd been in this helicopter rut for 7 years, and you can believe me when I tell you this was just one more addition to a long list of assignments I was not experiencing any joy in performing.

We'd left LP on a humanitarian mission to save the lives of four Lao soldiers for whom we felt a vague sense of responsibility. Each of us had made a personal decision to attempt this rescue during the briefing session and the only thing that could cause a cancellation of that commitment would be some evidence spotted in the LZ indicating it was a trap. Without such a sign there was no turning back.

We left LP with four on board. In addition to our crew of three there was the interpreter, Amnaj, who carried a radio in the hope he'd be able to make a last minute identification of these guys. We'd argued against him going along, citing the impossibility of him being able to make a positive identification in enough time for us to make a successful get-away if they weren't - and it just meant carrying excess weight, plus putting another man at risk, as well as further complicating the SAR phase of the operation if it came to that. For these reasons I'd always held a very strong dislike for having people on board who were not essential to the mission - but we were over-ruled by the customer and Amnaj came along for the ride.

The H-34 has a big, 9-cylinder radial engine in front, with a large cabin for troops and cargo behind it. The cockpit is above and slightly aft of the engine, and the pilot-in-command sits in the right seat so he can see what passes through the cabin door, as well as being able to see and operate the hoist mounted just above it. Looking out his side window, his attention intently fixed on the LZ, Bob kept us in a right-hand turn all the way down. Champanil with his Uzi, and Amnaj with an M-16, stood at the open cabin door searching for anything that looked suspicious. Filled with apprehension, I sat in the copilot's seat with an Uzi on my lap and, like the rest, hoped for the best, but anticipated the worst.   At around 100' above the zone Bob checked our descent and circled once or twice, giving it a final look to see if he could detect anything suspicious in the zone. None seen, he made an approach along the ridgeline, heading south, into the wind.

During all this time I never once saw the zone or the men we intended to pick up. Because the pilot in command, the hoist, and the cabin door were all on the right side of the aircraft the entire situation was biased to that side and the first indication I had that the shit had hit the fan was a great cloud of grey smoke rising above the engine compartment, immediately followed by a sudden descending, left-hand turn on the spot. Instantly I knew the smoke was from rapidly firing rifles, and that the engine, unable to swallow that much lead, was dead. As we turned 90 degrees to the LZ a swarm of bullets came buzzing through the cockpit, and time seemed to pass in slow motion as they shattered all the glass on the instrument panel in front of me. I saw the visor cover from my helmet pass before my eyes and didn't realize until a moment or two later, when the flow of blood from my forehead completely blinded my right eye, that I'd collected something in the turn. "Ooh shit," I said to myself, as we came down softly on the wheels. Bob and I looked at each other for a split second then each of us turned and bailed out of the cockpit. I just swung my feet out the window and jumped, crashing against the wheel strut on the way down.

We'd done a 180-degree turn before landing, and the bad guys were now on my side and still shooting. They seemed to have those guns from the old cowboy movies (the ones that never seemed to run out of bullets) and because of their proximity to us, the noise they made was all the more frightening. We were so close when they opened up on us I'm sure they had to duck as the nose and tail swapped ends and that big buzz saw of a tail rotor came their way.

At the cabin door I could see that Amnaj was intact and that Champ, although he'd taken a hit in the leg, was still on his feet and eager to make tracks. Without a moment's hesitation the four of us bolted straight ahead into the tall, thick grass, and a moment or two later Amnaj and I were separated from Bob and Champ by the shear density of it.

Trying to make a hasty getaway through a dense cover of elephant grass, with stalks as thick as a blacksmith's thumb, is not an easy task. You practically have to bulldoze your way through it, and then you leave a broken trail that anyone could easily follow. So when Amnaj and I stumbled onto what appeared to be a narrow, over-hung, animal trail, we abandoned our blind, headlong rush through the weeds and opted to follow it.

In 1965 I'd done a three-day jungle survival course at Subic Bay in the Philippines, but it was known to be a guided walk in the park and an excuse to get away from Vietnam for a week. It wasn't an attempt to simulate this sort of escape-and-evade situation and I suddenly realized how unprepared I really was for this. On the other hand, Amnaj had the appearance of a guy who'd had a lot of experience in this deadly cat-and-mouse game and for the first time I was glad he'd come along.

With him in the lead, we crouched down and slowly made our way along the trail that paralleled the ridge, frequently pausing and listening to determine whether we were being followed. We'd been creeping along the trail for about ten minutes when Amnaj turned and asked in a whisper, "You got a radio?" I shook my head from side-to-side, and jerking my thumb uphill, whispered, "It's in the helicopter." His face remained expressionless and his head nodded up and down a couple of times as he took in my reply.

A minute later he asked, "You got a map?" and shaking my head and indicating with my thumb, I again replied, "It's in the helicopter." Again, with an expressionless face, and his head nodding as he considered the news of yet another resource deficit, he silently slid a little further along the path. But we hadn't gone far when he again turned and asked, "You got a compass?" And the fact that I had to give another negative reply made me very uncomfortable - especially since a survival vest and radio were among the items I'd checked out of the Safety and Survival stores just before pre-flighting the helicopter back at Udorn.

There was a problem with the design and outfitting of the vests which made them heavy, hot, and generally uncomfortable to wear - and as a consequence, no one did. Instead, we subscribed to the unwise practice of dumping the survival gear in a heap behind the flight mechanic's seat at the cabin door with the expectation that when it came time to use the stuff the mechanic would simply stand at the door and pass out the vests, radios, and weapons in a calm and orderly manner. What we had now learned was that in this flight-for-life situation, with the guy in charge of our survival kits understandably distracted by a couple of bullet holes in his hide, and the very real likelihood of adding a few more to the collection, if it ain't on you when you bailout the window, you ain't gonna have it later when you really need it.

It was 1530 when I went out the window, and at 1545 I checked my watch to estimate how long the other aircraft would be able to stay with us. I figured they'd be able to stick around another 30-45 minutes before returning to LP to refuel and thought that as long as the aircraft were overhead we stood a better chance of getting away - that they'd distract the bad guys and perhaps help cover the sounds of our movement. When the planes left I expected the PL to get very serious about finding us.

By this time we were geographically oriented - we were on the east slope of the ridge (on the inside of the horseshoe) and could now look across the valley and see the village at LS-188. We decided (that is Amnaj formulated a plan, and I decided not to let him out of my sight) to continue down the slope another 25-30 yards, then turn south to parallel the ridge and eventually turn and climb to the top again, crossing to the west side before sundown. From there we would proceed to the valley below, then turn north toward the Nam U river, and hope to flag down the Baron in the morning. While my thoughts were busy with the moment-to-moment stuff my sidekick was already into tomorrow.

The Tangos began unloading their bombs, and when they ran out of bombs they started shooting up the area. Their attacks were returned by long, intense, bursts of automatic rifle fire from the top of the ridge to the south of us. And although we were headed in that direction we figured the Tangos were putting pressure on the bad guys who were probably moving a lot faster than we were. That thought was reinforced a few minutes later when we heard light, automatic fire that sounded farther away.

At 1615 I was aware of fast-movers (F-4 Phantoms) overhead. Then I saw a couple of A-1 Skyraiders (call sign Sandy), followed by an L-19 Bird Dog - the Air Force had joined the party. The FAC in the L-19 made a low-pass between us and LS-188 and collected a hole or two in the tail section from a burst of AK fire. Then a couple of Bells (HUEYs) and an H-34 arrived from the Plain de Jarres and the situation began to look a bit more cheerful for us - but only to the extent that we'd have aircraft on station to cover us, and we'd be able to get to the opposite side of the ridge before sunset. So we proceeded with that thought in mind, moving slowly and deliberately, stopping to hug the ground each time a plane dropped its bombs. The Sandys seemed to be bombing close to our position, and on one occasion a burst from their guns cut the air above us, and clipped the grass nearby. About a half hour later we were aware that the FAC was circling lower than the rest of the orbiting aircraft, and I used my Buck knife to cut off my T-shirt in case we needed something to attract his attention. A short time later the FAC descended to an even lower altitude and we debated the advisability of revealing our position before knowing whether it was safe to do so. Unsure of the security of our position we decided to stay hidden until we were more certain of the situation.

After three or four more orbits the FAC made a dive in our direction and I stood up and cautiously waved my T-shirt in the air as he passed only a few hundred feet in front of us. But he continued farther down the slope and out of sight. For a moment we were practically eyeball-to-eyeball and I thought, "If he'd been looking out his left side he may have seen us." Then he came around again and, since no one shot at him the first time, I waved my shirt a bit more enthusiastically. He came around a third time, and although he wasn't headed directly toward us, I was certain we'd been spotted. The helicopters began descending to a lower level and I could hear an H-34 continuing its descent nearby. It was in a right descending turn, and when it looked as though it was in position to make an approach to our location I was surprised to see it continue around and descend out of sight to a level on the slope below us. I figured the pilot must have spotted Bob as well, and it was more advantageous to get him first before coming to pick up Amnaj and me. I thought it must be Bob because the last time I saw Champ was at the cabin door when we all started down the slope together. While trying desperately to push through the thick grass he'd stumbled and fallen, and as he regained his footing it looked to me as though he'd been shot in the chest as well as the leg. About five minutes afterwards a dozen or so shots were fired above and slightly north of me, and I thought that Champ, slowed down by his wounds, had been found and killed.

I heard the increasing roar of the H-34's engine as it climbed away from its pickup and thought, "We're next," but it turned away and made another descent even farther down the slope. Amnaj kept asking whether I thought we'd been seen, and I repeatedly assured him of my conviction that we had. All the while the H-34 was making the pickups the Bells were flying directly overhead, not more than 100' above us. I could see the flight mechs leaning out their cabin doors and couldn't figure out why they didn't acknowledge my signal. They were flying east to west, toward the top of the ridge, and I thought perhaps they had seen us, and wanted us to move up the slope because the few small trees around us might complicate a hoist pickup. We then began a frustrating climb that almost put us in a panic. We would, literally, advance three steps and slide back two.

Until then I'd exhibited a sense of calm that I would not have expected under these circumstances. But with the possibility of rescue so near, and with the thought that perhaps we had not been seen at all, our progress up the hill seemed agonizingly slow. We couldn't have moved more than twenty feet up the slope before Amnaj found a near level spot and started beating down the grass to completely reveal our position. We simply spread our arms and fell forward, taking down as much of it as we could with each effort. And when the first Bell made a pass overhead I waved my T-shirt for the whole world to see. The helicopter made a right circling turn, and a moment later was in a hover directly above us with the jungle penetrator already on the way down.

Amnaj had asked me how we would be hoisted aboard the helicopter and I told him that if the H-34 made the pickup the horse-collar could only accommodate one of us at a time. But if the Bell came for us the penetrator could hold both of us if we needed to make a fast exit. Now 96-Whiskey was directly overhead, and the penetrator was on its way down. The flight mech had unfolded one of its arms to show us what to do with the other two, and as I scrambled aboard I reached for Amnaj but it was too late - I was already on the way up on the longest 30 second ride of my life. Dave Crowell reached out and helped me aboard, then sent the penetrator down for Amnaj. The last few minutes of this experience were just as dreadful as the first few. Although I didn't want to spend another moment in that place I didn't relish the thought of being so completely exposed and helpless while clinging to the hoist, and then to have to wait another eternity while the penetrator went down for my sidekick, who got caught in the branches of a dead tree on the way up. When he was finally hoisted aboard, we headed for LP. Hotel-63 was already on its way, and I was delighted to learn that Champ was on board along with Bob. I looked at my watch - it was 1730. We'd been on the ground exactly two hours.

Because of Champ's wounds, as soon as they arrived at LP the customer put him and Bob on a C-123 and sent them back to Udorn. When 96-Whiskey arrived a short time later, Amnaj and I jumped out, shook hands and said good bye – I never saw him again. At the customer's office I washed the blood from my face and hands, then downing three straight shots of his Black Label that never touched the sides of my throat. High on adrenalin, and now feeling quite refreshed from the wash-up, I changed into clean clothes, jumped in the Baron, and returned to Udorn where it all began just a few days earlier.

Bob was in the Chief Pilot's office when I arrived, and when I entered we just looked at each other in shocked amazement. "Where the hell have you been?" he asked, "You look like you just stepped out of the shower!" He wasn't far off the mark either - I'd cleaned up pretty well. By contrast, Bob looked like he'd just had a scrap with a tiger. His face and arms were all scratched, and his shirt and trousers torn and dirty. "What the hell happened to you?" I countered, and he told me how, as he had bulldozed his way blindly through the elephant grass he'd been cut up by its sharp edges. Aside from Bob's scrapes and scratches, and thirty-odd bullet bits in my forehead, plus a huge bruise on my left shoulder where I'd ricocheted off the wheel strut he and I had come out of it in pretty good shape. Whenever I think about it, however, I'm absolutely astounded he hadn't been filled full of holes by all the bullets that had zipped through his window. Unfortunately, Champ wasn't so lucky. He spent some time recovering in the hospital and when I saw him again about a year later his arm and hand were shriveled and useless due to nerve damage from his chest (or shoulder) wound. In spite of that, he told me he was happily working at The Suan Pakkad Palace Museum in Bangkok, and was very thankful to still be alive – and so were the rest of the crew.

Champ and Bob Caron's rescue is told by Bill Long on page 191.

Postscript: As a result of this being published in the Air America Log (the Air America Association's newsletter) it was translated into Thai and published in a similar association's newsletter in Thailand. Amnaj happens to be a member of that association and, via the internet we were able to exchange letters and photographs. We truly live in a small, small, wonderful world.

Flight Mechanic
Frank A. DeVito

Udorn, Thailand

March 1966 – September 1969

Introduction

While I was in the Army, I was an instructor on the UH-34D helicopter. This was where I first heard about Air America from another instructor, Robert E. Lee. The pay was very attractive, $652 per month plus $180 living expenses. This was 1966.

Following my discharge from the Army, I traveled to Washington, DC, and met with H. H. Dawson. He told me that flying in Laos involved delivering school and hospital supplies. He did not mention hard rice, the CIA code word for weapons or explosives. He did say, "But maybe a farmer would shoot at you because your helicopter scared his chickens." I figured out later when people were actually shooting at me that he must have been kidding. There were a lot of people shooting at me and they weren't farmers.

They flew me from New York to Thailand first class. During the flight, I started a conversation with the guy next to me whose name was Jim Agnew. We discovered shortly that we were going to the same country, same company and the same flight mechanic job.

The flight was pretty uneventful. I do remember being awakened at 11 p.m. and asked if I wanted another drink. I was impressed.

We were met by Air America personnel in Japan and Taiwan. When we got off the plane in Bangkok, there was nobody to meet us. We got to town with the help of an Air America employee in a blue uniform. Eventually we were told that we could take the night train to Udorn or wait a couple of days and catch the Air America shuttle flight. We decided to wait the few days and take the shuttle.

We flew up to Udorn, Thailand. When we got off the plane, I called Air America to pick us up. I told the guy behind the counter, some operations manager, that Jimmy and I were the new flight mechanics.

He said, "So what?"

So what! I thought, *we just traveled 7000 miles to be told, "So What!" This is some place.*

My First Day

Once we got to Udorn, they put us up in a Thai hotel in downtown Udorn with Thai beds and Thai bathrooms. I got to know the Air America routine in about two or three days.

I told Jimmy I was going back to the base where the Air America compound and Club Rendezvous were located to have a few drinks. I walked into the bar and found a spot at the end. There was a group of guys nearby talking about flying helicopters. One guy was saying that if the pad was under fire, he would go in.

"I would slip the helicopter sideways and go down at 1100 feet per minute," he was saying, or something close to it.

That's fast, I thought. *Great, he might get in but the helicopter would not fly out that fast.* That much I knew. I was thinking, *this guy is a fool.*

I didn't know anything about anything except the guy was wrong. How the hell would he get out?

Me and Mee
Udorn, Thailand

Memorable Moments

I was flying with pilot John Fonburg and co-pilot Dick Theriault. John was a very, very smooth pilot and Dick was pretty good as well. On the second or third day of flying together, Dick asked John what he would do if the engine failed. The mountains and jungles were all around us. I perked up my ears to hear the answer.

He hemmed a little and then gave his answer. I was sure Dick was hoping for RPM and power settings or how many feet above the ground he should flare it out, etc.

All John said was, "I would head for the green leafy stuff."

++++++++++

Ron Dubinsky and I were flying out of L-54, Luang Prabang. Nam Bac, LS-203, was under siege and we were asked to parachute in three loads of hard rice. I was concerned as I did not know when to push the parachutes out, wind drift and all that.

They told us that a DC-3 had tried to make the drop but they got shot up. This was a Lao DC-3 which cruises at 175 knots or so. Helicopters cruise at around 85 knots. Why us? It's not like we're faster.

They said a Lao would fly with us to help. So this soldier marched up, looking good, with a big set of paratrooper wings on his uniform. He looked "real" good.

We loaded the helicopter with three stacks of hard rice with parachutes on top and we took off for Nam Bac. About two minutes out from Nam Bac, I asked the paratrooper when should I push out the drop loads and about wind drift. He didn't know anything and neither did Ron. I dropped a roll of toilet paper out the door to check the wind drift. I don't know where it went.

The parachutes were attached to the D ring on the floor. I told Ron to be ready for a hit on the right side if they didn't open. I pushed the loads out, one at a time. The first two hit well outside the drop zone. The third one might have hit within the zone.

I passed this information to Ron. "At least they didn't shoot at us," was my comment.

"Why would they?" Ron said. "We just air dropped them two loads of hard rice."

++++++++++

Tom Hoppe and I were working out of Nam Bac, LS-203. Ed Rudolphs and flight mechanic Boxi Bukai were also working the same area. About 11 a.m. we were told to refuel and fly into North Vietnam for a search and rescue. Tom had the lead.

About thirty minutes into the flight Tom said, "Oops. Wrong valley."

Ed comes over the radio, "Whaddya mean, wrong valley?"

Tom answers, "That's Dien Bien Phu straight ahead."

So we turned right and flew towards the mountains around the valley. We spotted the A1E Skyraiders a few miles off and we flew towards them. We were about 5000 feet above the A1Es when Hoppe decided to lower the collective and get lower.

"Where are you going?" Ed asked.

"I'm going down by the A1Es where it will be nice and warm." They wouldn't shoot at us next to the A1Es.

So we flew down to 500 feet above the A1Es and got into a circle with them. We spotted the parachute and asked if we should go in for the pickup?

They responded, "No. The Jolly Green is twenty minutes out and they wanted to make the pick up."

In the early part of the war, Air America did most of the search and rescue over Laos because the Air Force was not permitted to fly into Laos, not even to save their own men. Additionally they didn't have the helicopters to do the job. That deficiency in their plan was corrected later on and they took over the rescues. Sometimes we rescued them anyway because Air America was right there in the middle of the action and time was always of the essence when you were down in enemy territory. There was talk of some animosity between Air America and the Air Force pilots. Some downed pilots had never been told of Air America's existence, hence, they did not know who we were and were reluctant to be rescued by an unmarked aircraft. Some pilots had been told that Air America pilots received a 10K bonus from the government for every pilot they rescued, which was totally untrue, but the Air Force pilots resented it and preferred not to be rescued by us. On the other hand there were plenty of rescued airmen who were extremely grateful, not caring who the hell pulled them out of harm's way.

This day we stayed put. The USAF Jolly Green made the pickup and we flew back to Nam Bac.

++++++++++

We were working at L-54, Luang Prabang, when we were told to stand by for a T-28 which was coming in with a "hung bomb," meaning the bomb was meant to be dropped but did not release and was just hanging down below the aircraft. We had been in the process of shuttling troops to a pad nearby and some of them were standing next to a rain ditch and were told to, "Take Cover." But everybody doesn't look at danger the same way. One guy was standing up with his fingers in his ears in case the bomb went off. You couldn't make this stuff up.

++++++++++

Working out of LS-36, Na Khang, pilot Ed Rudolph was told to take a guide and go to a new pad, drop off some hard rice and pick up the wounded. Ed had not been to the pad before and had never worked with this guide. So Ed flew out and he pushed the helicopter to the right.

The guide said, "No. No. No. Go Back."

Ed resumed course.

A few minutes later Ed pushed the helicopter to the left.

The guide said, "No. No. No."

Ed resumed course again.

So after testing him like this, Ed felt the guide must know where he was going.

Twenty minutes later, Ed spotted the pad. As he looked over the pad, he got the feeling that something wasn't quite right. He slowed down and set up an approach about 300 feet out.

The enemy below opened up on them.

Later I asked him, "What did the guide say?"

"Enemy. Enemy."

Ed didn't need the guide to tell him that was the enemy. There was plexiglas flying everywhere.

++++++++++

Pilot John Ford was flying with flight mechanic Frankie Claveria, an older Filipino guy. Frankie reported they were getting shot at. John asked where the fire was coming from hoping to hear a clock position.

Frankie answered, "It's coming from the ground, Captain."

++++++++++

A group of helicopters assigned to work the area were all shut down at LS-36 one day waiting for the rain to clear. There were several H-34Ds and Bell Huey 204s. We were gathered around one of the 204s where some of the crewmen were inside playing cards. One of the pilots started to complain about the LS-36 customer who thought he was carrying too light of a load.

With that, Dick Elder asked him if he knew where you would find sympathy in the dictionary.

The pilot didn't know.

Dick told him, "Between shit and syphilis."

You very seldom heard anyone getting cut any slack.

++++++++++

John Fonburg and I were flying out of LS-20A, Long Tieng. We were carrying four or five soldiers and some hard rice out to the area known as the Plain of Jars. This area was usually under the control of the Pathet Lao but we had very recently taken it back.

We were asked to take a load out to a forward pad. This was new ground for us. We were flying down the valley when John spotted some men on an outcropping 400 feet in front of us. So he called down to me to find out if they were the good guys or the bad guys. I asked one of the soldiers to stick his face out the door to see if they were good guys or bad guys. About that time, the guys on the outcropping opened up on us with small arms.

I pushed the mike button and asked John, "Does that answer your question?"

We zigged and zagged and got out of there.

+++++++++++

The super soldier. Dave Ankerburg and I were teamed up this day at L-11, Pakse. At about 10 a.m., we were told to fly this soldier and some fresh food out to a gun position across the Plateau du Bolovens. When we got there, we put the food and the soldier out and to our surprise the four soldiers who helped unload the helicopter jumped in. They gave me a thumbs up so we left.

Dave hit the mike button and said, "One soldier replacing the whole gun crew. He must be "Super Soldier."

Don't Take Off

Pilot Jim Williams and I along with Pilot Ed Rudolphs and his flight mechanic were working out of L-54, Luang Prabang. We each had a load and called the L-54 tower for clearance to take off. We were told to stand by and wait for a flight of three T-28s to land. So we turned the helicopter facing the runway to keep an eye on them. The next thing I knew Ed was coming around and his tail rotor and pylon were completely broken off and on the ground. I asked Ed years later, "What was your flight mechanic telling you?"

Ed said, he was looking out the back into open air and yelling, "Don't take off. Don't take off."

Well Ed didn't need the flight mechanic to tell him that. He had no tail rotor control and was facing up thirty degrees.

Ed had no explanation for the tail of his helicopter breaking off. Udorn maintenance never determined the cause of the incident. The aircraft was fresh out of overhaul with no signs of corrosion. It was disassembled and shipped back via C-123 to Udorn. Maintenance had it back in the air within two or three weeks.

Steve Nichols and Jack Eby, Maintenance Supervisor, inspecting H-33

Nakhon Phanom

We took off from Vientiane. We were scheduled to fly an infil out of Nakhon Phanom (NKP) Airbase. Infil meant putting troops in around the Ho Chi Minh trail behind enemy lines. Exfil meant picking them up which was far worse. You never knew what might be waiting for you at the pickup point. Sometimes it could even be a set up.

On this mission, there were three helicopters with two pilots each and one flight mechanic.

We landed at NKP and our three unmarked helicopters taxied to the spot the Air Force assigned to us. I have to say I liked taxiing through the ramp area. The Air Force mechanics who were working on their helicopters would always stop to look at us. It was great. I was out of the military and they were still in.

The pilots went to the briefing. I checked out my helicopter and topped it off with gas. Then I took off for the PX to have an ice cream soda.

About an hour later the pilots came back. Bing Bengtson who was the lead pilot got us all together. The first words out of his mouth were, "Boys, you better put your sleeping bags in the automatic position."

Now, it was against Air America rules to have a gun but everybody had two. We got around the rule by taking our guns apart and rolling them up in our sleeping bag. One time I was outside the operations area in Udorn where the aircrews park their bags before or after a trip upcountry. One bag really stood out. You could see the outline of an M-1 or carbine rolled up in the sleeping bag, standing tall.

Bing went on to tell us that there would be three propeller A1Es and four fast movers to cover our three helicopters. We never see the fast movers as they are in other air space.

Co-pilot Gene Rainville asked if we were going to Hanoi to plant the Globe and Anchor, a reference to the Marine Corps emblem.

We ran the mission flawlessly and not a shot was fired. But we were ready.

Steps to the Pak Ou
Caves overlooking
the Mekong River

Mee (Bear)

I bought a baby bear who I called Mee, the Thai word for bear, from a radio operator at the Luang Prabang landing site for $20.

I kept Mee for about two and a half years. She grew very, very big, and eventually she became too big to manage. I remember she kept tearing up her cage.

So one day, we packed her up and flew her upcountry to a safe haven and set her free.

In Conclusion

I would like to thank all of the pilots with whom I flew for bringing me home.

The maintenance people, Thai, Chinese and Filipino, in Udorn were great.

And to two men who nursed me through lots of "oops," Tom Kothe and Jimmy Hyder, thank you.

Stick pin given to me on a flight to Hong Kong on the Convair 888 known as The Golden Worm, circa 1967/68.

Flight Mechanic
Gary W. Gentz

Udorn, Thailand
February 15, 1966 - August 30, 1970
April 7, 1971 - June 15, 1974

Vietnam 1964

Introduction

I was born on January 21, 1945, in Postville, Iowa, to William and Jean Gentz. Except for six months in 1949, I lived in Iowa the first eighteen years of my life.

I lived in Giard, Iowa, from 1947 until October of 1956 where I attended a one-room country school until the seventh grade. We moved to Dubuque, Iowa, in October of 1956 where I attended 7th and 8th grade at St. Raphael's Grade School and then went to Loras Academy for my freshman year and Wahlert High School for my three remaining years of High School. After graduation, I worked on a farm until November of 1962 when I was laid off for the winter.

I enlisted in the Army in January of 1963 and went to Fort Knox for basic training and then to Fort Eustis for Single Engine-Single Rotor Helicopter School in April of 1963. After graduation in October, I went to Vietnam for 13 months, then to Fort Lewis, Washington, for my remaining time in the Army. I was honorably discharged on January 14th of 1966.

A month later on February 15, 1966, I went to Air America and was sent to Udorn. I was twenty-one years old.

Gary Gentz
Laos, 1967/68 Huey 205D

On a Wing and a Prayer

Compared to most who flew for Air America, my time in Laos was relatively uneventful. However, on one flight, I came very close to "buying the farm" and it had nothing to do with the enemy.

I was flying in an S-58T. Phil Peyton was the pilot and I forget who the co-pilot was but we were flying a mission to insert troops. The insertion point was south of L-108, Muong Soui, and we picked up the troops at LS 20A, Long Tieng. We had 12 troops on board and were holding at about 9,000 feet south of the landing zone because our air cover was not in position yet.

We had made about three orbits when we went into blade stall. Phil took the appropriate action to get us out of blade stall when all of a sudden one blade flew out of track which looked like about two feet. The 1 per vibration was very bad so I told Phil to drop the collective, which he was probably already doing. He called mayday and we started descending. The track was now about six inches out as we continued the descent.

The troops were all looking at me because with the blade being this far out of track, the vibration was pretty bad. I tried to look calm but I am not sure I was because I was pretty scared. We got about half way down to about 6,000 feet and I told Phil to pull in a little collective. When he did, the blade again flew out of track and the vibration really got bad.

By then we all figured out we had something very wrong with the rotor head or blade. I told Phil not to pull in the collective until the last possible minute but to let me know when we were about one minute from landing so I could get the troops in the door.

He had picked out an old hilltop site that was at about 3,000 feet above sea level. He told me we were one minute out so I got the troops as close to the door as I could get them, which did not take much effort. He made a real tight landing pattern and when he was on short final, I opened the door. When he pulled the collective, the vibration really intensified. Dust from the floor was flying around inside the helicopter and the vibration was REAL bad. I pointed out the door and told the troops to jump which they did. We were at about ten feet.

We made it to the ground finally, and my knees were really shaking. We shut down and immediately had other helicopters and fixed wing aircraft overhead.

I got up on the transmission platform and started looking over the head. We knew it had to be above the swash plate, since one blade was out of track. I really looked the head over but couldn't see anything wrong?????

We decided to fly down to LS-20A to get a main rotor blade and a tracking flag. We flew down in a Huey 205 and got the blade and one mechanic and flew the blade back to the site with it laying crosswise in the Huey with the trailing edge forward. We got back to the helicopter in about an hour. We tracked the blades and found the blue blade was six inches out of track at flat pitch. We quickly changed the blade and started the helicopter back up and we could see instantly that it was still out of track. I then got back up on the deck and REALLY looked over the head starting at the swash plate, pitch link and bolts and pitch horn. I got about half way up the horn when I saw a FAINT line across the horn. It had cracked!!! We then loaded up the removed blade and flew back to LS-20A and then back to Udorn.

Maintenance at Udorn got together a team to go back up the next day to change the pitch horn. I went on scheduled time off!

Apparently what had happened was the Army had overhauled the rotor head. The pitch horn had a steel sleeve in it which was pinned to the horn. Apparently, the Army was not removing the sleeve during overhaul and when they stripped the paint during the overhaul process, the stripper got between the pin and the horn that I believe was magnesium and caused corrosion to set in. So the crack started on the inside and when it had progressed far enough, it broke, but not totally, luckily for us.

Fresh Meat for the Troops

This event occurred during the floods of 1966 as I recall. The Mekong had overflowed its banks and the heavy rains had washed out many roads.

We departed Udorn and as we were flying past Vientiane, we were called by the operations manager to do a short mission. We were to fly to a Lao military camp that was east of Vientiane and pick up some fresh meat for some troops since the roads were washed out and the troops in the field were running out of food.

So we got the coordinates and the signal and found the camp in short order. We landed near the signal. I do not remember who the pilot was. After sitting on the ground for a few minutes, here came three troops being led by an officer. They were leading a small 300 to 400 pound water buffalo. They stopped 50 feet or so away from the helicopter and the officer pulled out his pistol. After a few more minutes of discussion, he shot the water buffalo between the eyes! However the buffalo did not go down. Instead all of his joints locked and he was standing as stiff as a board!

Now the discussion really got serious.

After a few more minutes, one of troops was sent away and came back with what looked like about an eight foot two by four. More discussion that was followed by the soldier hitting the water buffalo beside the head. All that managed to do was knock his eye out of his socket.

More discussion!!!

Apparently someone in one of the buildings was watching this and finally another officer came out and shot the buffalo behind the ear and he went down. We then loaded him after great effort and hauled it away to the troops.

Another success story!

The Flying Bear

We were working out of LS-85 when we got a radio call from the customer to go over to a pad east of 85 and pick up a bear. Charlie Weitz was the pilot. He asked for confirmation that we were to pick up a bear and it was confirmed.

We flew to the pad and landed. The troops had the bear in a large box. When they carried it to the helicopter, it would not fit inside the cabin of the Bell 205 crosswise as it was too wide. To do so, I would have had to remove the aft facing four-man seat and leave it on the pad. So instead, I loaded the box on the left side of the helicopter beside the transmission. It was sticking out of the side of the cabin into the air stream but most of it was solidly in the cabin. I secured the box the best I could and Charlie said he would fly as slow as he could. So off we went.

About five minutes into the flight, the box started moving. I guess the bear was getting excited and he was jumping around. All of a sudden, the top and left side of the box flew out of the helicopter. I quickly looked into the box and the bear looked back at me. I guess he got scared and started backing up.

At the same time I was telling Charlie what happened and to slow down. We were lucky the box top didn't hit the horizontal stabilizer, tail rotor or other part of the helicopter.

The helicopter slowed down but the bear backed up some more and slipped out of the aircraft. He was now standing on the skid tube.

Now it got like a Laurel and Hardy routine!

Charlie asked what was going on, why was I telling him to slow down and what was the bear doing?

He immediately started going to another pad in the area to land, why I am not sure. In any case the bear was getting tired and we weren't at the pad yet.

All the time, the questions and answers continued!

The bear had his claws into the plywood on the bottom of the box and was hanging on for dear life. Slowly but surely he started losing his grip. This was not good as we were not at the pad yet. I moved over to the door to watch the bear. We were now on short final approach to the pad. All of a sudden the bear slipped and let go, falling from about 50 feet. He was spread eagle as if he were trying to fly but SPLAT, he hit!

We landed at the pad. Some of the soldiers went down to the bear and the rest to the helicopter. I signaled for them to bring the bear up to the helicopter. Finally four of them brought the bear up. He was alive and his tongue was hanging out but he wasn't moving much, totally having the wind knocked out of him. So we loaded him onto the helicopter and flew on to LS-85. As we were landing, the soldiers came running to the helicopter in anticipation of seeing the bear. We landed, I opened the door, they looked at the bear, looked at me, looked at the bear and back at me. I signaled for them to take the bear out of the helicopter.

We took off. The customer called Charlie and he explained what had happened.

What was our motto? Oh yeah, "You call, we haul."

Another successful mission!

A REAL Rescue

I was flying in a Huey 205 with Dick Casterlin. We had stayed at LS-20A, Long Tieng, and were on our way to LS-85, Phou Pha Thi, with another Huey 204 piloted by Ted Cash. We were about ten minutes south of LS-85 when we heard a mayday that pilots were bailing out of an aircraft over LS-85.

We continued flying our route when we observed the parachutes in front of us. We circled the chutes until they were on the ground. One chute landed on the east side of a valley and the other landed on the west side.

Neither one of our aircraft had working rescue hoists.

Ted went after the pilot on the east side of the valley and he managed to get close enough to the ground that the pilot could get a hold of the skid and they got him on board.

The one on the west side landed in an area that had some relatively short jungle foliage but we couldn't get any lower than about ten feet. So I motioned to the pilot to hold tight and we flew up to LS-85 to get some rope and a person to help me pull the pilot on board. We flew back to the area and found the pilot with no problem. We tied a loop in the rope for the pilot to put his foot in and motioned to him what we were going to do.

I finally got a good look at the pilot and of course he looked to be about 6 foot 4 inches and about 250 pounds. I figured with all 190 pounds of me and the 140 pound Lao, we could hoist him up the ten feet. So we started pulling him up, we got him about half way up when the Lao got tired and sat down on the seat. There I was trying to hold the guy up. I managed to get my foot against one of the seat legs and screamed at the Lao to get back on the rope, which he did.

We finally got the airman up to where he could get a hold of the skid. This helped us to pull him up and he managed to get on the skid. We were then able to pull him on board.

Another successful Air America rescue!

The Bombing of Site 85

Site 85 was located near the top of Phou Pha Thi, a 5500 foot flat top mountain about fifteen miles from the North Vietnamese border. The Air Force built and staffed a radar installation on top of the mountain to assist in bombing raids on Hanoi and other key areas of North Vietnam.

On January 12, 1968, an attempt was made by communist forces to destroy the radar installation by attacking the site with four Russian colt bi-planes. During the raid, one of the colt bi-planes was shot down by an Air America flight mechanic from his Huey and a second bi-plane was brought down by ground fire from Site 85.

The shooting down of the Colt aircraft at LS- 85 was only part of the story. Most people never knew that Air America had people on the ground during this attack. This is that story.

It started in Udorn. I was flying in a Huey 204B with Phil Goddard as the pilot. Deadheading (hitching a ride) in the aircraft were Dick Elder and Norm Grammer. We were going to fly directly from Udorn to LS-85 where a "Special Mission" was scheduled for 3 p.m. that afternoon. Once we got ready for the mission, Dick was going to fly as pilot in command in the 205 that Ted Moore was currently flying and Norm was going to be the co-pilot in our aircraft.

As I recall, we arrived at LS-85 about 10 a.m. Since we had several hours to kill, I serviced the aircraft with fuel and after looking it over, Dick and I decided to take a tour of LS-85. We spent the next hour walking around the top of the mountain. We walked to the Air Force site but it was surrounded by barbwire so we weren't able to get to it. But we looked at everything else.

Pilot Dick Elder at crash site of a USAF CH-3 Jolly Green Aircraft, LS-85.

About 11 a.m., we got back to the customer's quarters and since I was getting hungry, I put a can of soup on the stove and laid down to read a Playboy.

Living quarters on top of Phou Pha Thi

About ten minutes later, I heard machine gunfire and a loud explosion! I jumped out of the bed and headed for the door. When I opened the door, I saw something burning about 50 feet in front of me and I heard an aircraft. I looked straight up and saw an aircraft flying north to south over the site. I knew this was not normal, so I headed for the helicopter to untie the main rotor blades.

As this was going on, the pilots were running to the helicopter. As I was untying the blades, I noticed machine gunfire hitting the ground about 50 yards in front of me and saw another aircraft coming in from the north. I got the blades untied and ran to an area west of the helipad and got down behind some logs. Dick was already there. I was lying down, and as the aircraft flew over, Dick stood up and starting shooting at it with his pistol! At the time it seemed very funny because through all the noise, I could hear the relatively slight sound of his pistol going off among all the other ground fire and noise.

By then, Phil had gotten the aircraft started and we ran to the helicopter. We got in the back and as Phil was getting the aircraft up to rotor speed, Dick climbed up into the co-pilot's seat. As we took off, we were right on the tail of one of the AN2s. Phil quickly closed the distance. I am not sure how close we were, but it was close, 100 feet or so.

He told me to get into position to shoot at it. I had to tell him I couldn't since my weapon was in the baggage compartment in the tail boom! In addition, I saw another AN2 aircraft coming in behind us. Since we were in a dive at high speed, it wasn't simply a matter of slowing down by climbing. With a Bell teetering rotor head, it takes a while to slow down and climb without losing the rotor head. In any case, we lost our chance to be heroes! We flew around long enough for everything to quiet down before we landed at LS-85 and refueled.

To this day, I think that three aircraft attacked LS-85 and according to the North Vietnamese, a fourth aircraft stood by in an orbit inside North Vietnam.

In any case, we found the aircraft that had crashed into the jungle and Phil managed to maneuver the helicopter down into the trees so I could take pictures of it. We could clearly see what looked like tubes in the burnt fuselage that held the bombs they dropped.

After this, we flew over to the other crash site and took more pictures. This aircraft appeared to have been flying low and looked like it clipped a tree and crashed.

We worked around LS-85 for the next three days.

We did not try to salvage the colt that was shot down by Glenn Woods as it was badly burned. We left it alone.

On the second aircraft that crashed into the trees, I winched up the three dead crew members from the aircraft. We flew them back to LS-36, Na Khang, and they were subsequently flown back to Vientiane where they were put on display. I also saw the HH-53 work to get the wreckage out of the crash site and back to LS-36. They had a hard time doing it because the aircraft was so heavy. They had to strip some of the gear before they could complete the mission. The customer gave me an AK-47 out of this aircraft.

AN2 Russian Colt Bi-plane Crash Scene

Shot up in Thailand

As I stated in one of my earlier stories, I was really pretty lucky as far as ground fire goes. An H-34 received a hole in one main rotor blade pocket from a shot from a Hmong rifle but other than that, I never received any bullet or shrapnel holes in Laos.

Thailand is another story.

I was flying a training mission out of Udorn in a Huey 204B with Frenchy Smith as the pilot. We were giving initial check out training to a new pilot. We took off and flew to the hills that were located about 20 miles southwest of Udorn so the new pilot could do a confined site landing. We made our first landing with no problem. But Frenchy decided that the landing area was not quite confined enough so he told the new guy to go about two hundred yards up the ridgeline where another more confined site was located.

We went around, and on short final, I slid out of my seat to look at the landing pad and open the door a little bit to clear the tail, when I noticed individuals walking down a path leading into the pad. Then I saw they had guns. We were about 50 feet in the air.

I told Frenchy to go around and just as he started to go around, they opened up on us. The aircraft was hit 16 times, the new pilot received a wound in his forehead from a piece of flying plexiglas but we had no other injuries.

We headed back to the base and declared a mayday and reported to Udorn flight information center what had happened. We landed on the Udorn taxiway so I could inspect the damage. I saw no fluid leaking and all the gauges were normal so we hovered back to the Air America ramp.

In the meanwhile, Wayne Knight, the Chief Pilot Rotorwing, had a Chinook dispatched to the Thai Border Police compound and they loaded up some border patrolmen and flew them over to the site.

Apparently the U.S. Ambassador took exception to this. I am not sure about the final outcome of the incident.

Landing at LS-32

Near the end of the fighting, we had lost all of the ground north of LS-20A, Long Tieng, except for LS-32, Boung Lam. This position was relatively well defended with a main position and all of these fingers running in different directions with defensive positions that could cover each other with defensive lines of fire.

Air America fixed wing aircraft dropped food and ammunition into the "bowl" of LS-32 and as long as they stayed in a tight pattern, they never took any ground fire. About once a week we would have to fly in and drop off some passengers (few) and pick up people who wanted to leave. At the time I was flying in the S-58T. We were on one of these missions to go pick up people. I was flying with Scratch Kanach, again not sure who the co-pilot was. On the S-58T we had a full door width step that you could kick open in order to facilitate loading. Some flight mechanics didn't like it because if you were rushed during the loading process, the people could overwhelm you. But I always told the pilot, don't pay any attention to what you see outside the door, when I say go, GO!

Another problem we had was that when we descended into the bowl of LS-32, the enemy starting shooting in with mortars and other artillery. But once we descended below the lip of the bowl, they didn't know where we were going to land and since the area was very large, we had many landing spots.

In any case, this flight in and landing were uneventful. Scratch asked for eight passengers so when I got five on board, I told him to leave but he hesitated because he saw this mob outside the door. I finally screamed at him to takeoff. By the time I pulled the last one on board we had twelve, or so I THOUGHT! I had pulled the door closed but when I opened it a little bit so I could watch the ground for ground fire, I observed this old beetle nut chewing lady holding on to the step for dear life. I looked at her for a second then decided in a fit of compassion to go get her. I had to open the door all the way since she was at the back end of the step dangling off the back end. As I stepped onto the step to grab hold of her, I slipped and almost went out the door. That really pissed me off. I started screaming at her and reached down and pulled her on board.

Scratch wanted to know what was going on and I told him. Needless to say we had a talk after we landed back at LS-20A.

Plain of Jars Area

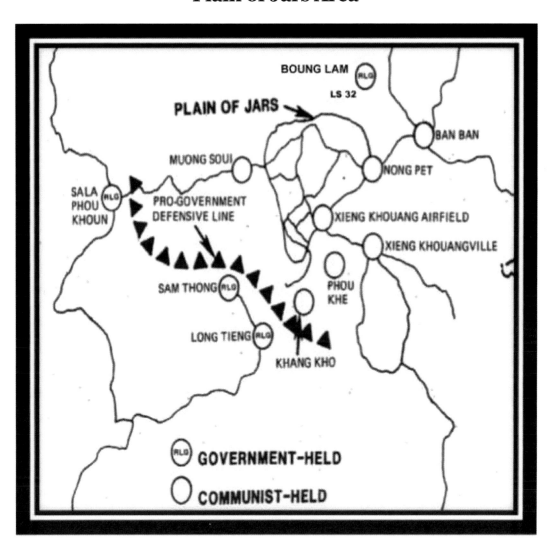

Based on an unclassified map in the National Security Archive
The War in Northern Laos, Victor B. Anthony and Richard R. Sexton
Center for Air Force History, MORI DocID 1255435

Flight Mechanic
Dennis L. Griffith

Udorn, Thailand
Summer 1965 – Summer 1967

Like most of us at Air America, I got my helicopter maintenance experience with the military. I served with the U.S. Army in Germany during the early years of the Berlin Wall. Upon discharge, I returned to Minnesota where I spotted the ad for flight mechanics with Air America. I applied and the rest is history.

These are my stories.

Under Attack

I remember a night at what I believe was LS-20, Sam Thong. There was a landing strip there, long enough for a large aircraft like a Caribou or C-123. We felt lucky to be there because they had a place to eat, a bed and a shower which was the best you could get in Laos, in my opinion, of course.

This night it had rained some and the laterite mud was yellow and really sticky and I was quite dirty. Along with our crew, there were a couple of fixed wing pilots remaining overnight at the site.

After refueling and completing the daily maintenance on my aircraft, I noticed the clouds were clearing and the moon was getting close to full. It was going to be nice tomorrow.

I thought that I would take a shower, go eat and then go to bed.

I checked out the shower and found that it was not what I wanted as it was not even warm. So I washed my hands and face and went to eat. I had a quick meal, checked the shower again which was now good enough. I climbed in, started to relax and hoped the hot water would hold out.

About two minutes into the shower, I heard gunfire. A firefight had started on the strip where the loads and stuff for the next day were kept. I could hear automatic fire and regular rifle shots.

That was enough for me.

I ran for the light switch knowing the bad guys would be coming and quite fast. Americans were top targets and there were several of us there to take.

One thing I found out was if you're wet it's very hard to dress, especially to pull socks on. My toes had kinks in them and then I jammed them into my boots. They hurt but that was minor. I could stand that. I knew, if I had to run through the jungle, I needed boots and I was in the survival mode.

It seemed to take forever to dress but I was finally ready.

The gunfire had increased and it was quite steady.

I left the shower building very low, sliding sideways through the door. I looked around for a good way to clear the area and noticed the lights on in the kitchen. The two fixed wing pilots were sitting at a table. I couldn't see what they were doing but they didn't look like I felt.

I thought if they're here and sitting in the light, I better connect up with them. Maybe we could leave together.

I eased toward the steps staying in the dark as long as possible. I went up the steps and sideways through the door.

I didn't know what to think when I got inside.

The two pilots were playing cards and the kitchen crew was cleaning up, getting ready for morning.

I cleared my throat and nonchalantly asked, "What's going on?"

One of the pilots answered, "There's an eclipse of the moon tonight. The indigenous people believe that a frog is eating the moon. If they make a lot of noise and scare the frog away, they save the moon."

I had a cup of coffee and went to bed.

Mortar Fire

Our assignment this day was to retrieve a wrecked Helio Courier aircraft. There were two helicopters participating in the mission. Our helicopter carried a few mechanics and their toolboxes. The other helicopter met us at the site. I'm not sure what their load was.

Coming in, we overshot the strip where the wreck was sitting and my pilot noticed where a couple of heavy shells had hit close to the aircraft on the strip.

After a little thought, my pilot decided to land on a knoll where a group of friendly soldiers had dug trenches and set up camp. When we landed the mechanics grabbed their toolboxes and took the trail to the airstrip.

The soldiers in the meantime indicated they needed rice and were hungry. So my pilot let the other helicopter pilot know and he left for food at another strip close by.

My pilot and I stayed by the helicopter watching the mechanics as they reached the wreck and started to dismantle it.

Soon, a couple of soldiers walked up to where we were and one of them held his arm up and made a quarter circle on his arm and pointed across the valley. My pilot and I couldn't figure out what he wanted and he could tell we couldn't, so he tried again. This time he held up his hand, opened and closed it three times and pointed across the valley. There was still no breakthrough. We were quite dumbfounded.

Shortly, we had an awakening that was real. A mortar round was on its way from across the valley. Everything was crystal clear now. The quarter circle he had drawn on his arm was in fifteen minutes they would start shooting.

Everybody at the helicopter was gone in a flash including the pilot and me, the flight mechanic. A trench in the ground was the place to be and we were as fast as anyone.

The shell hit close but not on target yet. Everyone sat up, popped their heads out and looked around. For some reason, I thought of prairie dogs but not for long.

"Head for the chopper," my pilot yelled. And we left our new friends in a hurry.

The pilot was cranking up the engine as I heard another shell coming in. The hit was off target but better.

The other helicopter was now over head with the food. So my pilot had him fly toward the mortar position as if we were calling in an airstrike. It worked. There were no more shells.

Then we looked around for the mechanics who had been with the wreck. We could see them coming up the trail but we didn't wait on the hill.

We moved to a spot down the trail that was good to go. We picked up everyone minus the toolboxes and sailed off for a different spot.

I really don't know if that little band of soldiers ever got their rice. I sure hope so.

A Tragic Incident

November 8, 1966, was just another day of load and deliver. We were working out of Nam Bac, an area we had recently taken from the Pathet Lao. It was the normal repetitious work that we did other than pump gas.

We had loaded quite a bit of heavier munitions onto H-41 when my pilot, Larry Wilderom, came up on the intercom and said we would have two passengers. Two young sons of John Perry, USAID coordinator for the area, wanted to ride along and see what we did. They were about eighteen or nineteen years old. We were not real heavy with stuff so the additional weight was no problem. They both climbed aboard, one in the co-pilot's seat and the other on the opposite side of the helicopter in the cargo hold with me.

The site we flew to was not far by helicopter. We circled the landing area and could see the signal indicating it was safe to land staked to the ground. The usual procedure for the signal was to lay it on the ground and then pick it up prior to the helicopter landing but staking it wasn't that strange because a lot of the safer sites did that to keep the signal from blowing up into the rotor blades when the helicopter landed.

We landed on the strip at the far end and started to taxi toward the encampment area. I thought that kind of strange. We normally off loaded where we set down, and the troops collected the load and dispersed it. This wasn't a normal delivery but I didn't know why. I just wanted to dump and go.

We hadn't been on the ground but a short time when the shooting started.

Larry turned the helicopter toward the right and was getting airborne. When the left side was exposed to the bad guys, the passenger sitting opposite me was shot through the side of the helicopter through his back into his stomach. I also felt something shake my back when we were turning. I felt no pain and the adrenalin rush was on.

I could tell the helicopter wasn't moving that well but we were leaving. That was good enough for me. As we left, the underside of the helicopter was exposed and I could see wood flying around in the cargo hold from the sheet of plywood that was always on the floor to protect it from the cargo we moved every day.

I thought of trying to help the boy that was wounded and then I felt my leg shake. I saw a little blood but no pain. The bad guys were aiming at the middle of the helicopter and not the area where the mechanics sat.

Mechanics always sat looking backwards and it entered my mind that I wouldn't know which way to run if we crashed and survived. I never saw where we were going, just where we had been.

The bullets stopped coming through the floor and I couldn't hear any more gunfire. I tried talking with Larry on the intercom, to no avail. Some of the radios were shot out.

I stood up and helped the boy across from me lie down on the seat. He really didn't look that good.

I also wrote a note to Larry which said, "You OK?"

He wrote back, "OK."

Now the short trip out was four times as long going back.

I heard Larry on the radio with a mayday. I realized only the intercom didn't work, or at least I hoped.

When we got back to Nam Bac, Larry set up to land and the engine quit.

Autorotation was required and we were doing fine. We flared for the landing and the engine fired up again. Torque took over and we landed going sideways, almost tipping over on the ground.

I thought if I jump out I also have a good chance to die. Sometimes the main gearboxes on choppers break loose and come through the cabin section. Then you have the main rotor blades, all 54 feet of them, to deal with. I stood at the edge of the door for just seconds before my better judgment took hold. Then I felt the helicopter rocking back down, stopping right side up.

Larry told me later that when the engine died on landing, he held the power setting at what he had and didn't back the throttle off. When we flared, pulling the nose up caused the engine to restart adding all that torque to our situation.

We landed and I tried to get the boy out that was with me. No luck. I wasn't sure of his status. I hoped he had only passed out.

Help was arriving now. Another helicopter piloted by George Carroll was with us part of the way back having heard our mayday.

He parked and helped us get the boy from the co-pilot's seat out. He too had been shot in the stomach.

A bullet had come through the pilot's side and hit the heel of Larry's boot.

Things were starting to calm down some at this time. George Carroll was asked to donate blood. I do not know who else was asked. I wasn't.

In the end, George did not have to donate blood. The boy who had been with me in the cargo hold had died.

The local medics gave me a tetanus shot which was a big mistake. I ended up with serum hepatitis.

I looked at the helicopter and all I could see were holes. One intake tube had a hole in it and apparently was one of the reasons the engine quit. I later heard that there were 141 bullet holes in the aircraft.

I headed for town in a DC-3 and, of course, to the hospital where I had surgery to remove the shrapnel from my leg.

I don't know how the surviving brother got to the hospital that day but he and I arrived back at Udorn the same day. We said, "Hi," shook hands and parted.

That was my last flight with Air America. Following the incident, I was assigned to ground maintenance and shortly thereafter left for home.

When I returned to the United States, I worked in aviation for a few years and then started working in construction. Today, I go fishing.

My fish and I
Northern Pike
37.5 inches long
17.25 pounds

Flight Mechanic
Loy "Rusty" Irons

Rusty Irons "hanging ten"
Na Khang, Laos, LS-36

I served in U.S. Army Helicopter Aviation for six years as a mechanic and inspector before I joined the civilian airline, Air America, in 1965.

I stayed with Air America for seven years as a flight mechanic. I Left in 1972.

****

As with all the aircrews, pilots and mechanics - the stories, close calls, humorous and tragic, are told at our annual reunions. Our version, other people's versions of our version, etc., makes for a few laughs and robust conversation over much libation "for those who crossed the Mekong."

****

These are my stories the way I remember them.

The Rescue at Phou Pha Thi

Phou Pha Thi is a 5500 foot mountain about 15 miles from the North Vietnamese border. When I arrived in Laos, there was a single rough landing pad, LS-85, on the side of the mountain close to the summit. During the rainy season, you had to fly through thick fog up the side of the mountain until you could see the plateau where the pad was located. The Air Force also had a navigational beacon in operation on the mountain. It was a beautiful spot with jungle foliage everywhere except for the summit where you could see for miles with an unobstructed view all the way to the airspace over Hanoi.

In 1965 as the war began to escalate in Vietnam and was spilling over into Laos, the Air Force found its bombing missions severely limited by the rainy season which ran from May to October in Laos. The solution came from advanced radar systems set up in South Vietnam and Thailand. These sites did not however reach the area surrounding Hanoi. The Air Force decided it needed radar closer to Hanoi in order to carry out more precise all weather bombing raids in that area. The summit of Phou Pha Thi was identified as the perfect location due to its elevation and proximity to Hanoi.

The Air Force built and staffed the radar installation on top of Phou Pha Thi, which became operational on November 1, 1967. There were two big problems with the location. The U. S. military was prohibited from being in Laos due to the 1962 Geneva Agreement and the area was extremely hostile. The Air Force resolved these issues by staffing the radar site with airmen undercover as civilian employees of Lockheed Aircraft Corporation. Additionally, as I recall, there were extensive plans to destroy equipment and evacuate the personnel in the event that the communists overran the installation. But even though the location was in an area of Laos where there was heavy enemy activity, no one really thought that the installation was at risk due to its elevation and configuration of the mountain which was nearly vertical on three sides and defended by Hmong fighters on the fourth side.

Lima Site 85
Photo courtesy of Gary Gentz

The first attempt to destroy the radar installation came by air. Four Russian Colt bi-planes that looked like World War I vintage attacked the site on January 12, 1968, causing very little damage.

The second assault by ground troops began on March 10, 1968. The Air Force had plenty of warning that the site was about to come under attack by multiple battalions of communist troops but did not want to give up the radar site due to its strategic value. Their failure to heed intelligence information was a fatal error. The installation that had been in operation just over four months and thought to be impregnable was overrun by communist forces on March 11. There were nineteen Americans at the radar site the night of 10 March.

I was on the first Air America rescue helicopter into LS-85 at dawn on March 11.

At the time of the attack my pilot, Ken Wood, and I did not know much about Site 85's situation other than it was HOT. We were scheduled to work the LS-36 area which included LS-85. In the early morning hours on the way to LS-36, we started getting radio chatter about LS-85. I do not recall what was said but the end result was that we were to evacuate the Air Force and CIA personnel from the mountain top.

There was a C-130 and several A1E Skyraiders already in the area when we arrived at 7:35 a.m. We could see the devastation caused by the bombing. A-26 Bombers and F-4 Fighters had been attacking the enemy all night, and just before our arrival, at daybreak, A-1E Skyraiders had hit the mountain with 20 mm cannons and dropped cluster bombs in an attempt to clear the way for us.

The rescue was pretty straight forward. Our aircraft could hover out of ground effect and we had the jungle penetrator hoist so we went after the people on the cliff. The other helicopters were directed to the pad next to the customer's position.

As we approached and I was thinking there couldn't be survivors with the Skyraiders dropping CBUs on top of their heads, we were contacted over the radio by one of the survivors. He and two others were still alive. They were in a small cave on the side of the mountain away from the landing pad.

Ken asked if they had any smoke to identify their position. He responded in the affirmative and shortly, purple smoke appeared from out of the mountain.

"I've got you," Ken acknowledged and moved the helicopter forward toward the smoke.

There was no landing area so Ken hovered close to the mountain as I lowered the jungle penetrator to the men below using about 100 feet of cable. I had no idea how many men were over the side.

The first guy up was seriously injured. I was able to lift him from the hoist and dropped it back down. The second guy up was Stan Sliz again immobilized by gunshot wounds to both thighs. As he was coming up, the cable swung out from the mountain and came back in, bumping the guy against the mountain. As the last man, Dick Etchberger, was strapping himself into the hoist, another survivor who had been in a different area of the mountain came running out of the fog toward Etchberger. He climbed onto the hoist with him, and I began hauling them both up. As soon as they were in, we broke hover next to the cliff and immediately got hit with approximately five rounds of enemy fire, one missing the engine fuel control by a hair.

I had not heard gunfire when I was operating the lift but as soon as I managed to get both guys in, I heard sounds like popcorn going off. Bullets started coming up through the floor of the helicopter before Ken got us out of range, one of which hit Etchberger who was sitting on the bench seat next to me. He was sitting on my AK-47, one of those guns we were not supposed to have. A round came up through the seat, through the stock of my AK, which I was unable to get back from underneath Etchberger. So I did not shoot back at anybody. I just played turtle and hunched over. A few minutes later, Dick slumped over against me and was leaning on me all the way back to LS-36.

The other two survivors, John Daniels and Stan Sliz were in desperate shape. Sliz kept fading in and out of consciousness and as he did I passed him a cigarette and when he passed out I took it back. Each time he woke up I would give him another one and take it back each time he passed out.

At LS-36 when we were off loading our passengers, we discovered that Etchberger was seriously wounded.

There had been five people in a cave that could barely fit two. They had been under attack for most of the night lobbing back live grenades that were thrown into the cave by the enemy. Two were killed, two were immobilized by wounds to their legs. Etchberger, a guy who had never been in combat in his life, spent the night fighting off the enemy with an M-16 and then, when he should have been safe, gets wounded on the rescue helicopter. Sliz and Daniel survived thanks to Etchberger's efforts throughout the night.

A second Air America helicopter went in about an hour later and took out wounded troops and CIA Agent Howard Freeman. An Air Force Jolly Green Giant brought out more troops a short time later. Simultaneously, a third Air America helicopter picked up CIA Agent John Spence and Sgt. Roger Huffman.

The last survivor, SSgt John Starling, spotted by one of our passengers as he was running for our helicopter was picked up by an Air Force Jolly Green Giant an hour after the others. Starling, immobilized from his injuries, was able to signal his rescuers with his flashlight. He had spent the last hours of the attack playing dead while the enemy walked around him killing anyone still alive.

Of the original nineteen Americans on the mountain that night, twelve were lost and seven survived. We also lost a pilot and his A-1 Skyraider. The plan to detonate the facility never happened. After the rescue and assuming the rest were dead, the Air Force attempted to level the radar site to destroy all technical and personal equipment left behind.

At the end of that day after turning over our passengers to the Air Force, I inspected my aircraft and discovered much to my dismay, she was still flyable. So we went back to work. I don't remember what we did but you didn't get paid for sitting on the ground.

Forty years later, I found out that Etchberger died of his wounds before he reached the hospital that day.

Ken Wood and I were reunited at the White House for the presentation of the Medal of Honor to Chief Master Sergeant Richard Loy Etchberger at the invitation of his sons. On September 21, 2010, Etchberger was posthumously awarded the United States military's highest decoration, the Medal of Honor for his actions during the battle of Lima Site 85 which resulted in saving the lives of his fellow workers. The medal was formally presented to his three sons by President Barack Obama.

The three day event was impressive. On day one, we were bused from our hotel to the White House, went through security, had hors d'oeuvres and talked to some interesting people, four stars on down. I took pictures of Madeline in different rooms inside the White House. I rescued some paper hand towels from the restroom (that's all I could find) and listened to the President talk. Note to the reader: I am a Republican.

On day two, we were bused to the Pentagon, had hors d'oeuvres and toured the 9/11 damaged area of the Pentagon (since repaired) which was very moving to see.

On day three, we were bused to the CIA Headquarters, had hors d'oeuvres and toured the Museum, led by the Director of the Agency Museum. This was very interesting. There's a picture of a helicopter doing the rescue on a wall in one hallway. I wanted to sign it, but.....

Some dignitaries from the Agency gave a little speech to the relatives and friends, a group of about fifty people, but did not mention Air America - silence to the end- that was very disappointing.

For three days our bus transport around DC did not stop at one stop light because eight to twelve motorcycle cops were leading our three buses (that was a kick in itself).

Following our Washington, DC, trip, we spent some time near Madeline's family home in Williamsburg, VA, and the Outer Banks. Overall it was a fabulous trip.

Madeline and Rusty Irons
The White House
September 2010

Ken Wood and Rusty Irons
Washington, DC
September 2010

Operation Pig Fat

November 1, 1968, the Hmong troops led by Gen. Vang Pao initiated an attack to retake Phou Pha Thi. The initiative called Operation Pig Fat was defeated.

Pilot Marius Burke and Rusty Irons circling LS-85 watching Gen. Vang Pao attempting to retake the mountain.

Rescue of Matt Luca

We were ferrying Gen. Vang Pao's troops in for an attack on LS-36 which had been previously lost to the Pathet Lao. There were five or six helicopters involved in the exercise. The weather was iffy and we had to sneak around hills due to the fog. Matt's pilot decided to go another way around the weather, got shot down in a rice paddy and landed. Matt had been shot in the foot by a round that had come up through the belly of the helicopter. While Matt was pulling out his survival pack, which we usually stuck under our seats for added protection, the helicopter exploded causing him to be severely burned. He fled the aircraft to a nearby rice paddy.

My pilot Steve Stevens and I were sitting on the ground waiting for the fog to lift when we found out they were missing, and in spite of the bad weather and enemy action in the area, my pilot decided to go in search of them.

As we searched the area, we spotted the smoke from a burning helicopter. H-34s will usually burn back to a folding point of the tail due to the magnesium in the fuselage. While circling the crash site we observed a body moving around in the wreckage which increased the urgency to land.

We went back to our landing point where Vang Pao was directing his operation and found out SPADS (Skyraiders) were inbound for air cover at the insistence of L-08, Vientiane, who always tried to get involved in rescues. Sometimes we followed their direction, sometimes not.

I asked for a gun as I did not have one at that time and Vang Pao grabbed an old British Bren gun from a ten-year-old soldier and gave it to me. I learned how to fire it as we headed back to the crash site. Several Lao soldiers had joined us and we were hell bent on effecting a rescue.

Back at the crash site we circled while Stevens talked to the Sandies who were going to strafe the far side of the rice paddy where there were heavy trees and brush.

After the strafing runs, we came in hot to the crash site. I wasn't thinking about getting shot. I was thinking about assessing the situation, doing what I could and getting the hell out of there. Adrenalin pumping, I jumped out, picked up a surviving soldier and put him on board. He was a mess.

At that same moment, Matt came running up behind me (if I had a smaller gun – enough said). It scared the living daylights out of me. Needless to say, I was very glad to see him alive. He was barely able to walk so I hoisted him into the helicopter.

Looking at the wreckage, I saw the pilot was still there plus about eight other blackened bodies. There was nothing we could do for them. We were out of there in minutes.

We flew Matt and the one soldier back to LS-48 where they were placed in a Porter and flown to Sam Thong.

After Matt recovered and returned to Udorn as a ground mechanic, he threw a party for Steve Stevens and me at the Club Rendezvous and everybody had a good time. (See Matt Luca's story on page 208)

Rusty Irons, Steve Stevens, C-123 pilot Bill Buckley, Matt Luca

Dick Conrad, Jim Peterson, Carolyn Eiler, Pat McCarthy, Roger Burdwood

Incident at Vientiane, L-O8

A pilot and I were sent to L-O8, Vientiane, to ferry an H-34, Commission International d'Control (CIC) helicopter flown by a French crew, back to Udorn for routine maintenance. On pre-flight, I found a beer can secured underneath an oil leak on the transmission deck. Not a normal fix but it did the job.

I don't remember if it was this aircraft or another but the story is true. The parking area for aircraft was covered with dried mud from the flood. The pilot asked operations to contact maintenance to pull us out to the taxiway so we could start up without blowing the dried mud all over the other aircraft in the vicinity. But no one ever showed up.

We waited a decent amount of time in the hot sun. Finally the pilot started the helicopter and we could see it wasn't going to be good. Just at low RPM, the dust was starting to rise. What made things worse was the next aircraft over was a nice clean Volpar twin engine beechcraft with the door open waiting for a VIP flight. My pilot pulled pitch right there.

Five miles into Thailand you could still see the dust cloud. The operations manager or somebody was screaming over the radio all the way to Udorn. My pilot just acknowledged his transmissions every few minutes with we were "Ops normal" proceeding to Udorn.

I don't know what our base manager or chief pilot ever said about it. Wayne Knight was always cool about things. You could not have asked for a better Charley Papa Hotel (Chief Pilot Helicopters).

I cannot say enough about management and the people at Udorn. We were a close family and the Club Rendezvous was our first relief after a tour upcountry.

Working seven days a week, the only days you would recognize were Wednesdays for Mongolian BBQ on the Club patio and Sunday Buffet in the restaurant, which served pretty good food at all times. (Except one time with Ted Cash at breakfast, but that's another story.)

One main reason that some of us lasted so long over there is that we had our weekends at one time during the month, six days of scheduled time off. We would get on a plane, train or car and head for Bangkok, Hong Kong or any other place. We came back refreshed and ready to go upcountry again.

Working Out of LS-36, Na Khang

We were working out of LS-36, the site noted for hostile action, ferrying refugees in the surrounding area back to LS-36. Pilot John Ford forgot to turn left at a certain ridge while making an "ops normal" transmission. We ended up close to the Plain of Jars, an enemy stronghold, and came under heavy ground fire. John got his head out of where it shouldn't be and turned around, heading for LS-36. We took seven hits down the middle of the H-34 from a hole in the main fuel line going into the carburetor, to wire bundles which cut all communications, and a number down the center of the floor. One hit my thermos bottle which scared the hell out of me as it was under my seat. Today that thermos sits on my computer desk to remind me that life is too short.

We had at least ten plus locals on board and no one was hit. Dumb luck.

With fuel running all over the hot engine and heavy fuel fumes, we coasted into the fuel pits at LS-36.

It was very close.

LS-36, Na Khang. Remains of a crashed helicopter
brought in to the site in the forefront
Photo courtesy of Gary Gentz

Crash with Pilot Dick Elder in XW-PFH

It was July 7, 1969. On our way back to LS-20A after working dawn to dusk at LS-36, we were tasked by the customer with dropping off a couple of cases of hand grenades at several pads on the way in. There was a rumor that the troops would hold on to a pad until the grenades ran out, then boogie out. Therefore, we tried to keep them well supplied with grenades.

We departed LS-36 with an American passenger in the co-pilot's seat. I was in the back with eight to ten boxes of grenades, which weighed 87 pounds each. I'll never forget the weight of those boxes.

On approach to the first pad at Houei Tong Ko, LS-184, Dick started to pull in power and discovered he wasn't getting it. I don't know what he was doing to correct the problem. All I knew was we were going sideways, down the hill about one foot above ground, cutting grass. We were doing okay until our skid caught a tree stump and flipped the helicopter over on its side.

Dick and the passenger both suffered broken backs.

Since I was not strapped in, ready to dump two boxes, I just rolled around with the 87-pound boxes of grenades. My helmet split in two. The crash knocked out three fillings and left a two-inch gash under my chin. The scar is now hidden by my second chin. When I woke up, my shirt was covered with blood, well maybe not very much. Dick was awake and lying outside of the helicopter as was the passenger.

I pulled out my new 4-channel radio. Can't say where I got it and declared a mayday. No one answered which was a big letdown. Finally, I got a hold of Crown or somebody as at that time of day everyone was returning to LS-20A.

They turned around a porter and the pilot landed on the "almost air strip," not yet approved for fixed wing aircraft. Before the plane landed, I got help from the locals to carry Dick and the passenger up to the strip on four-foot pieces of plywood to provide support for their backs. The plywood had been used to drop rice by parachute from big birds.

The porter pilot landed and said he could only take Dick and the passenger out. They had turned around a helicopter for me.

They had to pick up the tail of the porter to turn it around for takeoff. (All small bird pilots have hairy chests.)

I eventually got picked up by our other Bell helicopter within 15-20 minutes. In the meantime, I took pictures of the crash. Arriving at LS-20A, an aircraft was waiting for me with its engines running.

At Udorn, I was taken to the Air Force doctor. He sewed me up with seven to nine stitches and gave me some pain pills. I asked if I could drink with the pills. The answer was not just no, but hell no.

I made it back to the company club (like touching home base) and somebody rang the bell. The bell meant a free round of drinks.

I woke up the next day all black and blue from those 87-pound wooden boxes and with a dissolved mess of pills in my hand. It took about ten minutes to get out of bed. Then I headed for the club and the paperwork to report what I thought had happened.

Operation about Face

In August of 1969, General Vang Pao went on the offensive attempting to retake the Plain of Jars from the Pathet Lao. He succeeded in taking back Xieng Khouang, Muong Soui and several key towns in the southern end of the Plain of Jars.

We were working in support of Vang Pao's campaign, moving troops and ammunition. We landed on a bare hill, ready to drop off some hard rice when there was the biggest bang ever. The pilot and I both ducked, as if that were going to do any good. The helicopter had been hit by a 12.7 (50-caliber) bullet right between the two windshields. The bullet lodged in the wire bundle inside the cockpit that went to all the pilot's instruments. The shock punched out four or five instruments from their mounts and we lost a lot of them. The pilot pulled pitch and we got out of there. We made it back to our work area and I spent the next couple of hours splicing wires back together so we could make it back to LS-20A and then home to Udorn. For some reason, I always carried a good selection of splices, which came in handy. I guess it was my experience getting shot a lot. I wasn't called magnet ass for nothing.

Pilot Phil Peyton with General Vang Pao approaching in the distance

This photo was taken the first morning after taking the town of Xieng Khong Ville at the southern end of the Plain of Jars. Gen. Vang Pao was inspecting the area. The Pathet Lao had retreated from the area leaving behind large caches of arms, ammunition, equipment and medical supplies. Note the 37 mm guns on the trucks that were part of the extensive collection of material that was valued in the millions of dollars.

Operation About Face
Ground Situation on August 1, 1969

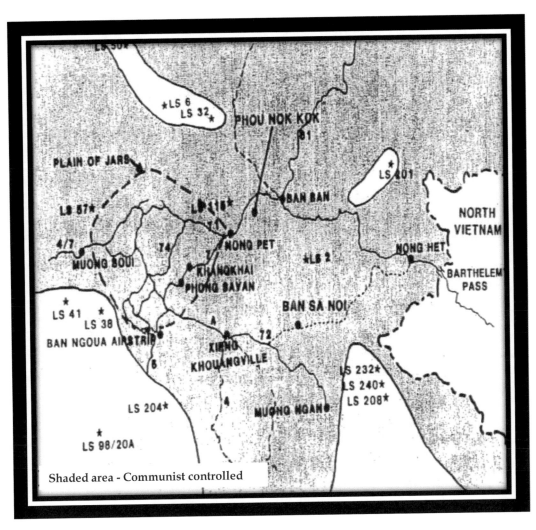

Based on an unclassified map from the National Security Archive
The War in Northern Laos, Victor B. Anthony and Richard R. Sexton,
Center for Air Force History, MORI DocID: 1255435

My Most Exciting Incident

On a flight from Udorn to LS-20A, Long Tieng, we had to stop at Vientiane, L-08, for a load from the customer, which was a routine thing. We picked up a load of 700-800 lbs of dynamite plus a box of blasting caps, which I was to hold in my lap and not to put anywhere near the dynamite. Okay!

On the way to LS-20A (fuzzy memory here), we were hit by ground fire. One round hit the engine rocker box cover. One round hit the right side of the oil tank and one round (thank heaven for V brace landing gear) hit the bottom of the brace. This one could have had my name on it.

I immediately ditched the blasting caps. I found out later that the customer was quite upset about that, but what the heck!

With the engine oil tank losing oil, you can imagine what the side of the helicopter looked like. We turned around and hauled ass for Vientiane. We made the lowlands when the oil pressure started down. The pilot landed in a rice paddy and I threw some oil into the oil tank. Made it another few miles and did it again. I forget how much oil we carried on board but we used it all.

In the meantime, we called in our plight on the company radio frequency and were answered by a C-46 who gave us an escort into Vientiane.

Vientiane had recently cemented their parking area and they were very proud of how clean it was. We knew this, so the pilot called ahead and requested maintenance to meet us with a BIG drip pan. Typical Vientiane – nobody got the word. We landed a safe distance from the fixed wings, shut down and proceeded to empty the rest of our oil on their nice new ramp.

As I always said, Vientiane never had a sense of humor with us helicopter guys. They were fixed wing, we were rotary wing and never the twain shall meet. Ha!

Working out of Long Tieng, LS-20A

After I quit flying, I was offered the job as helicopter mechanic in residence at LS-20A to help with inspections, expediting parts requests, etc.

Because they didn't want us to use our real names, my radio call sign while assigned there was Cecil C. Cesspool, the Crimson Crusader of Laos. While working at LS-20A, I rode around on a little Honda 50cc with a pith helmet and a small antenna on it. Made me feel like management. I got smiles from all the flight crews.

At the time I was working on the ground, Vang Pao was on the offensive on the Plain of Jars and we had captured a good amount of equipment. They needed somebody to go around and rig stuff to sling out such things as 37 millimeter guns on wheels, etc. For security they gave me a little kid with a big gun as my guard.

One day, I rigged two 37 millimeter guns for a dual sling by a sky crane, the first such helicopter I had seen upcountry. Later on they did other sling missions. In all this mess on the ground around us, there were a lot of unexploded cluster bomblets about the size of a baseball. The sky crane came into a hover for me to hook up the cable and here go all these little baseballs rolling all over the place and I'm standing on top of a 37 millimeter gun getting beat to hell by down wash.

I finished the job, picked up my guard who I think weighed all of about 60 pounds and tiptoed through a suspected mine field, ours and theirs. Since the positions had changed hands a couple of times, everyone had planted their own mines.

Soon after that I decided to return to the States.

Honda 50cc that I rode at LS-20A
On the left is Glenn Woods' piece of the Russian Bi-plane
that he shot down over LS-85

In Conclusion

I was going to write about the night life downtown at the Princess & Wolverine but I will let Steve and others off the hook.

There is a story about Roger (Trash mouth) Burdwood that I will share with you. Roger was sitting at the bar in the Princess and some Air Force 2nd Lt. was bad mouthing Air America (the first 2nd Lt. I ever saw doing that). Roger was the only one there. Well the Butter Bar 2nd Lt. indicated he knew karate and he would kick ass. So Roger decked him, putting him in the middle of the base drum of the band. Roger came up with the famous saying "Bar Stool" as in, you know karate, I know bar stool.

When I returned to the States, I learned to fly, soloed at 6.5 hours and endured a big earthquake in Los Angeles. I decided I could die anywhere and asked to rejoin Air America. I lasted for nine months in Saigon and was laid off there. The last two years in Saigon were a whole different Air America story. Marius Burke will have to tell that story.

I retired after 30 years as a mechanic with the Los Angeles County Fire Department. I still work as a consultant there a couple of days a week and always look forward to traveling with Madeline in our fifth wheel.

In my time with Air America to my knowledge, we never turned down a mission, rescue, etc. If it could be done, we did it.

"Anything, Anywhere, Anytime, Professionally."

Morning pre-flight at LS-20A with my unauthorized
AK-47 that took a round in the stock during LS-85 rescue

Rusty's Memorabilia

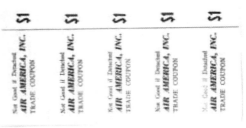

The five dollars I owed
Steve Nichols for almost
fifty years.

Max's Place on Patpong Road, Bangkok, was a favorite of Air America personnel. Sam, the proprietor, provided these cards to Taxi drivers so they could bring us back to his place.

Flight mechanic Bill Murphy, charming lady, Rusty Irons
Going away party for pilot George Carroll

Flight Mechanic
William Long

Udorn, Thailand

July 1969 – June 1974

Introduction

My first exposure to Air America was as a young 19 year old while I was in the Marine Corps. In April of 1962 my squadron HMM-261 was deployed to Udorn, Thailand. While there I would see the Air America helicopters coming in with strange looking crews in civilian clothes. I imbued them with super natural abilities and imagined that they could probably take the helicopter apart and put it back together blindfolded.

I left the Marine Corps and a year later joined the Air Force and in 1968 was once again in Thailand (Nakhon Phanom) with Air Rescue (Jolly Green Giants). My then girlfriend in Hawaii wanted me to get out and come back to Hawaii and get married. I decided to get out of the Air Force and return to Hawaii and get married.

While travelling back to the United States to get discharged, I stopped overnight in Bangkok and happened to see the Air America office. I stopped in to inquire about employment and they wanted me to begin immediately. The long and the short of the story is that I chose to go to work with Air America. Eva's loss was Air America's gain or vice versa and neither she nor Air America were ever the same again. We will let history decide who came out the better in that deal.

My First Trip Up Country

On my first trip upcountry as a flight mechanic, I was assigned to fly with Captain Elmer Munsell. Hal Augustine was assigned to give me my check out as a flight mechanic. We took off from Udorn and flew north. We were supposed to go to LS-118A, Nam Lieu, but the weather was getting bad so they told us to land in Vientiane and remain over night.

Shortly after landing in Vientiane, Hal said to me, "You'll work out okay," and he got on an aircraft headed back to Udorn. It was possibly the shortest check ride in history.

The next day we flew on up to Nam Lieu and worked there. At the end of the week Elmer was relieved by Capt. Jack (JJ) McCauley and I continued to fly with him. At the end of the first day with JJ, we got caught in the weather and had to land and spend the night on a hillside several miles from 118A. As darkness fell JJ began to ask me about my background and filled me in on his background. As we spoke we noticed flashing lights approaching from the distance. Since we were not sure if they were friendly or enemy and being unarmed and somewhat apprehensive about our security, I took a Ford wrench from my toolbox to use as a weapon if the need arose. When the people got closer to the aircraft, I slammed the door open and jumped to the ground ready to smash some heads. It was then that I noticed that they were Yao tribesmen from the area and that they had brought us blankets to keep us warm in the cold night mountain air.

We thanked them and settled in to get as good a night's rest as possible but every time I was about to fall asleep, JJ would ask, "Are you scared, kid?" and I would reply, "No, I'm not scared." This exchange continued several more times into the night until we finally fell asleep.

Much later we were awakened by the aircraft shaking. Then the shaking stopped and after awhile it would shake and stop again.

Once again we were apprehensive as to the cause of the shaking. Again, I grabbed my trusty Ford wrench, opened the door and dove to the ground, once more ready to fight for my life. It was then that I noticed the several burlap sacks under the aircraft. They contained pigs that we were delivering and I had put them on the ground so we would have room to sleep in the helicopter. The shaking was caused by the pigs moving in the sacks and bumping the bottom of the aircraft.

It was right then that I knew I was going to love this job.

My Shared Experiences with Chauncey J. Collard

Chauncey, at age 55, was the oldest active chopper pilot in the Vietnam War. In an article titled "The Last Day" written by Allen Cates for the Air America website, Cates wrote, "Chauncey Collard...piloted everything the Navy had since 1936."

Chauncey joined Air America along with his pilot friend Frenchy Smith on August 25, 1964. At the end of the Vietnam War he had been flying just short of forty years.

I was fortunate to fly often with Chauncey and many times we had some interesting moments that I have remembered for all these years.

There was the day we picked up four or five wounded "kids" from an outpost in Laos, north of Vientiane. It was late in the day, just about dark and storm clouds were beginning to form in the area. The wounded were all awake and some of them were even talking. The wounds varied from serious gaping stomach and head wounds to the less serious, but most of them were of the serious type.

As we flew them to Vientiane, the wind, rain and lightning intensified buffeting the helicopter in the darkening evening sky. Chauncey called ahead to Vientiane flight operations advising them of the situation and the condition of the wounded troops.

Considering the fact that Vientiane was staffed with both host country and third country nationals to whom English was a second language there were occasions when the salient points or the gravity of a situation may not have been as well understood as one would hope for.

We landed in Vientiane well after dark. With a few silent prayers of thanks for having made it through the bad weather and with the assistance of the onsite personnel, we unloaded the wounded from the helicopter in the front of the Vientiane operations building.

As Chauncey was taxiing away, I became aware that the wounded soldiers had been left out in the pouring rain on the ground. I was really concerned as they needed immediate medical attention. The Vientiane operations people had left them on the ramp and disappeared back into the relative comfort of their offices. Even though we had called ahead to advise them of the situation, there was no indication that anything was being done. After having flown into a dangerous area to pick up these wounded people and then flying through rain, thunder and lightning in the dark to get them to medical attention, I couldn't just leave them there lying on the ground in the rain.

Before Chauncey could get airborne, I told him over the intercom to stop. I jumped out of the helicopter, ran into the operations office and slammed my fist down on the desk of the guy on duty.

I do not recall my exact words but it went something like, "Listen you stupid mother-fuckers, you have people out there who are dying. Get your asses out of here and get these people to the hospital."

I do not know how many of those "kids" survived that day but I would like to think we contributed in some way to saving as many as we could.

+++++++++++

There was the time, just as we were landing near LS-14, a Caribou crashed during approach to LS-14, Pha Khao, Laos, on 4 February 72. They were carrying troops from Ban Xon, LS-272, to Pha Khao. Pilot Gordon V. Smith suffered spine injuries, co-pilot D. M. Houston fractured his skull, AFS M. S. Bailey received minor injuries, and kicker Khamouth Sousadalay was killed. Thirty four passengers were injured.

We landed about 50 yards up-hill from the crash site, Chauncey shut down the helicopter and I ran to the crash site to help where I could. The Caribou had pan-caked on the side of a hill and the fuselage was flattened so we could not open the doors and had to bust out the overhead cockpit window to extract the pilot. I picked up several injured people and ran up the hill carrying them to the helicopter. (I was in much better physical condition then).

+++++++++++

It was after dark and we had just landed at Udorn. We were taxiing to the parking ramp when I spotted a bright red glow showing on the horizon behind us. Chauncey couldn't see it so I called him on the intercom, telling him that there was a fire that might be a crash. In fact an Air Force F-4 had crashed on takeoff and burst into flames. Chauncey took off and hovered down the runway. At the site of the crash, it was dark and very smoky but I was able to spot a parachute and a man in the bushes waving at us. We picked him up but could not find the pilot. By then the Air Force choppers were on the scene and being low on fuel, we returned to base with the one crewman from the F-4. I don't think the pilot survived.

The next day I happened to be in the bar at the Air Force Officers' Club when one of the Air force pilots told me he wanted me to meet somebody. He introduced me to the man we had picked up, telling him, "This is one of the guys from the Air America helicopter that picked you up."

He looked up from his drink, nodded and said, "Oh," and returned to his conversation with his friends.

So much for gratitude.

+++++++++++

I was with Chauncey one day when we picked up nine Lao passengers in Luang Prabang and headed for Vientiane. About ten minutes into the flight, we heard a call for help from a downed Forward Air Controller (FAC) aircraft in our area. So off we went.

Since they were not privy to the radio traffic, the passengers never knew what was going on and that they were taking part in a search and rescue mission which lasted nearly an hour.

Eventually it turned dark and we had to return to Luang Prabang for fuel which was where we started. As we approached Luang Prabang the passengers noticed this and began to gesticulate in a concerned manner, telling me that we were not supposed to be there but should be on our way to Vientiane. I explained as best I could what the problem had been. After refueling we again headed south for Vientiane. It was dark and not a good time to fly in Laos but this was normally a safe route so I wasn't too concerned.

We were crossing some mountains following the main road south when the co-pilot, whose name I can't recall, remarked how poetic a scene was, created by the blinking lights below and the stars above. As I looked to see what he was talking about, I realized that the blinking lights were actually muzzle flashes.

I said, "We're being shot at. Turn right." However as I was looking to the right and front I saw more muzzle flashes.

"Never mind," I said through the intercom, "There are more of them shooting on my side." We were being fired upon by a truck mounted quad 12.7 mm machine gun.

Chauncey tried to speed up but with a full fuel tank and nine passengers, he only started to get blade stall.

Chauncey then put out a call on the radio, "Anyone still up? I might need help."

Captain Hutchinson was still airborne south of us and replied, "I will head your way." It all happened so quickly that I did not even have time to get scared. After a few minutes, we were out of range. Chauncey went back on the radio and told Hutch to forget it.

We never saw any tracers fired at us so there was no telling how close we came to taking a few rounds. We were not showing any lights so they were probably shooting at our sound, which would be behind us.

Chauncey and I had a great relationship and shared a lot of memories. He flew with Air America right up to the evacuation of Saigon on April 29, 1975. The stories of the Saigon evacuation can be found in the article, "Air America: Played a Crucial Part of the Emergency Helicopter Evacuation of Saigon," by William Leary and E. Merton Coulter on historynet.com.

Chauncey passed away January 11, 2012, at the age of 91.

Rescue of Champ Champanil and Bob Caron

It was February 1971. I was flying aboard an Air America UH-34D piloted by a single pilot, Capt. Harold Miller.

We had received instructions to return the aircraft to the Air America maintenance base at Udorn, Thailand. After having flown eight hours in support of the CIA Case Officer at LS-32, Boung Lam, we were proceeding south when we heard the distress call of mayday on the emergency frequency. As always, the hearing of the call of mayday was followed by an immediate racing of the heart and a tightening of the sphincter because we knew that another American aircrew was in trouble.

Even though we were over an hour's flying time away from the scene and other Air America aircraft were closer and already in route, Captain Miller turned the aircraft and headed toward the site of the distress call.

As we flew toward the scene, we were able to discern that an Air America helicopter flown by pilot Robert Caron with co-pilot Fred Frahm, while on a special mission to extract a CIA team, had been ambushed at the landing zone.

As we later learned from the crews, the Air America aircraft had a CIA assigned person aboard who was supposed to be able to make an eyeball identification and confirmation that these were the people to be extracted. When confirmation was made by the CIA assigned person, the pilot made his approach for the pickup and just prior to touching down on the area cleared for a landing zone, the "friendly" personnel on the ground fell to the ground and enemy troops came out of the jungle firing at the helicopter. The disabled helicopter made a forced landing. The crew consisting of pilots Caron and Frahm, flight mechanic Veera Champanil and a passenger leapt from the aircraft and sought cover in the surrounding jungle and brush.

As Captain Miller and I were proceeding, we could hear the radio chatter of other aircraft that had already arrived on the scene and of Crown, the Air Force Command and Control aircraft, well overhead. We could hear cries of, "look out, taking fire," and one crew calling to another that they had been hit by ground fire and could see fuel streaming from their aircraft. We heard other calls stating that there was no sign of any occupants in the aircraft or on the landing zone or any sign of survivors in the areas proximate to the landing zone.

Due to the heavy ground fire and no sign of survivors, it was concluded by Crown that the air crew had been either killed or captured and that they were calling off the rescue effort.

Captain Miller and I had just arrived on the scene when Crown made the call to terminate the rescue effort. Captain Miller began to turn the helicopter to head on home and as he was turning, I spotted the flight mechanic Veera Champanil waving a white cloth. I called this to Captain Miller's attention and directed him toward Champ's position on the ground.

As we came closer, I could see that he had been shot in the shoulder. While Captain Miller brought the helicopter to a hover, I lowered the rescue sling (horse collar) to Champ and motioned for him to put it on. I lifted him up and pulled him into the relative safety of the aircraft.

As Captain Miller began to pull away from the area, I spotted another person (Captain Bob Caron) waving frantically at us. I brought this to Captain Miller's attention and he brought the aircraft to a hover over Captain Caron. I lowered the rescue hoist and pulled him into the aircraft.

We headed for Luang Prabang where Bob Caron and Champ were loaded onto a C-123 and sent to Udorn. Co-pilot Frahm and the CIA assigned person (Code name Office) were rescued by Captain Ivar Gram, co-pilot Ted Cash and flight mechanic Dave Crowell and were brought into Luang Prabang shortly thereafter. Their crash and rescue story is told by pilot Fred Frahm on pages 117-125.

It was a good ending to a very long day.

My Broken Arm

I was flying with Captain Don Henthorn out of PS-22 near Pakse, Laos. We were ferrying troops and after landing, there was a whistling sound coming from the main rotor blades. Don said that he thought we may have taken a round through one of the blades. I told him to shut down the aircraft and I would inspect the blades for damage.

When Don had applied the rotor brake and the blades had stopped, I told him that I was going to climb up on the horizontal stabilizer to look at the blades. As I turned the tail rotor to bring the main rotor blades over the tail boom, Don saw a piece of plastic fall off the leading edge of the blade in front of him. He immediately realized that that had been the cause of the whistling sound. Without another thought, he wrapped on the throttle and engaged the blades at the same time that I was reaching for the tail rotor blade. The tail rotor blade hit my arm upward into the main rotor blade and the main rotor blade smacked into my arm followed by my getting hit on the top of my flight helmet by another main rotor blade and being knocked off the stabilizer to the ground. I was dazed and a bit confused as to what had just happened and my right arm was shaking and in pain. I walked up to the front of the aircraft and gave Don an inquiring look that asked what the hell was going on? He just motioned for me to get in the helicopter. I got in the helicopter and was rubbing my very sore right wrist as we took off. It was then that I noticed that my gold bracelet was no longer on my wrist. I told Don to go back and land so I could see if I could find my bracelet.

Don landed and I explained my problem to the troop commander. He barked out some instructions to his troops and they began walking around searching the ground for my bracelet. The thought crossed my mind that none of these troops were going to return an eight ounce gold bracelet which probably represented over a year's pay to them. But much to my surprise within a few minutes one of them brought my bracelet to their commander who in turn returned it to me.

As the day progressed, my hand began to swell and my wrist and arm became more painful. I wrapped an ace bandage around it and continued to work performing most chores one handed. Later that evening the pain had become much more severe and the swelling had greatly increased. The customer whose name escapes me decided that my arm was broken and that I should be sent out on a medevac flight to Ubon, Thailand. He fitted me with an inflatable cast which caused me to walk around with my arm raised in a perpetual Nazi salute.

Our flight was met by a U.S. Air Force ambulance that took me to the base hospital. As they brought me in, the doctor remarked in a voice that could be heard throughout the hospital, "Oh, this must be one of those spooks from across the river."

They put me in a bed and placed my arm in a bowl of ice to reduce the swelling prior to putting my arm in a cast. As I lay in the bed almost every patient and member of the hospital staff came walking by to see what "a spook from across the river" looked like. The next day they placed my arm in a cast and flew me back to Udorn.

When management saw my arm in a cast, they said, "You might as well go home. There isn't much you can do here with one arm."

So taking them at their word, I went home, all the way home to Massachusetts. The taxi from the airport dropped me at my sister's home and I walked up the steps and rang the door bell.

My sister opened the door, looked alarmingly at the cast on my arm and asked in a worried tone, "My God, what happened to your arm?"

I told her I had broken my arm.

She said, "Don't lie to me. Tell me the truth. What really happened?"

So I lied and told her that I had been shot to which she replied, "I knew it."

Proof once again that people will believe a lie over the truth

The Attack on LS-20A

One night while operating out of Long Tieng, LS-20A, in support of customer operations, I was in the customer hostel watching the evening movie. All of a sudden the movie stopped and the lights were turned on and one of the customers was there.

He yelled, "All you Air America people, listen up." He proceeded to tell us that they were expecting an attack that night and if anything happened we, the Air America people, should gather at the base of the karst across from the communications hut and that they would come by and give us further instructions.

We watched the movie to the end and retired to our sleeping quarters in the hostel.

Some time into the night I was awakened by one of the Filipino flight mechanics yelling, "Mister Bill, Mister Bill, we're under attack."

Still half asleep and a bit hung over, I got out of bed and turned on the light.

The Filipino flight mechanic again began yelling, "Mister Bill, Mister Bill."

A bit irritated I snapped back at him, "What do you want?"

He said, "We're under attack and the window shutters are open. Don't you think it would be a good idea to turn off the light to keep from attracting attention to our location?" If the term had been in vogue at the time, I would have said, "DUH."

I turned off the light and got dressed. We grabbed our customer supplied Uzi sub-machine guns and our survival vests and headed for the pre-arranged muster point at the karst across from the CIA communications hut.

As we stood at the base of the karst, we could see the 120 mm rockets coming in our direction but passing over our heads.

We waited and continued to watch the enemy rockets passing overhead, but nobody came to muster us or give further directions. It was then that the thought crossed my mind that if one of those rockets landed short, we could be in deep shit. As I thought about that I began to think about how we could improve our position. I eyed the communications hut which was so well fortified with sand bags that it was in reality a bunker that would afford much better protection from the rockets. I told the others with me that we should run across the road and take cover in the communications hut and to begin running on my signal. I gave the signal and we began to run.

Unknown to us there was a friendly 50 caliber machine gun set on the top of the karst from which we were running. Just as we began to run, the 50 caliber began to fire back toward the direction from which the enemy fire was coming. I did not know that it was friendly but rather assumed that it was an enemy gun and that they were shooting at us as we moved away from the karst, and they could well be closing in behind us.

My mind raced as I ran and in an instant I formed a plan. I knew there was a room in the back right corner of the communications hut with bunk beds. I decided I would run well ahead of everybody else, run into the room, dive under the bed and remain there for several days. Then I would sneak out in the dark of night and make my way south from Long Tieng heading for friendly territory.

Fortunately we were informed that the gunfire behind us was from friendly troops firing at the enemy across the valley. The attackers were rebuffed and I did not need to put my plan of walking from Long Tieng to Vientiane into action. But the incident gave me a keen insight into how the human mind works when confronted with situations that impact self-preservation.

I Can Smell the Cordite

I had been flying with Izzy Freeman at Long Tieng, LS-20A, when we received a radio transmission from Udorn operations with instructions to return to Udorn.

As we were flying south from Long Tieng, we heard a transmission from a Continental Air Services Porter that said, "Air America chopper heading south from the alternate." Izzy answered the radio call and the Porter pilot informed Izzy that a battalion-sized unit of the North Vietnamese Army had been spotted in the area and that he (Izzy) would be better served to gain more altitude. This was an area through which we had been transitioning on a very frequent basis during the past several days with no problems or signs of enemy troops, so Izzy took the message in a cavalier manner and continued south without taking the aircraft to a higher altitude.

Then he made the lighthearted comment, "Well here we are heading home as we are being decimated by enemy fire."

His nonchalant attitude got my goat, so I decided to teach him a lesson. I picked up my AK-47, pointed it out the door and fired off about twenty rounds on full automatic.

I never thought that an H-34 could climb that fast as Izzy pulled the collective up to his armpit and exclaimed, "Holy shit, they must be really close. I can smell the cordite."

I was laughing so hard that I nearly wet my pants.

Since that time, "They must be close. I can smell the cordite," has become the greeting line between Izzy and me whenever and wherever we meet.

Flight Mechanic
Matthew J. "Matt" Luca

Northern Okinawa, 1963

Introduction

I worked for Air America out of Udorn, Thailand, from October 1965 to April 1967.

My first introduction to Air America was in the spring of 1963. I was stationed at the Marine Air Facility on Okinawa.

I was sitting at the Whirlybird Bar one night when this fellow walked in. His face had red blotches and he was constantly drying his watery eyes. He said he was with an outfit called Air America and had been refueling his aircraft near some communist held area in Southeast Asia when they came under "unfriendly" fire. The aircraft caught fire and he was burned.

Our conversation was cut short when military police walked in and asked for IDs. He produced a passport, while I had my military ID card. The bar was posted as off limits and I was escorted back to my base without ever learning his name.

In 1965, I finished my first year at the Teterboro School of Aeronautics and received my Air Frame License. My second year would be for the power plant portion of the license.

A fellow classmate came to school one day with a want ad from a newspaper which read, "Aircraft Mechanics Needed. Overseas Assignment."

I decided to give it a try and within weeks I received a reply. The correspondence continued. *Who were these people?* Air Asia, Civil Air Transport, the names on the letter head were always different.

I was instructed to get immunizations, typhoid, para-typhoid and plague. *Where are they sending me?*

Finally the mystery was over. My next letter came with instructions for Udorn, Thailand, with Air America.

Taipei, Taiwan, stopover in route to Udorn, Thailand, 1965

Udorn

I was on my way and flying first class, too.

I laid over in Tokyo and then on to Taipei, Taiwan. At each stop I was greeted by an Air America representative and given instructions on where to stay and my next flight information.

I arrived in Taipei at the start of a Chinese holiday and had to wait four days until I could leave for Hong Kong and Bangkok.

Chinese Nationalist Parade
Taipei, Taiwan, 1965

My first troubles came in Bangkok. There was no one there to greet me and they wouldn't let me through customs unless I could tell them where I was staying. A Thai cabbie overheard me talking and approached me. He knew where the Air America office was downtown and also gave me the name of a hotel to give to customs.

At the Air America office, no one had any information on me. They told me to go back to the airport to Air America operations and maybe I could fly up to Udorn.

Operations at the airport told me there were no flights going out but told me if I went to the train station, I just might make it for the overnight trip to Udorn.

My faithful cabbie was still with me. Why not? I was paying him six US dollars plus tip on each trip. He was getting rich on me.

Luckily I caught the night train and arrived at Udorn early the next morning where I had my first samlor ride, a modern day rickshaw with wheels and pedal power.

I checked into the Udorn Hotel which was surprisingly modern, but at six US dollars a day, was kind of high. I would need cheaper accommodations.

I switched to a $3 a day room with no air conditioning and a Thai style toilet. It was facing the street on the second floor. Across the street was the Silhouette, a Thai business men's bar. There was a loud speaker outside and for the next two months, they played the same song, "Bridge Over Troubled Waters," continuously. Damn, I hate that song.

Taipei, Taiwan, 1965

Air America - 1965

My job with Air America was as a flight mechanic on the Sikorsky H-34 helicopter. The duties were mainly loading and off loading personnel and equipment of various types on flights into Laos. A second responsibility of a flight mechanic was to go on salvage and recovery of downed aircraft. Until a flight mechanic or pilot was officially checked out, he would receive training at Udorn. My first flight into Laos came in November 1965. Jim Peterson, another newly arrived flight mechanic, and I were flown upcountry to remove and bring back a wing from a Helio, a small fixed wing plane.

In between assignments, we reported to the main hangar for daily work.

In mid December 1965, there was a crash of an H-34, call sign Hotel 30. Every helicopter had its own call sign which was painted on the tail area.

Landing sites in Laos could range from an airstrip to accommodate cargo aircraft like C-123s to a small clearing on a hilltop just big enough for one helicopter to sit down on.

In the case of the H-30 crash, something went wrong on approach and the pilot overshot the landing zone and plunged down the hill. Luckily no one on board was seriously hurt. The chopper came to rest facing downhill and, except for the main rotor blades, was not too badly damaged.

I was sent to the site with Steve Nichols, a senior flight mechanic, and we made our assessment. Due to its size and weight, we did not have the capability to lift it out in one piece. We would have to dismantle it where it came to rest.

We recruited some Lao soldiers who were stationed at that site and had them cut out a clearing around the chopper.

After discarding the main rotor blades, we began to dismantle sections and components. Smaller and lighter parts were carried by the soldiers back up the hill and flown out on other helicopters. The entire operation would take about a week if all went well.

At the end of each day, we were flown back to the town of Luang Prabang. The hotel there was a favorite of Air America aircrews whenever they spent time in this area.

As the project continued, more help arrived to assist in the operation. Flight mechanic Dick Conrad was sent to aid with the sling operations. This operation involved another helicopter hovering above the site and ground personnel attaching larger objects to a cargo hook located on the underbelly by means of a cable harness.

The rotor head and transmission went out as a unit. Then the engine went without any problems. We were down to our final piece, the main fuselage section. The disabled helicopter had been secured and held upright by cables attached to nearby trees during the dismantling process. This was no longer feasible because we needed to have a quicker way to untie the fuselage during lift operations. We decided on a simple method of using rope through one of the cabin tie down rings, then wrapped the rope around a tree stump. One man would stand on top of the fuselage and the other would man the rope. As soon as the sling was attached, the man on top of the fuselage would jump off, hopefully clearing the wreckage. The rope would simply be let loose on lift off.

Conrad and I decided to take turns because no one wanted to stand on top to make the hook up. The process involved standing on the wreckage with another helicopter hovering over you, inches from your head. If something went wrong, there was little to no time to jump clear. I went first while Conrad handled the rope. Steve guided the pilot and gave the okay for lift off.

Success quickly turned to failure. The load was too heavy and the pilot had to release or risk crashing. We watched as H-30 fell to earth and tumbled down the hill.

Again we recruited the Lao soldiers to cut a new clearing and upright the fuselage. We would try again tomorrow.

The next day it was Conrad's turn to do the hook up while I handled the rope but first we had to lighten the load and take more components out of the cabin section. Another pilot and chopper was sent in. Although the same engines were in our helicopters they didn't perform the same way. Like two cars of the same model, one always performs better.

The hook up was made but as Conrad went to jump clear one end of the sling cable caught his boot and he came off head first. His ribs were bruised from the result of landing against a tree stump. Still he managed to scramble clear.

The load was still too heavy for the second helicopter and for the second time was dropped. Hotel 30 was now truly a wreck. Numerous dents and tears covered its once smooth outer skin.

We had an injured flight mechanic. Conrad was sent back to Udorn and we had to delay until a replacement could be sent up. On top of this the Lao soldiers refused to cut any more trees so we would have to do it ourselves.

Conrad's replacement arrived shortly and we continued with the operation. He introduced himself simply as Cris. He was a stocky built man of Filipino nationality. He told me he had been a flight mechanic before I arrived at Udorn. While on a mission upcountry, he had been shot while on the ground and severely injured. After his recovery, he was assigned to ground maintenance and hadn't been released to go back on flight status yet.

Our third try was successful. Captain Lou McCasland flew off with what was left of H-30.

Transmission and rotor head being lifted out

Dick Conrad, left, and Matt Luca having lunch at the H-30 crash site

Matt Luca observing Lao soldier's lunch of roast rat

April 1966

I had been flying missions in Laos for a few months. Flight mechanics would go out anywhere from six to nine days while the rules for pilots would usually be three to four days. The helicopter and flight mechanic would remain upcountry and a relief pilot would take over with no time lost. We carried aboard anything and everything that would fit inside. We supplied Lao Army outposts with food and ammunition. We flew in troops, carried out wounded and relocated refugees.

Some hilltops were small peaks and our pilots would make a fly over and the flight mechanic tossed out rice bags and other cargo.

I was on my return trip to Udorn when the news of another crash came over the radio. A flight mechanic by the name of Crisologo had been killed and his body was being flown back to Udorn. I was going over the name in my mind and then it dawned on me. Cris! It was Cris, the Filipino who had worked with me back in January on the H-30 recovery. He had returned to flying several months after his first accident and now it had claimed his life.

Unloading supplies at an outpost upcountry
Photo courtesy of Judy Porter

May 1966

From the last couple of weeks of April and into May, I found myself being scheduled more and more. I would return to Udorn and only get one day's rest and go right back out to Laos again. I didn't mind. We were in the middle of May and I had the most hours ever. My pay check would be the highest yet.

My next trip out was to Savannakhet in the southern part of Laos, usually easier and safer flying conditions. My pilot was Lloyd Higgins. The helicopter was H-42. On the third day we were sent up north. We were to link up with another group of choppers. There was a large operation going on up there.

It was the start of the monsoon season and that afternoon we found ourselves in a heavy downpour. Higgins decided it was too risky to make it back to our base at Sam Thong so he landed on a hilltop that was home to the Hmong tribe people of Laos who fought against the communist forces. The next morning when the fog lifted, we went on to Sam Thong. Higgins was rotated out and my relief pilot was John Wilmont. *Not much older than I am,* I thought to myself.

That afternoon we got caught in another heavy downpour. Wilmont got low and followed a small stream back to Sam Thong. I did not like flying in heavy rain with no visibility but at least I would have a warm meal, shower and bed for the night.

Rainy season Sam Thong, LS-20, Laos

May 19, 1966

The next morning at Sam Thong when I came outside, there was a line of helicopters, more than I was used to working with. We were going to transport troops of the Royal Lao Army. Some big push was going on to retake LS-36 which had been taken over by the communists. Moving troops into position was a lot easier because they were calmer. It was when they were retreating in the face of attack that things were chaotic as they fought their way onto the helicopters.

The plan was to take these troops to a staging area on high ground. The first run was completed without incident but heavy fog was rolling into the designated landing area so we had to choose another landing zone.

As fuel was burned off on each trip making the aircraft lighter, Wilmont instructed me to load two more soldiers. The second trip was into the rice paddies. It was a large opening and as the troops came off the different choppers, they ran in all directions instead of staying together. The pilots decided we would have to land closer together on our next run.

My cabin was packed on the third run. We were the second chopper in the convoy. As we were going in, the first helicopter radioed that he spotted tan uniforms on the ground and they were firing on him. He was aborting and leaving the landing area.

Tan uniforms! Usually worn by North Vietnamese regulars, I was thinking.

We were at the site and on a landing approach. We were going in.

Just as we started to set down, all hell broke loose. Shots rang out and we were being hit. There were loud explosions and sparks flying inside the cabin. I was trying to assess our situation but events were happening faster than I could think.

H-42 was bouncing about almost as though we were being dangled on a string. I sat down on the flight mechanic's seat just as we came to rest on the co-pilots side. I simply slid off the seat and onto the floor.

My first thoughts were, "*I'm not even hurt.*"

We were at a 45 degree angle and had not turned completely on our side.

Again they opened fire on us. Dozens of white holes appeared as bullets tore through the side. I was still lucky, crouched into a ball behind the fire wall and protected by the wheel and strut assembly.

All was quiet again. I could hear no voices. My depth perception was off. I was looking towards the rear of the cabin but all I could make out were piles of "green laundry" bags. But they weren't laundry bags. They were dead soldiers.

I have to get out, but how? If I go out the door, I'll be spotted and shot. If I try to knock out one of the emergency windows, I'll make noise and the shooting will start again. My other escape was up through the co-pilots seat and out that window, but that meant making noise again.

Everything had taken place in the space of a minute but it seemed much longer.

Suddenly I heard a voice. It was my pilot, Wilmont. "Luca, get the survival kit."

Without thinking of answering, I grabbed the kit and leapt out the door twisting 180 degrees, facing the front of the helicopter. No sooner than my feet touched the ground, bullets rang out. I ran but only got two steps when there was an explosion followed by a hot orange ball of flame. I threw my right hand up to protect my face and continued to run.

The survival kit was gone probably dropped when the shooting started. I still hadn't opened my eyes when I tripped and went head first toward the ground. I felt a hard rap to my right foot, a bullet had finally found me.

Then there was another bit of luck. The rains the day before had left a few inches of water in the rice paddies. This helped extinguish whatever clothing that might have still been on fire. More importantly, the water cooled my burns.

A feeling of horror came over me. My face is burned. My eyes were swollen shut and my lips were balloon size. I pictured an overdone baked potato.

Then the explosions started, one, two, three in succession. H-42 was blowing itself apart. Ammunition was cooking off from within it. I could feel objects landing on my backside and when the burning started, I flipped onto my back and let the water do its job.

Back on my stomach again, everything was quiet. It was time to assess my situation. Without lifting my head, I peered at my right foot. There was indeed a hole in the top of my boot. I touched my face again, this time with more thoroughness. It was stiff and warm but not really painful. My right hand had the most pain and when I lifted it from the water, there were sheets of flesh hanging from it. I put it back into the water.

It was about nine thirty in the morning. I was twenty-four years old and about to die in some rice paddy.

Why me? I thought. *Why not me?*

There was no one in the world that I would wish this on. I came here on my own free will and knew what the consequences could be.

Was the enemy still out there? I could play dead by keeping my face in the water and staying still. That would never work.

I vowed that if I ever got out of this rice paddy alive, I would never come back or cross the Mekong again. Crisologo tried it back in April and it got him killed.

The morning wore on. The water dried up and the heat was getting to my burns. I decided to crawl out of the rice paddy, staying close to the mud dikes that make up the sections of the fields. For the first time I felt a mild, dull ache on my left leg. It didn't hurt that bad so I forgot about it.

As I crawled, I came across my ball peen hammer and roll of safety wire. How odd. They had been in my toolbox and were now lying side by side. Next was a piece of human flesh about ten inches long. I picked it up. It was charred black but still pink on the inside when I twisted it. *This could have been me,* I thought, and tossed it away.

I heard the sound of a helicopter high above, circling about. I flipped onto my back and moved my white handkerchief slowly across my body right to left and back again. Then I heard another roar. This time it was Skyraiders, McDonald Douglas A1Es known as Sandies and used on rescue missions. They pack a punch with 50 caliber machine guns and carry an array of bombs, rockets and napalm. I watched as they turned and started their strafing runs. They were heading straight for me. *They're going to shoot me, sure as hell.* But instead they passed over and hit the tree lines and turned back for another run. I was near some bushes and threw my body into them. It was an irrigation ditch.

For the first time in hours I felt safe. I could hear the flapping of helicopter rotor blades coming in low and fast. They came in directly over my head and landed.

I'm saved.

As soon as it touched down, it lifted off again.

They're leaving me!

They moved up and landed at the wreckage of H-42 and the flight mechanic jumped out.

It was now or never for me. *Go, Go, Go,* I yelled to myself, as I ran for the rear of the chopper. I would travel several yards and fall because of the gunshot to my foot. But I made it. Just as the flight mechanic turned and tossed a Lao soldier onto the cabin floor our eyes met. It was Rusty Irons. The pilot was Steve Stevens. They had risked their lives to make a daring rescue.

I tried to step into the cabin but my foot gave out again. Rusty boosted me in and asked about my pilot, Wilmont. I said I didn't see him get out.

We took off. It was then I saw my left leg, the one with the dull ache. The explosion had torn my flesh away down to my calf muscle.

I was flown out to a small site and then flown to Sam Thong in a porter aircraft. Then I was loaded onto a Caribou. They laid me down in the cargo area. Father Lucien Bouchard, who everybody just called Father B, appeared. He was a missionary priest, who even back then, was a legend in Laos, living and working with the mountain tribes.

He asked me if I wanted to do confession.

When I hesitated, he said, "Don't worry. You're not going to die."

I said confession.

My ordeal was over. I would spend the next few months healing in various military hospitals. When I returned to Udorn, I transferred to ground maintenance. It was not the same again and in the spring of 1967, I resigned and returned to the States.

In spite of everything that happened, it is still to this day, some forty six years later, the most rewarding time spent with the greatest group of guys I will ever know.

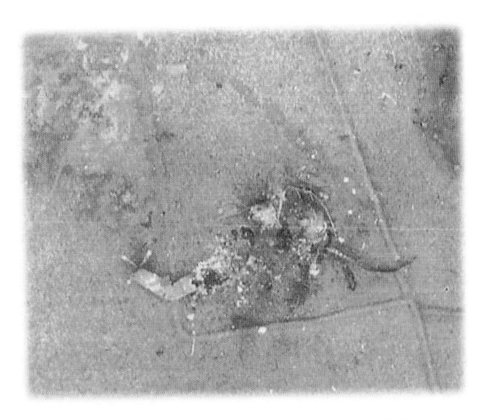

Crash site near LS-48 where pilot Bill Wilmont died
and flight mechanic Matt Luca was rescued by pilot
Steve Stevens and flight mechanic Rusty Irons.

Flight Mechanic
David L. "Mac" McDonald

My Honda S600

Udorn, Thailand
April 1965 to April 1967

In the early 1960s, I was working for Petroleum Helicopters, Inc., out of Louisiana doing offshore oil support and Columbia, South America, where I spent two years on oil exploration teams in the Amazon.

In those days, the helicopter world was small and I knew some of the pilots who had flown for Air America. I knew from their stories what Air America was all about. When I returned from Columbia, I heard they were hiring. Since I was always ready for new adventures and the pay was outstanding, I contacted H. H. Dawson in Washington, D.C., and was hired over the phone. Two or three weeks later, I was on my way to Southeast Asia.

Search and Rescue (SAR) at Sam Neua

On July 14, 1965, pilot Sam Jordan, co-pilot Dick Lieberth and I were doing routine work supplying outposts in the area around LS-36. I had been flying with Air America for about three months. My pilot was a seasoned captain but the co-pilot was new to Air America and was still being checked out prior to becoming captain.

Sometime in the late afternoon, we heard over the radio that a Navy plane had gone down near Sam Neua near the North Vietnamese border not far from our location. In fact, an aircraft from the USS Independence on a bombing mission over the Ho Chi Minh trail caught fire after a bomb exploded prematurely under the wing. The pilot and navigator ejected into hostile territory prior to the plane going down. There were no other aircraft working in the area with us and solo SARs were not permitted so we did not attempt a pickup.

Fortunately the pilot and navigator survived the night and the following morning the SAR operation continued. We were told that two other Air America helicopters would handle the rescue so we continued our mission of supplying outposts near LS-36, which was just as well as the airmen had gone down in bad guy country and they had a night to bring in reinforcements. This wasn't going to be an easy rescue. I was new at this and the co-pilot even newer.

A short time later, however, we were called to join in the rescue as one of the Air America helicopters attempting the pickup was shot up and had to leave the area.

Sam was told to fuel up at LS-36 which he ignored because we left for the pickup site without the added fuel. Sam was an experienced, unflappable pilot and I had complete confidence in him. At some point the adrenalin kicked in and I was ready for anything.

There were a lot of aircraft in the area. There was another Air America helicopter, an Air Force Jolly Green, several T-28s, a Caribou and Skyraiders. If the bad guys wanted something to shoot at, we were giving it to them.

We spotted one of the downed airmen fairly easily. We swooped down, the guy leapt in and we were out of there. He could not help us pinpoint the other airman, however, so we continued to circle and search. Radio communications from the ground were not clear and they didn't respond to our calls for more information.

Finally Sam spotted the guy near a clump of trees and moved the helicopter toward the area. We were in a hover over the trees when we saw flashes of gunfire nearby so Sam called for support from the T-28s.

Now we were under small arms fire, the Navy was laying down air support, Sam is hovering all this time at full power and I'm thinking about the fuel gauge.

Amidst this bedlam of gunfire, bombs dropping and Skyraider 20-mm cannons firing, I tossed the hoist cable out but it kept getting caught in the trees. Shortly I felt the airman on the horse collar through the cable and I started the lift which is very slow on a good day. I never saw him until he cleared the trees on the hoist.

Sam was trying to talk to me but I could only focus on the pilot who was not strapped into the harness but hanging on with only one arm through the horse collar with enemy ground fire popping off all around us. I had one thought in mind. Get the guy into the helicopter as fast as I could. I just couldn't release the hoist button to hit the mike button to respond to Sam.

Meanwhile the co-pilot is useless and the unflappable Sam is becoming flappable.

Somehow in the mass confusion of it all, Sam thought the airman was in the aircraft and started forward. We were probably up to sixty knots when he realized the guy was not in the aircraft. He was still hanging from the hoist some 50 feet below, swinging like a pendulum. It must have been a hairy ride.

When I pulled him in, the airmen hugged each other in relief. They were two happy guys.

We were desperately low on fuel and barely made it over the ridge to a friendly site where we pumped in a 55 gallon drum of fuel. We then took them to LS-36 where they transferred to the Caribou for the ride back to Thailand.

We went back to work.

Lt. Donald Eaton and Lt. Donald V. Boecker had been on the ground evading the enemy for nineteen hours. Today they are both retired Rear Admirals.

Engine Change Upcountry

Flight Mechanic Johnny Sibal

Hmong Audience

Pattaya

Air America Beach House

      Air America had a beach house in Pattaya, Thailand, located on the east coast of the Gulf of Thailand about 100 miles southeast of Bangkok. Pattaya was a small fishing village until the 1960s when American servicemen began arriving for rest and relaxation during the war years in Southeast Asia. It has since become a prosperous tourist area.

Wet submarine

The scuba club in Udorn built a wet submarine and Bobby Nunez drove it all the way to Pattaya, almost 400 miles, on top of his little truck. It must have puzzled the locals no end.

If I remember correctly, it didn't work well on its maiden voyage. It went to the bottom and overturned. We'd made the driving planes too big and water pressure wouldn't let the driver correct upwards. No one was hurt and we went back to the drawing board.

Takhli

An interesting two months for me in 1965 was when I was sent TDY to Takhli Royal Thai Air Force Base located in central Thailand about 150 miles northwest of Bangkok. I was to help the Air America mechanic there, first name Jesse, don't recall his last, with turning around Air America aircraft on secret flights that I knew little about but could draw my own conclusions.

The Air America pad was in a heavily guarded, secluded part of the base. Everybody wore civvies but they were obviously Air Force. The place was covered in antenna arrays and I had to sign a non-disclosure agreement about what went on there.

U-2 flights were staged out of there but we weren't supposed to say U-2. The joke was we could say "You Also."

Southern Air Transport DC-7s from Japan and Taiwan routinely came and went at night, after we refueled and did preventative maintenance. I didn't know their destination but suspected Pakistan as they were feuding with India at the time. They were mostly loaded with arms, munitions and once a Helio Courier. Sometimes they carried oriental troops, Taiwanese, I think, who were loaded and unloaded in darkness. Jesse and I weren't allowed near the aircraft until the troops left in covered trucks.

"Shower Shoes Wilson" used to fly in and out periodically in a black, unmarked C-46 bulging with radar domes and electronic gear. It was just him and one guy, a technician of some kind, I assume. Then they would leave for two or three days, come back to Takhli for fuel and soar off again.

At times Air Force C-130s would come in. We stripped all military ID off, and an Air America crew would take it somewhere. Who knows?

I came down with Malaria while at Takhli so I wasn't much help any longer. I think I was replaced by Dick Conrad and returned to Udorn.

You've probably heard all the Tony Poe legends. He was something else. Once at LS-118, we were sitting around the dinner table and he produced an unopened bottle of bourbon. He opened and drank from it, set it back on the table, pulled out a 38 and said the bottle better be empty before it got back to him.

The ear bounty stories are true. I saw them strung up in the radio shack at LS-36.

There will never be another job like Air America. It was an interesting time with great people.

After Air America, I returned to Florida, met my future wife and ended up as an Aircraft Maintenance Supervisor for the County of Volusia, Florida, where 33 years later, I retired, enrolled in Medicare and joined AARP.

Flight Mechanic
Richard S. "Rick" Strba

LS-50, Phu Cum/II, Laos
1968

We were at LS-50 for a school dedication in the village of Phu Cum. We had brought in about eight people both American and Lao including the legendary Pop Buell, a former Indiana farmer who worked in Laos as an agricultural advisor for USAID.

The pilot and I were invited to lunch but I told them I had to stay with the helicopter. The pilot went with them but returned in about ten minutes. I guess he looked over the lunch special and changed his mind.

My menu was hot beanie weenies, Vienna sausages and crackers cooked over 115/145 (aviation fuel).

I was twenty five when I joined Air America. I had served with the U.S. Marine Corps in helicopter maintenance from June 1960 to June 1964. Following the Marine Corps, I went to work for a freight airline called Zantop Air Transport. While there, I responded to a help wanted ad in the newspaper which read, "UH-34 Flight Mechanic Aircraft Maintenance Supervisors, Far East Aviation Company [with an 800 number]." After applying, I received a job offer and reported to work for Air America in Bangkok, Thailand, in March of 1967. Later I moved to Udorn, Thailand. From March of 1967 to May of 1970 were some of the most exciting times of my life.

These are my stories.

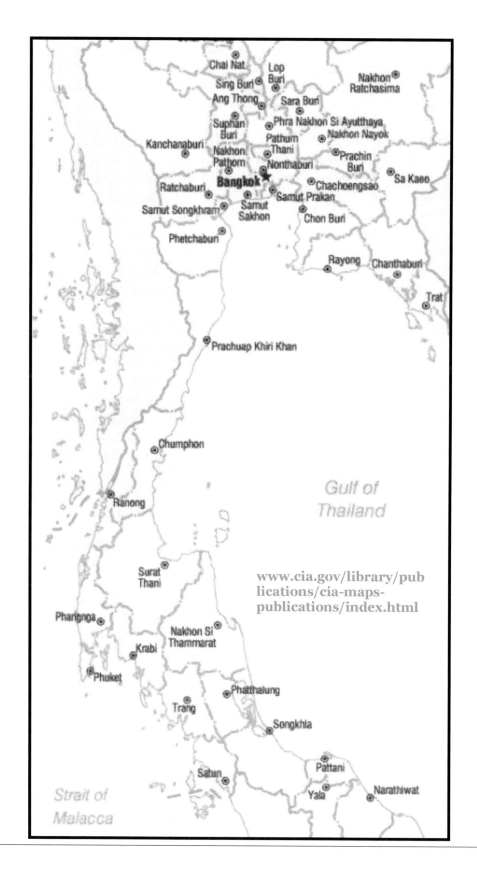

www.cia.gov/library/pub
lications/cia-maps-
publications/index.html

The Story of 803 - Ragan Field

803 was an Air America Bangkok based UH-34 Helicopter temporarily assigned to Songkhla, Thailand. Unlike most Air America H-34s, 803 was painted white. Previously, it was part of a fleet of white aircraft assigned by the United Nations as unbiased peace keepers in the region. However, every time they went out in the field and tried to get between opposing forces, everybody shot at the white helicopter. Couple that with the non-payment to Air America for maintenance, and it ended up with Air America getting one white UH-34D.

I was the flight mechanic on 803 for about six months. The pilot was Tom Moher.

For the first three months, we spent almost all the time in Songkhla. We were working for Janski & Bailey, a unit of Atlantic Research Corporation. Our job was to fly a group of eight engineers out to a camp in a remote jungle rain forest in southern Thailand where they were building an airstrip which could accommodate fixed wing aircraft like the Air America Helio Couriers. The guy in charge was S. Morgan Ragan.

We would leave the Songkhla airport at 7 a.m. It was about a one hour flight. We would leave the camp at 4 p.m. for the return to the airport in Songkhla. This was a Monday to Friday job with weekends off.

While at the camp, there wasn't much for us to do. We had a small cabin with two beds, a desk ceiling light and an air conditioner. Weekdays were early to bed and early to rise at 5 a.m. for breakfast. We would take a box lunch with Thai food that we would eat about noon. Tom looked at the food and said it probably came from the rain forest.

Weekends we would sit around the hotel pool or go to the hotel beach. If it were a beach day, we would have lunch at the beachside restaurant. Tom would always get beef and rice with extra beef and hot peppers. When we went back to the beach, Tom took the beef and peppers with him. He would walk around until he found a piece of wood or a banana leaf. He would roll up a hot pepper in a piece of beef and set it on the banana leaf, then wait for the beach dogs to come along. They would smell the food, pick it up and chew it a couple of times. Then they would jump up in the air, start running like hell, barking and yelping. Tom and I would be laughing so hard, nearly falling out of our beach chairs. The Thais walking by just stared at us. Maybe it was their dog or it could have been one of their grandparents, a belief in the Buddhist religion that you may be reincarnated as some other life form.

Customers on Air Strip Survey

Once during the three months at Songkhla, we had to go up to Udorn for a 90-day inspection. We flew to Bangkok where we were met by a relief pilot so Tom could spend his week with his wife Kathy in Bangkok. I went with the aircraft to Udorn. There was a little more night life than in Songkhla and I could sleep late.

Tom came up on Friday. We did a test flight on Saturday and left for Songkhla Sunday morning. It took about seven hours with a fuel stop in Bangkok. When we landed at Songkhla and taxied in, they had the 803 girls holding up their sign. That and the dogs were the best parts of being down there.

Monday we flew out to the camp. We had been gone a week. They were working on the airstrip, marking out trees, some of which were 150 feet high, and cutting them down. At least we had something to do, watching people work.

We knew that the Helio Courier was coming soon but the engineers wanted to do some tests using the helicopter while the rain was holding off. So Wednesday, two guys were out measuring the cabin door and the cabin and taking notes. Later they asked me how to start the auxiliary power unit. I showed them and they said thank you, my job was over. These guys were going to run all their equipment with aircraft power hooked up to cannon plugs in the cabin, no splicing wires. They were good. They knew what they were doing and they did it.

Because there would be an engineer in the co-pilot's seat and two in the cabin, I stayed on the ground during the tests. They had Tom flying a pattern over the trees at different altitudes from high to tree top level.

The air strip was completed just hours before the monsoon rains began. The runway, made from crushed rock, was about 750 feet long and 50 feet wide. In a 1968 Atlantic Research Corporation Newsletter, it said that estimates for the construction of the landing strip had been between $50,000 and $150,000. In the end, the actual cost for materials and labor came in at $2500, which was accomplished primarily through the cooperation and enthusiasm of the Thai people.

A few weeks later on a Friday, the Helio Courier arrived from Bangkok. It landed at 2 p.m.

At 4 p.m., they asked who wanted to fly back to Songkhla on the Helio. Everybody said they would take the helicopter. For the last time, the eight engineers climbed in. The last guy in was the man in charge, Ragan, who everyone called Reb. The Thai people had been so impressed with his work that they named the air strip Ragan Field in his honor.

Helio and 803 prior to last flight out from Ragan Field

About 20 minutes after takeoff, Reb told me to close the cabin door. He opened a box he had brought onboard. There were two bottles of champagne and nine glasses in it. When the cork popped, Tom called down and wanted to know what the noise was.

I told him about the bottle.

"You're not drinking?"

"They gave me a glass."

"Save me some."

A few minutes later I called up to him, "The bottle's empty."

"God damn. Who drank the last glass?"

"I did."

He became quiet.

When we landed and Tom was shutting down, everybody waited to say good bye and Reb gave Tom the second bottle of champagne.

Tom showed it to me and said, "We'll drink it tonight."

"No," I replied, "Take it to Bangkok and drink it with Kathy."

The next day we flew to Bangkok where I was dropped off first at the Siam Intercontinental Hotel. Three months was a long time to be in a rain forest in Thailand.

I said, "Well, we're back in the big city."

Siam Intercontinental Hotel
Bangkok, Thailand
Photo courtesy of Roger Wollstadt

The Siam Intercontinental Hotel

Whenever I was in Bangkok I stayed at the Siam Intercontinental Hotel. It was expensive but I was only there for ten days or so out of a month so I figured, what the hell, why not go first class and live a little better?

One night in Bangkok, a group of about ten Air America guys were at Max's Bar on Patpong Road. We worked hard and we played hard and this night we were pretty rowdy as was the norm. About 5 p.m., I decided to go back to the Intercontinental Hotel for happy hour where it was a little more civilized. To my chagrin, the group decided to go with me. I knew this wasn't a good idea but Tom had hired a car with a driver for his visiting family so we all piled in and went to the Intercontinental. They trooped into the lounge and proceeded to drink and carry on in their usual manner, singing songs and telling jokes. Our group was being so rowdy that people started to leave and after a while, I tired of their behavior myself, told them so and retired to the quiet luxury of my room.

They continued to drink and run up a heavy tab. At some point in the evening a bell boy walked through the bar paging a Mr. Wilson. He carried a sign with Mr. Wilson's name and room number on it. The Air America guys all called for their checks, which they signed with Mr. Wilson's name and room number.

The next morning when Mr. Wilson, who did not drink at all, checked out, he was presented with an enormous bar bill. He immediately freaked out and management was called. The lounge manager quickly figured out what had happened and called up to my room, demanding that I come down immediately and pay the bill.

I paid the bill but I was fuming. I called Tom and told him I was going to hunt them down one by one and make them pay me back. I never invited them over to the Intercontinental again but they showed up anyway.

Night Missions Out of Nakhon Phanom

Tom and I with co-pilot Ted Cash were flying 803 on a night mission out of Nakhon Phanom (NKP). It was a classified mission. We had a couple of customers, a secretary for the group and the director for the project.

We were out in the woods halfway between NKP and Nakhon Sawan. The only navigational aid was the ADF. It was real late at night with thunderstorms all over the place. We figured we wouldn't get much done that particular night and should return to the base for the night.

When we took off from the compound where we had been working, the pilots made the classic mistake of night flying, instead of flying due north toward the base, they did a 180 degree turn and headed south. We were heading toward what we thought was NKP dodging thunderstorms and bad weather. It was black as the ace of spades. Apparently the pilots were not watching the navigation instruments very closely. We passed over a small town on the river and started following a road which would lead us to NKP. That is if we had been going in the right direction. We followed the road and the lights kept getting closer and closer Pretty soon we were about 100 feet above the lights but the pilots were reading 3000 feet on the altimeter. I could tell from their comments that they were lost. I mean real lost.

It finally dawned on them that we were going in the wrong direction and were in the mountains. They followed the lights up the mountain and located a top secret camp up there called Camp Cloudy. There were lights all around it. We flew around the base and made our approach onto what we thought was the landing strip.

Tom landed and shut down. Just about the time the rotor blades stopped, this voice came over the loud speaker, "Helicopter, you have landed in our mine field."

I heard this thumping from the cockpit and I looked up and Tom was banging his head on the cockpit sliding window.

They told us to start up and follow a jeep that would take us to a safe place to land inside the fence. Tom let Ted fly the aircraft into the confines of the base. When we landed, there were about ten American soldiers waiting there, weapons ready. 803 was white with an American flag painted on the tail pylon. What puzzled them was the time of night. It was about 11:30 p.m.

I was always the first out of the helicopter unless we were in Laos. It was easy for me, one foot on the landing gear and the second on the ground. I barely got on the ground when Ted came around to start the bullshit show.

Ted introduced himself and said, "We are on a special inspection tour of US military bases in Thailand for Secretary of Defense McNamara." The civilians with us all carried DOD ID cards which loaned credibility to his story.

They took us to a club where Ted just continued this line of bullshit about this was the best base we had visited and how badly we had been treated at other bases and their base really knew how to treat VIPs and so on. He asked about the quality of their food supplies and did they have everything they needed, and on he went. It must have worked because they gave us the VIP sleeping quarters that night. Breakfast was all set up for us and they gave us a really great meal and then they took us all on a tour of the whole base. We climbed into the helicopter and off we went. I never heard if the shit hit the fan or not.

www.cia.gov/library/
publications/cia-
maps-publications/
index.html

Thailand

Refueling at U-Tapao

For about five years 803 was assigned to a military research group out of an academic think tank from the States. They were here to clean up the guerilla warfare and insurrection in Thailand and give the Thai government some of our excellent technical and military advice on how to cope with their situation. What a joke.

On one particular mission we were sent on a two day assignment with a retired special forces major who had a heavy liking for his booze. Every time we took him out we had a problem because of it. This time was no different.

He met us in Bangkok in the early morning and we flew out to Lopburi, an abandoned Japanese military camp that Bill Lair had turned into a training camp for the Thai Police Aerial Reinforcement Unit (PARU). There were three groups of Special Forces people conducting all the training at the site.

When we arrived, the major, who we will call Steve, got off. There was a hand shaking and back slapping ceremony with his friends while we shut down and Tom and I went over to the little club for coffee. While there, Steve and his friends came in and started pounding down the beer. It was still morning.

About 10 o'clock Steve came over and said he wanted to go to the Marine detachment at a remote spot in southern Thailand. "I have to pay a visit there and do some work."

Tom said, "Hell, that's the other end of the spectrum. They do more work at the other camp due south, southeast." Tom was not too anxious to make the long trip especially with this guy.

"I just want to go over and say Hi to my friends."

Tom said, "Aw, shit. Okay."

One of Steve's Special Forces buddies, a captain, decided to go along.

We arrived at the site about 11:30 a.m. and shut down. Steve and his captain friend said they wanted to go in to eat lunch and would be back about 2 o'clock and ready to go.

So Tom and I found a place to eat and returned to the aircraft promptly at 2:00 p.m. We waited. We waited. We waited. 3 p.m. rolled around and still no customer. We were getting pretty ticked. There was a hard and fast rule against flying at night in Thailand. It's not conducive to a long life.

Along they came about 3:30 p.m. and piled into the helicopter. A couple of border patrol police chiefs had joined the group. They were loaded to the gills. Steve and his Special Forces captain friend had the Governor of the Southern Province of Chonburi in tow with three of his red beret guards. They were really bombed and they had a couple of bottles of some kind of

Chinese wine with them. They were singing, toasting, shaking hands, walking arm in arm and swearing to be companions for life against the pinkko communist bastards and so on.

Tom was really getting pissed off, but I couldn't stop laughing and that was getting him more pissed.

As soon as they were boarded, we were airborne. Tom told me we had to go to U-Tapao Air Base for refueling. He was anticipating a real bad scene. He was hoping they would fall asleep but, from where I was sitting, there was no chance of that. They were drinking more wine. The Governor was trying to jump out the door. The others were dancing back and forth, yelling at each other or rolling around on the floor.

I told Tom what was going on and he responded with, "That's just great. I want to get into U-Tapao, refuel and get the hell out."

To expedite our time on the ground at the Base, Tom called the U-Tapao tower and said, "This is Air Force Helicopter 803 inbound with a code six on board." A code six was the Air Force VIP code for a Governor of a Province. "We want to refuel and get back in the air immediately to return to Bangkok."

They said to hang on. They would get back to us. They called back to confirm there was a code six on board.

"Yes, we have a code six on board with his guards and we want to refuel with an immediate departure. We do not want to hang around the base. We want to be back in Bangkok before dark."

"Okay. Can do. Call us when you are two miles out."

I heard Tom say, "Thank God for that."

At two miles out Tom called the tower again. "U-Tapao tower, this is Hotel 803. We're two miles out."

"803, you're cleared for landing." They told us to land on the parallel road to the south and taxi to the refueling pits on the southeastern end.

We were just touching down when Tom told me there were two staff cars pulling up, one with the Base Commander flag.

It got worse. When we taxied up, Tom pulled up short and locked the brakes. Right in front of us was a ten man Air Force Honor Guard. The base commander and a colonel got out of their cars and they were all standing there expectantly waiting to see what was coming out of our helicopter.

They did not have to wait for long.

Tom started the shut down because we were almost out of gas. He said later he considered leaving but he just didn't have enough fuel.

While we were shutting down, Steve fell out of the helicopter face first right in front of the whole group. Next came the Special Forces captain, who stepped over him and damned near tripped. He leaned back on the helicopter, holding on for dear life. They both kept blinking their eyes trying to focus on all the military brass and the honor guard in front of us.

Tom continued the shut down as if everything were normal.

The Governor got out of the aircraft, trying to remain upright. His body guards got out with their little submachine guns and stood around the Governor. They didn't know what was going on. Were they going to arrest the Governor or what?

The honor guard snapped to attention. They all looked kind of shocked by the whole thing.

The base commander started forward and stopped, started and stopped again. He put his hands on his hips, trying to figure out what the hell was going on.

Tom completed the shut down.

Steve got up from the ground and walked over to the base commander and had some words. The Special Forces captain was still hanging on to the helicopter trying to focus in and listing about 35 degrees to the left. Steve started giving everyone the finger, saluting them and telling them to all piss off.

Someone explained to the Governor that this was an honor guard for him. He was very pleased. He grabbed Tom's Air America cap, the one with the wings on it, from the helicopter, whipped it on his head sideways and proceeded to inspect the troops. He tried to take their rifles from them but the guards were having none of that. He proceeded down the line, shouting orders in Thai and weaving back and forth. I was expecting him to fall down at any minute but so far so good. Steve joined him, chatting to the honor guard as they moved down the line.

I was still in the helicopter doubled up with laughter. Tom was still in the pilot's seat just shaking his head.

The Air Force commander approached the helicopter, rapped on the side and yelled up at Tom, "What the hell are you and where are you from?"

"Sir, it's a long story, but if you will just refuel me, I'll get these people the hell out of here. I'm stuck with a bunch of VIPs who've been drinking and I just want to get them back to Bangkok.

"I'll tell you what, you son of a bitch, I'll take your name and your number and it will be the last time you get airborne again."

"I'm sorry. I'm not at liberty to give you my name and number. You'll have to check with the customer over there."

"I got your number, you son of a bitch. I'll get your name." The guy was furious.

Tom said, "Look, this isn't my god damn fault. I'm just the pilot."

This just made him madder.

Meanwhile on the ground it was turning into a real circus. The Governor had just fallen on his ass in front of the honor guards who were having trouble maintaining their poise. I could see them starting to grin as a prelude to outright laughter.

Our Special Forces captain came over and said something to the commander which apparently enraged him even further if that were possible. He must have made a threatening move toward the Special Forces guy who struck a karate pose and told the commander to back up, which he did. Then our guy climbed into the helicopter and passed out on the seat. The commander ordered him out of the helicopter but he just laid there.

Then the Commander said, "I'm calling the military police and I'm locking everybody up."

At that point Tom intervened with, "If you do, you're going to have a very embarrassing situation. You would be locking up a Thai Province Governor. It will really get to be a hairy scene and you're going to be in deep shit."

The commander and his colonel discussed it, thought about it and fumed a little. "Get them the hell out of here. Get out."

We got the Governor back on his feet and into the helicopter. Steve turned and saluted everybody and climbed into the helicopter.

The commander came up to Tom and said, "Don't you ever, ever, ever dare come back here again. If you ever come back here and we can get our hands on you, we will."

We refueled and off we went. We flew all the way back to Bangkok and then Steve told us he wanted to go back to Lopburi for a big party they were having that night. We arrived at Lopburi about twenty minutes after dark. By the time we got to the party location, everyone there was dead drunk and asleep. So much for the big party at Lopburi.

Porter on the Air America ramp, Chiang Mai, Thailand Airport

803 Flight to Laos

Tom Moher and I left Bangkok about noon to fly to Nakhon Phanom (NKP) Royal Thai Air Force Base where we were to meet the customers the following day.

Upon arrival at NKP, I fueled the aircraft and completed the overnight service in preparation for the next day. Then Tom and I walked over to the transit barracks office to get a room for the next two nights. It was great staying on the airbase compared to a hotel in downtown. Additionally our room was just down the street from the Officers' Club. The first time I was at the NKP Officers' Club, I bought a membership for $30 which was a good investment as they serve "back in the States food" and the membership card was also good at the Bangkok Officers' Club.

The next morning, we flew to the NKP civilian airport, a short distance away. We landed, shut down and awaited the Thai Airway C-47 from Bangkok.

The plane arrived shortly and we saw five or six guys carrying small bags or suitcases and briefcases. They were planning on visiting a number of villages in Thailand over a two day period. The leader walked over to Tom and gave him a list of the villages he wanted to visit.

We took off shortly and flew to the first village on the list which was about one hour north of NKP.

While on the ground waiting for the customers to do their thing, Tom said, "This guy isn't going to make all the villages in two days. He'll go back to Bangkok and blame me."

We left for the second village flying southwest. We landed and off they went.

They came back and we were off to village three. When we landed, it was after 1 p.m. Tom told them we needed to go to NKP to refuel and would return to pick them up.

We landed back at NKP and called for fuel operations who said it would take a while as they had six of their aircraft ahead of us. So we waited. Finally, I suggested that Tom go to the Officers' Club to get our lunch. I gave him my order and money and he walked off with his head down. Tom took all this dealing with the contractors way too seriously.

About forty minutes later a jeep pulled up and Tom hopped out. He had managed to get a ride back.

"Are we ready?"

"No fuel yet," was my response. His reaction was like someone shot his dog.

He had bought a cheese sandwich, fries and a 7-up and I knew his stomach was bothering him.

About the time we finished our lunch, the fuel truck rolled up. As we topped off and the fuel guy was rolling the hose, Tom was doing a battery start, I was signing the fuel slip, and the rotors were engaging.

Back at the village where we left the contractors, the leader asked me, "What took so long?"

"The air force had six planes ahead of us and their aircraft come first."

He just looked at me and shook his head.

We got to village four, completed business and the leader of the group asked to go back to NKP. In route, he asked, "Could we start early tomorrow morning?"

"How early?" was my response.

"7:30 a.m."

I asked Tom and he said it was okay. We returned to NKP and the Officers' Club.

The next morning we got to NKP airport before 7:30 a.m. and they were waiting for us. We loaded up and headed to village number five which was the last one on yesterday's schedule. We landed and shutdown. Took off from village five to village six where we shutdown. Took off from village six to village seven. Before we landed Tom told me to tell the leader that we were going to refuel, which I did. We dropped them off and took off a few minutes later. Tom told me that we were not going to the airbase for fuel.

"Where are we going?"

Tom said, "Thakhek."

"They won't give us fuel. The aircraft is the wrong color." 803 was white and Air America helicopters were generally camouflage green.

He said, "We'll just take it."

"There'll be people there."

"No, they'll be at lunch."

There were times when I quit being a flight mechanic and became Tom's henchman. Then it dawned on me. He was bull shitting me.

As we were flying along, I was looking out the door. I could see the airport across the river. Tom made a sharp right turn and nosed the aircraft down. He swung around and landed next to the fuel dump."

He said, "Get two drums."

I rolled the two drums to the cabin door. We hoisted them on board and I was trying to get a strap to hold them in place when the crew bell went off.

I plugged into the **intercom and heard** Tom say, "Look out the door."

To the right there was the road from the airport to the town and down the road, coming fast and furious, were two army jeeps. We were airborne heading back to Thailand.

Our people thought we would be gone another two plus hours so they went to lunch. About half way through their lunch, they heard us landing so they hurried back to the soccer field to watch us pump fuel.

We went on to the last three villages and still had time to get the people back to NKP airport to catch Thai Airway back to Bangkok.

We still had to go back to the NKP airbase for fuel and Tom wanted to make a chow run to the Officers' Club. It was almost 9 p.m. by the time we got to Don Muang Airport.

As for the fuel from Laos, I never thought much about it and I don't think Tom did either.

About a month or so later, we were going to the Air America base at Udorn for maintenance. We landed and Tom called operations to let them know 803 was on the ground.

Operations responded with, "Okay and, Captain Moher, you must see the base manager."

I asked, "Is it your birthday?"

Tom said, "No."

I didn't think much about it. Tom and the base manager, Clarence Abadie, went back years.

About an hour later Tom came by and asked what I was going to do?

I said, "Go to the club, then later, head downtown."

He said, "Sounds good."

"By the way," I said, "What did Abadie want?"

"He told me that 803 would never cross the river or go into Laos again."

"I told you 803 was the wrong color. You should blame it on the International Control Commission."

Refueling 803 somewhere in Thailand. I'm on the pump.
Tom Moher is under the poncho holding the hose.

Reunion at Chiang Khong

While flying 803 out of Bangkok, Tom Moher and I flew numerous diplomats, dignitaries and pedantic types for various contractors and agencies. Tom had been doing this for five years and his patience with the people was waning. Mostly he found them pretentious, egotistical and in rare cases, downright stupid. The over educated were the most unbearable. They could talk theory for hours but could not apply it.

As Tom put it, "They had the common sense of an ant."

Over time he became hardened and embittered towards them. In my case, I was professional while working with them but in the evenings on my own time, I could be a little blunt.

It was a Sunday morning when we left Udorn for Chiang Mai in northern Thailand. We landed about noon and Tom waited until I did the overnight service on the helicopter. Then we left for the hotel.

Monday morning, we left the hotel to go to the airport to wait for Thai Airways from Bangkok with our new group of contractors.

The C-47 taxied up and our hotel van drove over to the aircraft to take their baggage. As they came down the stairs, they walked directly over to the helicopter. Something that would be unheard of in today's security climate. There were five in the group. They were wearing brand new jungle fatigues, boots and hats. Tom thought they looked ridiculous. We were going to be with this group for a week.

Today we were to stop in villages to the west and north of Chiang Mai without flying into Burma. After Laos, Tom was watching the map real close. Everything went all right and we got back to the airport a little after 4 p.m.

I thought this group might be okay. They liked to quit early while it was still daylight. Little did I know that in two hours I would be eating those words.

The contractors left for the evening. I was working on the aircraft waiting for the fuel truck when Tom came up to me to say that one of the contractors wanted to have a drink with him in the hotel bar at 6 p.m.

"Leave me out," I told him.

"Just one drink, then we'll leave."

"Okay," I agreed.

When we got to the hotel, it was almost 6 p.m. so I went into the lobby men's room, washed up, combed my hair and walked to the bar. Tom was sitting on a stool with nobody else around. Tom said that the guy had called down and told him he couldn't leave his room so he wanted us to come up there and have a drink. I should have known better but we went up to the room.

When we got there, this guy said, "I couldn't meet you in the bar because the Russians have just invaded Czechoslovakia and I must stay close to the phone in case the ambassador needs me."

Well of all the pompous stories I'd heard from these people, this was the mother lode and I lost it. I don't recall my exact words but fucking asshole was mentioned several times along with jerks, idiots, etc.

The next morning, we went out to the airport for an 8 a.m. takeoff. When the people showed up, there were only four of them. Our drinking buddy of the previous night was missing.

Tom asked, "Are we waiting for someone?"

One of the contractors responded, "No. Mr. X is going to catch the 10 a.m. flight to Bangkok."

So I said, "He mentioned last night that he might have to go to Czechoslovakia." These people just looked at each other and Tom had a hard time climbing up the side of the helicopter because he was laughing so hard.

I found out later that our drinking buddy was a retired Army major who worked as a State Department security officer. Part of his job was talking to people like us and others to see what kind of information we were giving out. I was further told that if he was wearing engineering boots that was where he kept his tape recorder.

Off we went. Each day was the same, we would stop at a village and the contractors would disappear into the village for hours while we waited in the hot sun. They would return and we would go to the next village and do it all over again. Once they posed on the Burmese border, sprinkling dirt on their clothes, holding their interpreter's rifle in various poses and pointing to the Burma sign. This went over real well with Tom. He finally told them that it wasn't too smart for Americans to be seen carrying weapons on the border between Thailand and Burma. They also asked us to fly them into Laos but Tom refused and so did the Embassy when they asked for permission.

Sometime during the trip this group found the rations that we stored in the back of the aircraft for emergencies and ate them. Tom read them the riot act. They said they were sorry but did not offer to replace the food.

Close to the end of the week, we were going near the golden triangle where Thailand, Laos and Burma come together on the Mekong River. We landed at several villages and about 3:30 p.m. we left the last village on the list for an overnight at Chiang Khong. Chiang Khong was a sleepy village across the Mekong from Ban Houei Sai, Laos. Ban Houei Sai had an old French fort left over from the Indochina wars or colony days.

Part of the fort was used as a hospital by the Tom Dooley Foundation. They had an American doctor and several American nurses along with two or three American volunteer Pan American flight attendants who taught the local people English.

There was an airport in Chiang Khong but we had to land on the school soccer field for security reasons. The soccer field was in town so we had to walk back and forth to our hotel which was nice by 1968 standards.

French Fort at Ban Houei Sai, Laos

We checked in, got a couple of bottles of cold beer and went upstairs to our rooms. Tom's room had a balcony with chairs facing the river. It was relaxing watching the boats going up and down the river and back and forth to Laos.

About 7 p.m. and after a few big Singhas, the local Thai beer, we decided to walk down to the restaurant on the river. It was early. After we arrived, we had another couple of beers. Then the four contractors showed up and asked to join us.

Sure, I didn't care. In one more day, we would drop them off in Chiang Mai and they would fly back to Bangkok. Tom and I, in a couple of days or a week, would get another group of soil samplers.

We ordered dinner and then later, around 9 p.m., when we were talking about going back to the hotel, a group of Thai's walked up to the front of the restaurant. I was looking at this one guy and was thinking, *he's big for a Thai.* He was pointing at Tom and me. When he walked up, I saw that he was not a Thai. He walked around the table towards Tom, yelling, swearing and laughing. Tom got up laughing as well. It turned out to be Tony Poe, the infamous CIA agent who lived among the Hmong people in Laos.

Tony said, "Get up. I want to sit down and talk to Tom Moher."

I started to get up and Tony said, "Not you." He told the contractor next to me to get up and find another chair.

Tom and Tony had met when Tom was flying for Air America in Laos. Tom left Laos to fly in Thailand and Tony thought he had gone back to the States. They reminisced for about 10 or 15 minutes. Then Tony started looking around the table at our people.

"Where did you get these people?" he asked Tom.

"Chiang Mai. We're taking them around to some of the villages in the area."

Tony looked right at them and said, "Stay in Thailand. Don't come to my site. You people are no good. You're bad people. You're evil." Those were the nice thing he said about them.

Shortly Tom said to me, "Look at that table," and he nodded his head toward the group that had been with Tony when he came in. They were looking at the four people at our table. As it turned out, they were Thai police and a Lao army officer. The four contractors did the right thing. They got up, paid their bill and left.

We sat and bullshitted for another 30 minutes until the Thais and the Lao came up and said they were leaving. Tony said he had to leave with them because the Lao had the boat back to Laos (thanks to USAID).

On the walk back to the hotel, Tom said, "I know I'm going to get written up about this incident with Tony."

I said, "Don't worry. You didn't do anything."

Turns out, I was right. Tom didn't get written up. I did and in about three weeks the white helicopter for me became green and Bangkok was only for R&R visits.

After about a month of flying out of Udorn, I got a trip to LS-118A, Nam Lieu. That night about 6 p.m., I walked up to the house where all the overnight crews stayed. I walked in and Tony Poe was holding court.

He saw me and said, "You been here before?"

I said, "No."

He said, "I've seen you before."

"I saw you in Chiang Khong with Tom Moher."

He gave me a big smile and said, "I told you those people were bad. They wrote me up. I got a letter from the ambassador about that night."

About a year later, I was working out of Luang Prabang. After securing the aircraft for the night, I went to the hotel. Walking up the path past the bar, I noticed two Air America pilots at a table with the State Department security officer from out of my past wearing his engineering boots. I got my key, threw my bag on the bed and went back downstairs. I came up on his right side and said to the pilots, "Watch what you say. He probably has a tape recorder in his boot." The pilots looked at me and then got up and left. The asshole just stared at me. I went to get a beer and when I turned around he was gone too.

When I think back, my blow up with this guy probably saved Tom his career. Tom really loved to tell a story.   He probably would have told him everything that had happened in the last eight years.

Beechcraft C-45 on the Air America ramp Chiang Mai Airport, Thailand

A C-47 Lao commercial airliner on the ramp at Ban Houie Sai Airport

Landing Short of the Pad

We were working out of LS-20, Sam Thong. My pilot was Tim Woozley. While making an approach to a pad in the area, Tim was a little low. The tail wheel hit the lip of the slit trench used as part of the fortification, shearing off the tail wheel. Tim held the tail up while I off loaded and then we returned to LS-20.

We had called ahead and the onsite mechanic had set out a couple of tires to rest the tail on.

Tim called the skyline radio site to pass on to Udorn maintenance that we needed a tail wheel assembly. Udorn maintenance had parts and people ready to go upcountry on a moment's notice to assist flight mechanics upcountry to repair their aircraft.

About four hours later a Thai mechanic showed up with the parts and we made the repairs. The next day we were flying again.

L-19 Day Trip

An L-19 bird dog was flying up the Mekong River from L-11, Pakse, when the engine started running rough. Lucky for him there was a large sand bar that he was able to land on.

L-19 Bird Dog and Lao Officers stranded on sand bar near Pakse

I was doing functional check flights that day when they told me to preflight one of the helicopters. I do not recall the call number of the helicopter. Shortly a pilot whose name also escapes me showed up. A few minutes later the orange cart, an electric powered ramp vehicle, showed up with a Thai mechanic and a couple of boxes of parts. We loaded everything and off we went. The pilot was smart because he flew east to the Mekong then turned south and followed the river until we spotted the aircraft and people on the ground. We landed and shut down. I told the mechanic we would bring the boxes. The mechanic picked up his toolbox and off he went. The pilot and I brought the boxes.

On the ground with the plane, was the pilot in his flight suit, a big Lao officer in uniform and a standard size Lao, probably a bodyguard. I suggested that we all go back to the helicopter and sit in the shade while the repairs were made. It was very hot which was probably why the river was drying up, exposing the sandbar.

The mechanic worked on the aircraft for about an hour or more. Then he climbed into the cockpit and started the engine. He let it idle a few minutes then added power. He did his checks and shut down the engine.

We walked over as he was closing the engine cowling.

I asked, "You done?"

He said, "Yes, I just have to do the logbook."

I picked up his toolbox and a box of parts and walked to the helicopter. My pilot and the mechanic came up and we watched the aircraft taxi to the end of the sand bar. The pilot ran it up and let the brakes go. It took a long run but he got airborne before he ran out of sand.

We took off for Udorn. When we got back, we checked with operations for any more flights. Nothing was scheduled and it was time to head for the Club.

Flight Mechanics relaxing at the Club Rendezvous
From left: Steve Nichols, Willie Parker, Johnny Sibal,
Joe Gaculais, Champ Champanil, Joe Siathong

Bodies

We left LS-20A, Long Tieng, for LS-108, Muong Soui. The pilot was Ron Allendorfer. When we got there, the customer, who went by the name of Jack the Fac, told us over the radio that he wanted us to pick up a body from another site. Ron told him that he wanted to talk to him first and we shut down. Jack came over in his Army major's uniform. I guess he was a real Army major. They talked it over and we started up and off we went.

Ron located the pad and a guy came out and put out the signal that meant it was safe to land. As we started in to land, the guy picked up the signal and moved off the pad to the side. That was always a good sign, someone standing out in the open. A better sign is when there are eight or ten people standing around.

Everything was going good until we got about 40 feet from the pad. Then there was a loud pop with smoke and the guy standing off from the pad went flying through the air. Ron added power and off we went.

Ron said, "We're under mortar fire."

When we got back to LS-108, Jack was outside to meet us. I guess his people called him from the site.

The story was that at night enemy troops would tie grenades to trees and run a wire or string to another tree. When someone or something like rotor wash from a helicopter landing caused the pin to pull, BANG. It could have happened that way and he wanted us to go back to the pad.

He said the magic words, "I'll fly back to the site with you."

Ron asked me, "Do you want to go back?"

I said, "Sure, if he comes along."

We landed back at the site and picked up two bodies. We flew back to LS-108 and dropped Jack off. He asked us to take the bodies to the hospital at LS-20 which we did.

Close Call

I came back to Udorn from upcountry after a six day trip on a Sunday night. I picked up my mail and went over to the club. Geza Eiler, the chief flight mechanic, was there.

He came over and said, "I put you on the schedule for tomorrow."

"Why?" Normally after a six day trip you would have a day off.

Geza said, "I need a flight mechanic and you're the only one in town. I'll get you back as soon as I can."

Monday, I got picked up at my residence by the company van to go to the airbase. We took off for L-39, Savannakhet, in H-50 with pilot Jerry Booth. We worked the area around L-39 until 2 p.m. when the customer released us. While we were refueling, Jerry called Udorn operations for instructions. Ops told us to go to LS-20A.

That was clearly not what I wanted to hear.

We took off. About an hour later, we get a call telling us that when we arrive at LS-20A, I was to change aircraft with flight mechanic Montano Centeno and return to Udorn for maintenance.

I had Tuesday off. I checked the schedule for Wednesday and I was on it.

Wednesday, we took off for the Vang Vieng area. I rarely worked there and not much went on up there. About 11 a.m., while working the area, a message came over the radio that H-50 landed short of the pad at Khang Kho, LS-204, crashed and burned. H-50 was the aircraft that I had changed with Centeno on Monday night.

Later that night we learned that there were no survivors. Pilot Jerry Booth and Montano Centeno both died and H-50 was completely destroyed by fire.

Geza, I think I told you this before but I'll say it again. Thanks for getting me back that Monday.

Geza Eiler
Chief Flight Mechanic
Air America

Harvey's Rock

We were working at LS-20, Sam Thong. The pilot was Harvey Potter. We landed and taxied over to the USAID warehouse to pick up another load.

The customer approached us with five or six people made up of Americans and two Lao, and handed me a note and said, "Take these people to this village, wait, and bring them back here."

I gave Harvey the note and told him what I was told.

We got the people onboard and off we went.

We found the village on top of a big hill. There was no pad, no landing strip and no signal. We circled a couple of times and then Harvey told me to get one of the Lao down below and ask him if that was the right village.

I got a Lao, sat him down by the door and pointed at the village. I shook my head up and down. He looked at me, shook his head up and down, and smiled. He was home, I guess.

There were some paths running down the hill to a large field so Harvey landed about 50 feet from the paths. On landing, we ended up with a nose up angle. I didn't think anything about it. The people got off, said they'd be about an hour, and walked up the hill toward the village.

We stayed by the aircraft and about 45 minutes later, our people were back.

I got the APU started and got the people onboard. I'm standing outside with the fire extinguisher, which is standard procedure, ready for the engine to start, when Harvey waved me up to the cockpit. I climbed up the side to where Harvey was pointing to the forward tank fuel gage. It was empty. The fuel had drained back into the center and aft tanks due to the pitch of the aircraft.

Harvey asked, "Any ideas?"

I responded with, "We could call for a couple of drums of fuel."

"Not a good idea." Harvey apparently wanted to keep this a secret.

I got the people off. I told them the engine wouldn't start. I didn't tell them why. They just walked away and stood at the bottom of the hill with the Lao spectators.

Harvey's idea was to push the aircraft back on level ground. Maybe the fuel would drain back to the forward tank enough to start the engine.

We each took a side of the aircraft and walked back in line with the landing gear, maybe 60 or 70 feet, looking for holes, big rocks and tree limbs where the tail wheel would travel. The grass was up to our knees. I got four soldiers for each landing gear, let the brakes off and we pushed back for about 35 or 40 feet. Then the left gear hit a rock stopping the aircraft.

Harvey went through the motion of digging with a shovel. One of the soldiers took off running. I looked around for the Americans. I guess when they saw us pushing the helicopter they went back up the hill.

The shovel arrived and Harvey started digging around the rock. I went and sat in the cabin for about ten minutes then went back to give Harvey a break. As he was digging around the rock, the rock was getting bigger.

Pilot Harvey Potter with his rock

"Harvey, we'll never get that rock out."
"You're right," he finally acknowledged, "I'll call for some fuel."
I started the APU and started to walk the shovel back to the troops when I heard the engine cranking over. Our efforts had paid off. The fuel had drained back into the forward tank.
We took the people back to Sam Thong. They got out and walked away.

Harvey Potter was well liked by everyone. He died on March 2, 1970, from injuries in the crash of an H-34D, H-46. The accident took place on February 25, 1970, southeast of Luang Prabang. The crew consisted of pilot Harvey Potter, flight officer John W. Beardsley and flight mechanic Joe Gaculais.

Beardsley was a newly arrived, fully qualified H-34 pilot who was undergoing his area training with Potter, a close friend. They were carrying two 55-gallon drums weighing about 800 plus pounds and five passengers.

The designated landing site was one of the worst upcountry. The pad with an elevation of 4850 feet was on such a steep slope that it would have been unsafe to land any way except up-slope. Beardsley was at the controls when on approach to the landing site he allowed the rotor RPM to get too low while overloaded for the altitude. H-46 crashed and burned.

Initially Potter and Beardsley were able to exit the aircraft and walk away. Their polyester uniforms had burned away leaving them in their T-shirts and shorts that tend to resist burning. They were picked up by Ed Rudolphs and transported to a spot where they boarded a C-130 that transported them to Udorn. From there they picked up a flight to the burn center in Tokyo, Japan. From all outside appearances they were not that badly injured and were mobile and talking. Potter died on March 2 and Beardsley on March 10 in the hospital in Japan.

Four of the passengers died in the crash and one survived with minor burns. Flight mechanic Joe Gaculais suffered serious burns and spent several months in painful therapy before he could return to duty.

Following the fatal crash, the landing site was abandoned for another site a short distance away.

Harvey Potter was one of the best.

Dien Bien Phu

We were working an area near L-54, Luang Prabang. The pilot was Bob Davis. We were to work until 1 p.m. and then standby for a special mission. There was a second H-34 coming down from Ban Houei Sai and two pilots were flying up from Udorn. On all dangerous missions, Air America assigned two helicopters with a pilot and co-pilot. Routine missions were normally flown with just a pilot and no co-pilot. I knew I was in for an interesting trip.

The pilot briefing was set for 2:30 p.m. and take off was 3 p.m. Bob and I landed a little after 1 p.m. The pilots from Udorn were already there. We all jumped into a jeep and went to Luang Prabang for lunch. We got back about 2:15 p.m. The second helicopter had landed with flight mechanic Mick Forest. We had both worked in Bangkok at the same time but in different jobs. I was with 803. Mick was advisor to the Thai Border Police.

3 p.m. came and we took off. After about 40 minutes, Bob called down and asked me to look out the door to see if I could see a river.

"Yes."

"Can you see hills farther out?"

"Yes, again."

Bob said, "That's Dien Bien Phu."

There was nothing there, just big open grass fields but that was in 1968. Today they have a museum and a bed and breakfast. Now it's a tourist attraction.

Back to the story, we were flying north now. About 15 minutes later a Helio Courier aircraft flew past us. On board, they had an American customer and probably a Lao that knew the area and could talk by radio to the people that were to be picked up, making sure they were the right people. The reason you have to make sure these people are the right people is because you can't tell by the way they look. They are dressed in Pathet Lao uniforms from their boots to their hats with AK-47s, magazine belts, bamboo grenades and Chairman Mao buttons.

We continued on for another 15 or 20 minutes. Finally we got the okay to make the landing. We started a slow descent. The other helicopter stayed up high. He was our search and rescue aircraft in the event that things did not go well for us. The Helio was gone. He was probably five miles away circling to fool the bad guys.

We were still at about 2500 feet when at the 1 o'clock position we saw red smoke coming from a nearby hilltop. Bob went into autorotation heading straight in. He made one of the smoothest landings I've ever had. The hill was covered with elephant grass which grows five or six feet high. When the rotor wash hits, the grass just lays down and makes a swaying spooky motion. Our people walked to the helicopter. They didn't seem to be in a hurry. I would have been. I think there were seven. The guy in the middle had his hands tied behind him and a rope around his neck. I got them in, told Bob we were ready and off we went back to Luang Prabang.

When we got back to Luang Prabang, the other H-34 flew down the strip, landed and taxied to the ramp. We landed at the end of the runway where there was a small military covered truck waiting. When we parked, the truck backed up to about six feet from the cabin door. The people in their fancy uniforms got out and into the truck.

I made up my mind that I would have a couple of extra scotches at the Lang Xang Hotel bar that night, a good hotel and the best bar in Laos.

LS-36 Evacuation

It was February 1969. We were working out of LS-36, Na Khang, which was a large Lao military base in northeastern Laos. We worked there for two days carrying supplies and troops to surrounding outposts. The air strip was closed to large aircraft like C-123s and Caribous, they could only do air drops. Helicopters and small fixed wing aircraft could still land.

I think it was about ten days later that LS-36 was attacked and overrun. The North Vietnam army and Pathet Lao, most of the time, would attack from two or three sides and leave a back door for the troops to bug out and I didn't blame them one bit. But then we had hundreds of troops to locate and evacuate. Hopefully when they ran, they ran together and they had a radio so they could talk to other groups and aircraft flying in the area.

I would have thought that by the second day the American advisers would have a good idea of how many troops and their location and could guide them to a safe area for helicopter pick up.

So there I was on March 3, 1969, leaving LS-20A with pilot John Ford and co-pilot Ted Cash. There were five or six H-34s including one search and rescue (SAR) aircraft participating in the evacuation. When we got to a large clearing, there were three T-28s circling to provide air cover. There were two groups of soldiers about 200 feet apart so you could land and load two aircraft at a time. We were the third or fourth aircraft to land. This turned out to be the easy part.

There was an American on the ground with seven troops, all traveling light.

The troops scrambled into the cabin and the customer who stayed on the ground said, "Go."

We took off and were circling over the trees to gain altitude. I don't know how high we were. A guess would be 1200 or 1500 feet. Suddenly there was a big bang to my right. Dirt and dust and small bits of paper flew everywhere. I thought my aircraft had been shot to shit.

A 12.7 round, which is a really big bullet, had hit the forward tank fuel boost pump housing, missing me by inches. The bullet had traveled up through a 4x8 foot plywood sheet which was there to protect the cabin floor. Over the months the plywood collected dirt and dust which exploded everywhere. Ted kept a small map case on the cockpit floor. The round continued through the aircraft hitting Ted's map case on the floor of the cockpit causing bits of paper to float around and added to the drama. The bullet missed Ted's seat bottom by inches and exited out under the left cockpit side window.

Then it really got scary.

When the round hit, John nosed the aircraft over and we headed down with power on. I looked up and saw the engine rotor tachometer in the red. As we were flying south, we were losing fuel. It was pouring out in a steady stream. The SAR helicopter was following us at a safe distance. John thought we had enough fuel to make LS-50, a small landing area at Phu Cum II, and we did.

The SAR H-34 landed along with us and shut down. The flight mechanic was Frank DeVito.   Together we examined the holes and Ted's map case, secured the aircraft and flew back to Sam Thong where the pilots got a ride back to Udorn and I stayed overnight to wait for mechanics and parts to work on the aircraft that we had left at LS-50.

Supplies being dropped to Lao troops at LS-36
prior to the site being overrun by enemy troops.

H-62 refueling at LS-36, Na Khang

UH-34 at LS-20, Sam Thong undergoing engine change.
Note A-frame of Pat McCarthy fame in background.

Mines on the Ho Chi Minh Trail

This was the biggest operation I was ever on.

We started out from Pakse site PS-22 at 12 p.m. on a Sunday. There were seven helicopters, six H-34s, two of which were for search and rescue, and one Huey and one Porter. We carried ten soldiers and five boxes of mines.

PS-22, a landing site near Pakse

We flew about 20 minutes and landed in a large open field near a tree line somewhere close to the Ho Chi Minh trail. The troops got out and grabbed their boxes. Each box had a rope on each end so there were two men to a box. Each soldier had a small pick and an entrenching tool. Off they went through the trees.

The helicopters all took off and returned to PS-22. When we landed, my pilot said two barrels would top off the fuel tanks. We were almost finished with the first barrel when the Porter came flying down the runway at about 50 feet above ground waving his arm up and down. My pilot got on the radio and the customer said he wanted all aircraft to be on the runway ready for takeoff as soon as he got confirmation that the A1E's were in the air for air cover.

His people were under attack.

Shortly we got the word to take off and hold at an area until they had a landing zone. We didn't circle for long before we saw five or six A1Es circling. We were told to fly south toward the circling Porter until we could see what looked like a dirt road. Then we were to turn and follow the road north in a line. When the customer would call for color smoke, the first aircraft would land short of the smoke for pickup and so on. I think we were the third aircraft to land. The Huey is always the first to land and that was all right with me.

As soon as our wheel hit the ground, three or four soldiers jumped aboard. While we were sitting there which was only seconds, you could hear rifle fire and the A1Es dropping bombs. They had to be close because the aircraft rocked side to side and dirt, grass and small branches were coming down, hitting the blades. Two more soldiers jumped on and I had just about had it. I looked out the door and two more were running toward us. As soon as they climbed onboard, I told the pilot to go before a big branch or rock hit a rotor blade. There was no place for an SAR aircraft to land if needed. We took off right down the trail, climbed over the trees and headed for PS-22.

I always wondered, with all the aircraft there flying, sitting on the ground and taking off, why nobody took a hit. Maybe with the air cover, the bad guys figured why be a hero and get a bomb dropped on you.

UH-34 at Pakse with four T-28s in the background

Customer Shoots Hole in Rotor Blade

We left Udorn to fly to LS-20A, Long Tieng, to pick up cargo. My pilot was John Fonburg. We landed at LS-20A and were told to go to a loading spot and shutdown, which we did. A truck pulled up to our aircraft and an American customer got out. I had to lift the cabin passenger seats up to make space for the cargo. A couple of Lao's loaded and stacked four hundred boxes of M-16 rifles. The customer climbed up the side of the aircraft to give John a list of sites to land at in the Ban Xieng Lom, LS-69, area. This was probably the worst area in Laos for bad guys as the base camp was about three miles from the North Vietnam border.

Once our cargo was loaded, the truck left and the customer climbed into the cabin. We took off and flew to the first outpost and landed. As usual the Laotians mobbed the helicopter around the cabin door to see what we brought them.

The customer told us to shutdown. He would be about twenty minutes.

John said, "No, we're not shutting down here."

I repeated this to the customer.

A couple of soldiers climbed in to pass out the rifles as the customer and a Lao officer counted them. Then they stopped unloading and started loading old M-1 Garand and M-1 carbine rifles. I didn't have room so I lifted the four seat section across from my seat. There was one seat left in the cabin for the customer to sit on. He came back and climbed aboard and off we went to the second outpost where we landed and the same thing happened. The people on the ground mobbed the aircraft so the customer moved them back and everything went on like the first stop.

Soon we're flying to our third stop. As soon as the wheels touched the ground, the customer released his seat belt, leapt up, opened the door and jumped out. He held his M-16 up to the sky and fired off three or four rounds. That did the trick. The mob stopped but the customer had failed to notice that the rotor blades were still turning. The guy didn't think anything about what happened.

To the pilot, I said, "John, we have to shutdown. I have to check the rotor blades."

Sure enough, the customer had hit one blade. The bim indicator was showing black.

The good thing was that we had 300 plus M-16 rifles on board so if the aircraft were un-flyable, they would come for the cargo. If this had happened on the ramp at Luang Prabang, we wouldn't have flown the aircraft until we got a new blade. But John was an old timer and he wasn't going to spend any more time on the ground in this area than he had to.

I told him we couldn't change the blade here because the pad was only a small hill flattened down to land on. We would have to go to Sam Thong.

We started up and waited for the customer to come back.

When he returned, I said, "We have to go to San Thong for maintenance because you put a hole in one of the rotor blades when you fired up into the air."

After taking off, I told John to radio Skyline to tell Udorn that we needed a main rotor blade at LS-20.

About 3 p.m., a Caribou landed at LS-20 with our blade and two mechanics. We borrowed the USAID forklift and changed and tracked the blade. John called Skyline to call Udorn and tell them the aircraft was back in service and to check our schedule. Skyline said we were secure for today and were to work out of LS-20A tomorrow.

While we had been waiting for our blade to arrive someone had removed all the rifles from the aircraft.

The next day we went to LS-20A and they sent us somewhere with troops and boxes of ammunition.

My days of gun running were short and over.

Loose 105 rounds carried from L-108 airstrip to gun artillery position. They came two shells per box and weighed 120 pounds, which was probably more than a Lao soldier weighed. They would remove the rounds and would most likely sell or trade the wood from the boxes.

North Vietnam Army prisoner being transported from An area near the Plain of Jars to LS-20A, Long Tieng

Search and Rescue

Search and Rescue missions were the most challenging as they were dangerous and had the most at stake. You usually had little notice, no coordinated plan and went for it on a wing and a prayer.

I was working out of Pakse, L-11, with pilot JJ McCauley. In the morning we worked out of the Pakse Airport carrying people, rice and other cargo. About noon we were finished so we refueled and flew up to the Bolovens Plateau to a site with a long runway.

A large transport aircraft landed and part of the cargo was boxes of 105 artillery shells. They had an outpost on the east side of the plateau with one 105 gun. Our job was to resupply the outpost, including the shells.

About the second trip when returning to the airstrip, we got a call from another H-34 that was working Savannakhet. He said he was going on an SAR for a downed pilot south of Saravane. He asked us to be his backup.

I told JJ that we didn't have a hoist.

He called the other aircraft back. The other pilot said he had a hoist.

We met with the other H-34 and followed him until he started down for the pickup. The pilot was in a large open field and was signaling with a mirror. The H-34 touched down for a second or two then took off quickly. We both headed west until we broke off to return to the plateau. When we landed the customer called and said he was coming down. We were done for the day.

JJ responded, "Take your time. We have to pump a couple of barrels of fuel into the aircraft."

There is no better feeling than a successful SAR unless you're the guy rescued.

Regretfully, not all SARs end as well.

On July 4, 1969, I was working out of LS-20A, Long Tieng. I remember the date because it was Independence Day but I don't remember who the pilot was.

We were empty, heading back to 20A, when an alert came over the radio that a pilot was down at specified map coordinates. My pilot checked his map and said it was on the Plain of Jars or close to it. This was a highly dangerous area occupied by the communist Pathet Lao.

In the meantime another H-34 came on the radio and said that he was going to check it out. So that made it clear that we had to go too. Air America required two helicopters on all SARs. Had time permitted, we would have added a co-pilot to each aircraft. As it was, both aircraft were single piloted.

As we were flying to the spot on the map, off to right of us we spotted the other H-34 coming across about a half mile ahead of us. So it looked like we were going to be the backup again. My pilot called the other aircraft and asked who was flying. The answer came back "The Indian." That was

Don Henthorn who said he was part Cherokee. I don't know if the Indian label was his idea or if another pilot, Dave Ankerberg, had given it to him.

We got to about a mile of the designated spot and the pilot on the ground came up on his radio.

"I see you," he said. "I'm at the base of the ridgeline in a wooded area near my parachute."

His parachute was out in the open and we could see it. It was near some trees where we presumed the pilot was hidden.

Don said that he was going down a little and moved in toward the chute.

As backup, we held our position.

People may think a mile is a long distance but at 3000 feet above ground level on a clear day, you can see a lot.

Don got to maybe a half mile from the ridgeline and started circling. He called the pilot and said he had to see him in the open before he would come in. On the next pass close to the ridgeline, the enemy opened up on Don's helicopter. There were a lot of flashes which was more than two or three bad guys with AK-47s.

The last words the downed pilot said to us were, "My hands are up. They are coming down for me."

As we continued to circle, the parachute was dragged into the trees. At that time we left the area to return to LS-20A. We never made visual contact with the downed pilot. From the time we made radio contact with the pilot until we left the area was about fifteen minutes and we were the only two aircraft in the area. Our SAR was over. There is no worse feeling.

When I got back to Udorn, I contacted an Air Force major that I knew and told him the story. He knew who the guy was and gave me his name, Col. Patrick Fallon. He was the vice commander of 56th Special Operations Wing, Nakhon Phanom RAFB, Thailand.

In September 1969, Ho Chi Minh became ill and died. The North Vietnam Army and the Pathet Lao pulled back to the North Vietnam border and Gen. Vang Pao took back the Plain of Jars. We were busy flying missions very close to Xieng Khouang or what was left of it. I would guess the US Air Force came back and leveled the town.

Colonel Fallon was never found. His current status is listed as Killed in Action-Body Not Recovered. A memorial service was held for him on June 22, 2012, at Arlington National Cemetery with a missing man flyover by the 56th Fighter Wing, Luke AFB, AZ.

Last Flight

We left Nam Lieu, LS-118A, to return to Udorn with pilot Ben Van Etten. We stopped at L-25, Ban Houei Sai, for fuel on the way and then, at the request of the customer, picked up two American "hitch-hikers" at a dam site near Nam Ngum.

It's about a two hour flight and most of the time the pilots just followed the Mekong south, then cut over to Udorn. We were about an hour and a half into the trip at about 6000 feet above the ground. Ben had the aircraft on the automatic stabilization equipment with collective friction on, homing in on the Vientiane aerial direction finder. He was reading a book.

Suddenly, the engine cut out for a few seconds and we dropped like a brick about 2000 feet. Ben went into autorotation and called in a mayday. Then the engine came back on for a few seconds but was running very rough and back firing. Then it quit. There was dead silence and we were dropping from 4000 feet.

Ben continued his autorotation downward. As he told me later, while descending, the right side (pilots) windshield fogged and he needed to look out the side window to see the landing area. Initially, during the descent, he didn't spot a good landing area. He thought we might have to land in the trees and the crash would be blamed on "pilot error." Fortunately, he spotted a rice paddy with a single tree in it. Just prior to touchdown, he lost sight of the tree and was concerned that we wouldn't make the open area and would hit the only tree in the rice paddy. Fortunately we missed.

We landed in a large dry rice paddy near a small town about thirty miles from Vientiane. Fortunately for us, it was a fairly safe place. Ben called Udorn and told them that we were okay and gave them our location.

About this time, people started to gather around and then the village police showed up. They didn't say anything to us. They just kept the people away.

About 20 minutes after we landed, we heard aircraft engines. I fired off two flares. That was the first time I ever did that but it worked. The aircraft changed course, flew over, circled twice and then continued up north. A short time later an H-34 landed. We transferred our stuff to the other helicopter. I closed the door and windows and we all flew to Udorn. We gave the American "hitch hikers" one heck of a ride which I expect they remembered for the rest of their lives.

That was my last trip upcountry. About six days later I was in Bangkok for a few days then back to the United States.

I've heard some people say that Air America was the best job they ever had. I know it was for me. It was paramilitary work done mostly with old military aircraft in a hostile area. We did the same things that the U.S. military did in Vietnam and sometimes we probably did work that the military didn't do. Things went pretty well because we were mostly all long time civilians who wanted to be there. The operation was set up very well. The aircraft maintenance was tops. We did have some engine problems in the H-34 helicopter but considering the engine was designed before World War II, what could you expect? The brightest spot was that the pay was three times more monthly than I made in the States. Plus for special missions requiring two pilots with air cover, we were paid a bonus.

Why did I leave after 38 months? I had to for medical reasons.

In those 38 months, I made lifetime friendships and great memories and have incredible stories to tell.

Two USAF CH-53 Jolly Green Giant SAR aircraft taking off from LS-20A

Air America porter crash at LS-20, Sam Thong, Laos

Chapter III
The Stories of Those Who Did Not Return

By

Stephen I. Nichols

Pat McCarthy replacing the gear box on an H-34 at LS-20

Franklin D. "Jesse" Smith

Jesse Smith was a good friend and had literally met me at the door when I first arrived in Udorn. He also met me at the door the morning they rescued me after a night in the Mekong River

Following the accident into the Mekong River, I was grounded. It was standard procedure to ground the mechanics following a crash. You would normally stay grounded until you bitched about it because management needed ground maintenance people just as much as they needed flight mechanics. If you never chose to fly again, management was happy to accommodate you on the ground.

It was during this time that I took a flight with pilot Sam Jordan and a new pilot, Dick Lieberth, who was in the process of being checked out as captain. The reason for the flight was twofold, a check ride to qualify Lieberth for solo operation and to look for an old wreck site upcountry. We landed and walked around the area but found nothing. Upon returning to the aircraft, the new pilot took the controls, and when starting the aircraft, he oversped the engine. I was ticked because this required me to do an immediate overspeed inspection that involved oil sumps and screens and magnetic plugs. Simply put, it was just a hot oily mess. Besides no one wanted to tear down a helicopter engine at a remote site because anything could go wrong. The heat and humidity of the day added to my aggravation. Everything checked out okay, so I put it all back together and we had an uneventful trip back to Udorn.

The following morning, I was on the flight line when Jessie came up grinning as usual. He was scheduled to fly to Pakse with the new pilot who had been checked out with me the previous day. This would be the pilot's first solo trip.

Jesse needed a new door track for the aircraft that he planned to install when they arrived at Pakse, so we walked to the supply center together to get the track.

As we walked back, I said, "Jesse, watch this guy. I don't think much of him. Yesterday, he oversped the engine and I had to inspect the whole damn thing."

Jesse laughed, "He's fine. Don't worry about it."

I remember him walking away like it was yesterday with the track resting on his shoulder, looking back to laugh at me one last time.

They departed for Pakse in southern Laos where they picked up two customers to show them around. As they took off from a pad at L-44, Saravane, soldiers who witnessed the accident said the blades coned up and they went into the trees. The engine was pushed back some 42 inches. There were no survivors. John Aspinwall went to the scene to investigate the accident for Air America. He said if the soldiers had not witnessed the accident and pointed out its location, the aircraft would never have been found due to the triple canopied rain forest type foliage. Upon investigation, John determined the crash to be as a result of mechanical failure. He surmised that the pilot, during takeoff, had pulled the mixture lever from rich to normal, but at the carburetor, a little serrated arm had slipped so it actually went from normal to idle cut off. When the engine cut off, the helicopter was too low to perform any kind of safe autorotation.

With things like this you never know for sure. I only know Jesse did not come home that day. He died in the crash of H-32 on October 12, 1965, along with two CIA agents, Mike Deuel and Mike Maloney. The pilot survived the crash but died before rescue.

Romeo B. Crisologo

We had been sent upcountry to recover a Helio Courier that had been ground looped off the side of the runway. Ground looped in some cases means the pilot was coming to the end of the runway and to avoid hitting something or going over the side of a mountain, he would dip one wing into the ground and swing the plane around in a half circle. Sometimes this was accidental and sometimes intentional. The pilot in this incident was Dick Crafts of "wood chipper" fame.

A Helio Courier is a single engine light plane perfectly suited for confined off-airport operations. Super Courier, a more powerful derivative, was used by Air America for liaison work, light cargo and reconnaissance. Its ability to land on very short runways made it ideal for landing on mountain tops throughout Laos. Helios remain very popular among bush pilots in Canada today.

The crew I was with that day was pilot Sam Jordan; co-pilot Alex Nattaline, a Brit, and flight mechanic Rudy Serafico. Cris Crisologo and I had been picked up at another site and were along for the ride. We were flying in an H-34 that was the newer style 148 series with an ejector fuel system where, if you parked it on an upward slope with a low fuel state, the fuel would drain to the rear, and you could not start the aircraft because the fuel booster pump couldn't pick up enough fuel to provide positive fuel pressure to the engine.

While the mechanics assessed the damage to the Helio, Sam, our pilot, proceeded to set up his picnic table for lunch with the red and white checkered table cloth like right out of an Italian restaurant. He placed the contents of his wicker basket on the table and ate his lunch. This was a ritual with Sam. He always brought his picnic basket in an attempt to retain a bit of civility from his previous life. I thought it must be great to have someone pack a lunch like that for you. To us he looked a little strange in the middle of a dirt runway.

While he dined, the rest of us decided to turn the helicopter around so we could get it started when we were ready to leave. We put Rudy in the pilot seat to man the brakes while the rest of us pushed the tail around to turn the aircraft 180 degrees and point it down hill. However, when we started turning it around it nearly got away from us and would have gone over the edge of the runway and slid into the ravine. We would never have been able to fly it out. Apparently the helicopter had one weak brake which we did not notice until we needed it.

We did what we could with the Helio Courier and were off. We had fun that day, Rudi, Cris and I.

Cris Crisologo with the Helio Courier ground looped at a site in Laos

Cris was a truly remarkable person. Early in his career with Air
America, he had suffered serious injuries. He and his pilot were caught in

bad weather and landed in a clearing where unbeknownst to them there were enemy troops nearby. When the weather cleared, he was standing next to the aircraft as the pilot fired up the engine. An enemy near the tree line took aim and shot Cris in the shoulder. When he fell to the ground, the pilot took off leaving him there. He evaded the enemy probably because they thought he had left in the helicopter. No one came back for days which he didn't understand. He told me himself that he waited there bleeding and in pain until he gave up and was getting ready to commit suicide by drinking massive amounts of water when a helicopter made a low pass over the area. He signaled the pilot who picked him up.

Air America patched him up and found him a job in the system. If you were injured or incapacitated in any way, Air America would always find you a job, usually one of your choice even if it required extensive training. Cris, however, came back to Udorn and wanted to return to flying. He had suffered extensive nerve damage that affected the use of his left arm but still he kept asking to go back to flying. Management finally sent him out on a test flight with the chief flight mechanic where he passed all the tests and was returned to his previous job as flight mechanic.

A short time after our trip upcountry to recover the Helio, on April 9, 1966, Cris was killed near Ban Pak in western Laos. They were taking off in H-14, an H-34, from a site surrounded by trees, carrying a broken down 75 mm pack howitzer and a couple of soldiers. They probably did not use enough power to get through transitional lift and went back into the trees. The howitzer gun barrel came forward and pinned Cris down and he could not escape when the H-34, which is highly flammable due to its magnesium skin and high octane fuel, burst into flames.

The two pilots and other passengers survived.

Abandoned temple
Nam Bac
Photo courtesy of MacAlan Thompson

Patrick F. "Pat" McCarthy

I was in the dining hall holding back tears and thinking, *I better change this conversation fast.* Pat McCarthy, a good friend, had died that day.

Pat was from Ireland, a little guy with red hair. He was already at Udorn when I arrived in 1965. He was a seasoned flight mechanic with Air America with previous experience as an aircraft mechanic in Vietnam with the Marine Corps.

When our paths crossed, which was not that often due to flight schedules, Pat and I discussed money and investing. With flight pay, we were making good money. Why else would you work in a job where people were shooting at you and you weren't supposed to shoot back? The more flight time you had, the more money you made. We were averaging 180 to 200 hours a month by this time and the money was very good.

Pat was not like the rest of us. Flight mechanics were generally a loud, obnoxious bunch especially after a few drinks after hours. Pat was serious and conservative, not a big spender and not one for the ladies. While most Air America personnel bought huge motorcycles, Pat bought a Moped size bike. He saved and invested his money wisely. In fact, when he died, I believe he had a substantial amount of money saved.

Pat was with the Marine Corps in Vietnam before he joined Air America. He had the self-discipline and values of the Corps and followed all the rules. One such rule that he followed and I did not was requiring the Hmong troops we were transporting to unload their rifles before boarding the helicopter. This involved removing the magazine and checking that there were no bullets in the chamber. This process might be okay for highly trained U.S. troops but some of the Hmong guys were just barefoot kids who were poorly trained and a little scary around weapons. Unlike Pat, I left well enough alone and just let them board. As things happen, Pat was going through the gun checking routine when a bullet was fired, passing through the transmission attachment bracket about a foot behind the pilots head. I rest my case.

Hmong Troops being transported upcountry

One day while I was at LS-20 for some reason I can't remember, Pat landed with pilot Tom Hoppy in an H-34 that had a large crack over the main gear box attachment lug. They decided not to go any further and to replace the main gear box at LS-20. Udorn sent a replacement main gear box unit built up as a quick change unit which included a main rotor head and servos already assembled. All we needed was some form of A-frame tripod to lift it high enough. The helicopter stands about 14 feet to the top of the rotor head.

We noticed a pile of fresh cut 2 by 8s waiting to be used for the new hostel for overnights at the site. As we were eyeballing the pile, the new hostel manager came over and made it quite clear we were not to touch it.

The minute he boarded the Caribou and lifted off toward Vientiane, we were on to the lumber. Pat and I with the help of Rico, an Air American machinist/welder, and one other guy built the nicest tripod in all of Laos. We were banging six inch nails into this beautiful teak wood with no reservations whatsoever. We were able to have the helicopter flying within a day. The tripod remained on the side of the runway at LS-20 for years like a monument to the ingenuity of Air America flight mechanics.

A-frame tripod used to change out the main gearbox upcountry. Pat
McCarthy on top. Rico in front of helicopter. Steve Nichols and
unidentified worker right.

It was unusual for Pat and me to be off duty at the same time. In fact
it was rare for any of the flight mechanics to be off at the same time. I had
roomed with a guy once and only saw him once or twice a month.

It was in November of 1968 when Pat approached me and said, "Let's
go to Hong Kong for the week."

"Nah," I replied, "Too much trouble. I hate the train ride to Bangkok.
Too much hassle."

"No, no. We can fly Royal Air Lao out of Vientiane," he said.

Royal Air Lao was an airline with one airplane, a DC-6 that the CIA
found, it was rumored, abandoned in the mud in Malta. Mechanics were
able to make sufficient repairs to fly it to Taiwan where it was overhauled
and brought to Vientiane, operating as Royal Air Lao. There was little
connection with Air America except that we were probably their best
customer and our pilots were known to fly the plane.

I had never flown Royal Air Lao but had heard a lot of good things
about it so I agreed to go along. We hopped an Air America plane from
Udorn to Vientiane, a thirty minute flight. When we arrived in Vientiane,
we discovered that we needed some form of visa stamps to get in and out of

Laos on this aircraft. If we were in Udorn, we could have easily obtained the necessary paper work but this was a different place and would normally take two weeks to obtain the VISA stamps from the immigration office. Apparently Pat knew people because he disappeared with our passports and returned in minutes with the necessary papers to board the airplane.

The plane had a nice interior with gorgeous Lao stewardesses. The flight was direct to Hong Kong and appeared uneventful. Upon arrival we were transported by the crew bus along with the pilots to downtown. In route, we heard the pilots saying how they had lost all electrical power for a short time at the outer islands.

Pat and I had a good week in Hong Kong. Now months later, I was sitting across the table from one of the AF Contract Monitors in the Club discussing the accident that had taken my friend Pat's life.

One of Air America's more common missions was the transport of ammunition for the Royal Lao Army. We transported so much, so often that it became routine. We thought nothing of sitting on guns, sacks of grenades or 125 Howitzer rounds while in flight. I can remember grenades breaking loose from soldiers' web gear and rolling around under my feet. I can also remember sleeping on piles of 105 howitzer rounds. It was also rumored that some of the Lao fighters would straighten some of the pins in the grenades making them easier to pull when under fire but also making them highly susceptible to accidental explosion. Unfortunately we may all have been lulled into a false sense of security.

That fateful day, December 7, 1968, Pat's helicopter was at LS-107, Houei Ma, unloading ammunition that included grenades. The crew consisted of pilot William Frazer, flight mechanic in training Bernardo L. Dychitan and Pat. They were providing support to Vang Pao's operation to retake Phou Pha Thi. While unloading a sack of grenades, it is believed that a pin dislodged and exploded igniting the other grenades and the other ammunition on board. The blast destroyed the helicopter, killed the three crew members and eight Hmong fighters and injured numerous others in the vicinity of the blast.

To this day I remember one of my last conversations with Pat in my office at Udorn

"Pat," I said, "Why don't you quit flying and come on the ground? You're going to get killed doing this shit." Using the "kill" word was just not done in our culture. I don't know why I said it. I had only heard it used once before and that was directed at me.

Pat just laughed, "When your time is up, it's up. There's nothing you can do about it." And he moved on.

Pat was flown home to Ireland and buried in St Patrick's Cemetery, Dunmanway, West Cork.

Royal Air Lao

Pat McCarthy and Avionics Technician
Photo courtesy of Orville Mock

Glenn R. Woods

On August 14, 1969, I received word that Glenn Woods' Bell 204B helicopter had crashed upcountry and there were no survivors. I immediately sought out one of my best mechanics, Gary Gentz, to go to the crash site to help determine the cause. In a weird set of circumstances, Gary and his wife were at Glenn's home visiting with his wife and I had to notify him at the house without alerting her. This was one of the most difficult moments of my time in Laos.

We brought the wreckage back and reconstructed the helicopter on chicken wire. The damage to the aircraft was unbelievable. We concluded that, for some unknown reason, the helicopter rotor head must have over tilted, broke the mast and then the disk turned 90 degrees and sliced the aircraft in half down the length of the aircraft. Glenn was in the copilot's seat and was killed instantly.

I have only good memories of Glenn, one of which is our trip to Macau, China, in January 1968.

Glenn Woods left and Steve Nichols at the Stone Table, Macau, where in 1844, the 'Mong Ha' Treaty was signed between China and the U.S.A.

Macau is one of the two administrative regions of the People's Republic of China, the other being Hong Kong. It is located west of Pearl River Delta. It borders Guangdong Province to the north and the South China Sea to the south. Macau, formerly a Portuguese colony, was handed over to the People's Republic of China in 1999. The population is predominantly Chinese.

We were both in Hong Kong at the same time for R&R. We had not traveled together to Hong Kong but were at the same hotel when Glenn approached me and said, "Hey, will you go to Macau with me? I want to do some gambling."

I gave my usual, "Nah, I don't think so. Don't you need your passport stamped?" I probably gave more reasons for not going. I don't recall. I didn't gamble and I did not like to spend money as I was saving to buy a farm when I returned to Connecticut.

Like most of my friends, he just ignored my, "No, thank you."

He said, "Give me your passport. I'll take care of it." And he did.

We took a hydrofoil called the Flying Flamingo over to Macau where we were met by a Filipino man who said for $20 bucks he would show us around the Island. Since we did not have a clue where or what we should see, we jumped at the offer.

It turned out to be a great tour of the area including the ruins of St. Paul, a French Fort, the house of Sun Yat Sen who is known as the Father of China, the Treaty Table, the Buddha Shrine and numerous other attractions that we would have never seen without the guide. After that Glenn took his allotted $100 to the Casino and lost it in about three minutes. But all in all, it was a great trip and I was glad we went.

Glenn also had one of the more interesting experiences in my time with Air America. As I may have said before, the weather can make flying in Laos extremely dangerous. When visibility is poor, pilots go up over the clouds and fly by speed and time to go a specific distance. Then they find a hole in the clouds and drop back down hoping for the best. This time the pilots with Glenn as flight mechanic were flying one of the new Bell 205 Hueys. Evidently they somehow miscalculated their distance, so when they came down through the clouds, they looked around but could not recognize the area. They saw little white farm buildings and knew they were not in Laos anymore. It looked a lot like China and in fact they may have flown into China. The United States was not even supposed to be in Laos. China was out of the question. They shot back up through the clouds and headed back south. They flew until they ran out of fuel and landed on a sand bar in the Nam Tar River. They jumped out and ran into the underbrush for cover getting pretty torn up from the brush. They were picked up very shortly by Air America helicopters.

Now we had a very expensive undamaged helicopter abandoned in Nam Tar Province a few miles from Nam Tar City which was under enemy control. Air America did not take losing an aircraft lightly.

I was in the club at Udorn when I was approached by my boss, Jack Forney, Director of Tech Services. "Steve, you need to retrieve the helicopter at Nam Tar. Taipei wants it back."

I had downed several drinks and I already knew we had recon pictures of the helicopter with dugout canoes pulled up to the sand bar and camouflage brush on the aircraft which meant the Pathet Lao had already taken possession of it. In my opinion this was a suicide mission.

"Not me, Jack. I'm not being paid enough," was my response.

"The bar isn't the place to discuss money, let's go outside," he said calmly. Jack was always pure business.

Outside, he said, "Taipei wants the aircraft back and someone has to go. It doesn't have to be you but you need to get a crew ready."

I agreed as I really did not have an option. It was either that or go back to the States on the next plane. After considerable thought, I decided to send one of my mechanics who was already on thin ice due to his inability to meet some of his early morning commitments. He was a good mechanic. He just didn't like to get up in the morning. I called him in and explained that he could wipe the slate clean if he would take this assignment and he readily agreed.

The team leader and volunteer for the operation was Harry Fawn, Bell Maintenance Supervisor. I assigned two other mechanics to go on the mission but I do not recall the logic behind the selections.

This crew of four was to be transported in on a USAF Pony Express helicopter. They were to take the aircraft apart and sling load it out. As parts were dismantled and attached to a sling, they were to call in an Air America helicopter that was situated out of sight. The helicopter would come in and transport it to a site where a fixed wing aircraft, I think a C-123, would pick it up and transport it back to Udorn. They had propeller driven Skyraider A1Es for support.

Everybody on the crew knew the mission was a bad idea but Air America never considered an assignment too dangerous to try. Harry later told me that he had it all planned out in his head. The pony express had a ramp on the back which opened up and a small side door toward the front of the cargo compartment. He stayed up front so that when the ramp opened he would be the last one off.

"Wouldn't you know it," Harry told me later, "When the plane landed, the crew chief, opened the small door next to me instead of the ramp door making me the first one off the aircraft in a big white mechanic's suit."

They had all been issued guns but if you weren't used to handling a gun, it was of little comfort. One of the mechanics in his haste or fear accidently cooked off a round and everybody ducked for cover. There was no return fire from the enemy. They found the enemy had abandoned the aircraft after an attempt to destroy it by breaking the windows and smashing the control panels. All they really had to do was throw a grenade in it but apparently they did not think of that. Our people were able to retrieve the aircraft without incident and returned with bragging rights to another Air America success.

A painting of Glenn hangs in the CIA headquarters in McLean, VA. Not his portrait but one of him leaning out of an Air America Huey as he shoots down a Russian Colt bi-wing aircraft with an AK-47. Glenn Woods was the first and only person that I know of to ever shoot down a fixed wing aircraft from a helicopter.

In 2007, the CIA celebrated the 60th anniversary of its founding. In conjunction with the anniversary they commissioned several paintings to commemorate important milestones in its history. One such painting by aviation artist Keith Woodcock was commissioned and donated by Marius Burke and Boyd Mesecher. The painting titled "An Air Combat First" depicting the incident now hangs in CIA Headquarters.

An Air Combat First
www.cia.gov

The history behind the painting is as follows. On January 12, 1968, LS-85 came under attack in Laos. LS-85 was a top secret Air Force radar site built on top of Phou Pha Thi, a 5,500 foot mountain very close to the enemy territory in Northeastern Laos. Some thought it should never have been built there but the Air Force needed a radar station closer to North Vietnam for support in orchestrating bombing attacks against the North Vietnamese. About fifteen air force personnel manned the station which soon became a primary target for the communists. The personnel were all Air Force volunteers under cover as employees of Lockheed Aircraft as the United States military was not supposed to be in Laos.

On the day of the attack, pilot Ted Moore and Glenn were approaching Site 85 with a cargo load of ammunition when they saw the smoke from the attack and saw two Russian Colt bi-planes that looked like World War I vintage attacking the site with two others standing by. Moore took chase and having the advantage of height, positioned the aircraft above the Colt where Glenn, leaning from the Huey, shot the plane down with the AK-47, the personal weapon that he was not supposed to have. The one I sold to him. Gary Gentz was on the ground at Site 85 that day and tells his story on page 146.

The other plane was brought down by ground fire from Air America and other Hmong troops already on the ground at LS-85 before the attack began. The other two planes escaped back to North Vietnam.

Glenn remains in Udorn, Thailand, where he chose to be buried.

Montano L. Centeno

Montano Centeno was killed with pilot Gerald A. Booth on 17 July 1969 in a landing accident at Khang Kho, LS-204, a site overlooking the Plain of Jars near Pa Doung, LS-5. The aircraft, H-50, was completely destroyed by fire.

I did not know him well. He was an older Filipino flight mechanic who once told me he was working to put his son through medical school.

Centeno with pilot Wayne Gentry had the distinction of being aboard Sikorsky's UH-34, H-15, when it passed the 10,000 flight hours mark.

Every flight mechanic has a special story to tell, some more than one. Centeno told me this story.

On a trip upcountry in H-15, he was in the flight mechanic's seat and a Hmong officer was directly across from him. They were cruising along engaged in conversation when a sniper's bullet hit the officer in the head and he fell off the seat dead right in front of Centeno.

Like all flight mechanics, he did an outstanding job for our country. He lost his life for his efforts.

Ernesto M. Cruz

On January 10, 1971, an Air America H-34D helicopter crew consisting of pilot Bill Foster, flight mechanic Ernie Cruz and flight mechanic trainee Reggie Boston was moving troops and ammunition in the Long Tieng, LS-20A, and Sam Thong, LS-20, area in Laos. Cruz was a seasoned Filipino flight mechanic whom I remember as a quiet guy that never rocked the boat at all. He just did his job, quietly and well. Boston was a relatively new guy and I believe this was his first trip upcountry.

This story is reconstructed using an audio tape made by Bill Foster while recovering from his injuries at Brooke Army Medical Center in San Antonio, Texas. The tape was made available to me courtesy of Joseph Lopes.

Their mission was to carry Thai troops and ammunition between Sam Thong and a landing pad at a Thai outpost, about four kilometers away. They were working as a single helicopter and single pilot on this mission since the enemy threat level was not significant and other Air America helicopters were working in the area. Weather and visibility were good.

There were a couple of customers at Sam Thong overseeing the loading of ammunitions and troops. It looked like some of the munitions that were being loaded were not in the original containers. This was a concern, especially with hand grenades where the pin could be pulled inadvertently, something that I can identify with as transporting ammunition had become a laissez-faire event for all of us.

Foster's other concern was that the landing site markers were permanently placed rather than displayed as the helicopter approached the landing pad. The landing site should have been marked with predetermined colored signal to tell the pilot that the site was safe for landing. The signal was to be put out for the pilot to see and verify, and as soon as the helicopter started to land, the signal would be removed. Without such an arrangement it's possible that the outpost could have been overrun and not safe to land there. All the pilots took exception to the permanent marker and Foster had reiterated this concern earlier in the day to the Thai outpost Commander.

The accident occurred on the seventh and last trip to this outpost. The helicopter had landed and the crew and Thai soldiers were in the process of unloading the cargo. The area had been safe throughout the day and there was no problem landing at the outpost. The helicopter had been on the ground for about two minutes when an explosion occurred in the cargo compartment. A flash fire from the explosion entered the cockpit from the cargo compartment burning Foster who managed to escape with serious injury to his arms, legs, face and eye. Foster remembers little about the explosion. He was in the right seat waiting for the cargo to be unloaded. He was wearing the Air America flight uniform which included cotton pants and a short sleeve cotton shirt with his flight helmet on, without the visor down. He was wearing only one glove because he thought he had better control of the cyclic with a bare hand, a mistake he regrets due to injuries he sustained on his right hand.

Foster has no idea how he exited the helicopter. His next memory was rolling on the ground trying to extinguish his burning shirt and pants. He had lost vision in one of his eyes so vision was significantly impaired. He was aware that the helicopter was still running but was blazing and exploding so his urgency was to get away from it while he was still conscious. He felt he was not physically capable of trying to save anyone that may still have been in the helicopter. So he ran up the hill to get behind the Thai fortifications not knowing at the time whether personnel there were friend or foe. Once in the Thai encampment, which was friendly, Foster did a quick evaluation of his condition and explored options to get out of there. He knew other helicopters were working in the area so he needed to get to a safe location where he could be picked up. Having limited sight and no idea if and where mines or trip wires might be, he grabbed a Thai soldier and pushed him in front of him, hoping the soldier would know how to get outside the encampment without blowing up. Soon after exiting the perimeter a Huey approached, hovered and Foster was pulled into the helicopter.

Just prior to the blast, Boston had been sitting in the flight mechanic's seat looking out the door. The explosion happened between the flight mechanic's seat and Cruz in the back. The first explosion knocked Boston against the bulkhead and ignited his clothing. He saw a hole in the side of the aircraft about two feet in diameter. The flames were shooting toward the back of the aircraft where Cruz and a Thai soldier were sitting. According to Boston, Cruz and the Thai retreated to the back of the aircraft toward the tail cone to get away from the flames. To me that would have been suicide and a seasoned mechanic like Cruz would have known better so I expect that they were blown back into the tail cone by the blast and probably knocked unconscious, as Cruz would have known his only chance would be to come back through the flames at any price.

The second blast blew Boston out of the door of the helicopter with his gunner's belt still on. He managed to get his gunners belt off and as he attempted to return to the aircraft to help Cruz, a third explosion threw him further from the aircraft. He was able to extinguish his flaming clothes and crawl to safety as the entire helicopter was now fully engulfed in flames and, due to the high octane fuel, burning furiously. It was too late for Cruz and his Thai companion. They never made it out.

In minutes Air America helicopters filled the sky around the disaster.

One helicopter piloted by Ken Wood with flight mechanic Benny Shafer landed close by and Shafer picked up Boston and carried him to the helicopter. They took off and then spotted Foster some distance away where he had retreated to escape the exploding aircraft. He had managed to get to an area where the helicopter could hover close to the ground. Foster ran to the helicopter and was yanked in by Shafer. They were up and out of there within seconds, heading for Udorn.

It was never really determined whether the explosion occurred first in the cargo compartment or if the helicopter was hit by mortar fire or a rifle propelled grenade causing the ammunition to explode. I was not involved in the investigation as I was working at that point with the Twin-Pac conversions. Boston thought they had been hit by a mortar round from outside while Foster thought the explosion had come from the cargo compartment or below the helicopter. Boston said the explosion occurred inside the aircraft not below and that he heard what he thought was small arms fire which, in hindsight, could have been their own ammunition exploding. After listening to their story, however, and based on my experience, I think that the left side of the fuselage was struck by a rifle propelled grenade that ignited the gas tanks causing the flash fire that shot up through the cargo area and into the cockpit. Then the ammunition ignited in a series of explosions.

Severely burned, Boston and Foster were transported back to Udorn and then on to Japan. After ten days of ice baths in Japan, they were both transported to Brooke Army Medical Center in San Antonio, Texas, for skin grafts and recovery.

Ernesto M. Cruz, the Thai soldier and seven other local personnel in the vicinity of the aircraft were killed that day.

The remains of UH-34D H-78 at TG 7525 in January 71
Photo courtesy of Ward S. Reimer

Gone But Not Forgotten

Many flight mechanics were hired at Udorn in my last two years with the company. I was heavily involved in the Twin-Pac conversions during that time and I no longer sought out the new guys to welcome them aboard. In truth, I did not want to get to know them. We had lost a lot of people some of them very good friends. When a new flight mechanic introduced himself, I could barely look him in the eye knowing that he might not return from the next flight out.

Alfredo J. Alor, Feliciano C. Manalo, Valeriano P. Rosales and Manu Latloi were people that I never really got to know but that does not make their ultimate sacrifice any less important to me and I will share what little I know and what I have read in various sources.

Alfredo J. "Freddy" Alor was killed in action on May 19, 1972. On approach to a landing site near LS-289, Khong Sedone, Laos, the helicopter, H-92, was hit by small arms fire causing the engine to fail. The pilot autorotated into a tree congested rice paddy. Flight mechanic Alor was hit by the main rotor blade as he exited the aircraft. One passenger was injured. Passenger and crew were rescued as the aircraft was being destroyed by mortar fire.

Feliciano C. Manalo was killed in action on July 16, 1972, when his helicopter, H-52, came under large caliber enemy fire while attempting an emergency medevac of local troops near Pakse, Laos. Pilot Emmett Sullivan with co-pilot Jess Hagerman were coming in low to the landing zone when a machine gun opened up on them on the left side. Sullivan turned away and started to climb. They took a 12.7 mm round from the left side striking and killing Manalo instantly. He had just returned from accompanying Freddy Alor's body back to the Philippines.

Valeriano P. Rosales was killed in action on April 7, 1973. He was flying in Bell UH-1H, 17006, with pilot Chuck Osterman and co-pilot Terry Clark. They were flying a peace team from the International Commission of Control and Supervision (ICCS) from Hue to Lao Bao, South Vietnam, on a peace-keeping mission. There were two aircraft transporting about 12 to 15 ICCS and North Vietnam Army people to a site just south of the DMZ. The aircraft was clearly marked as ICCS and was on a prearranged flight schedule and flight path. In a valley in the area of Huong Hoa, South Vietnam, they were attacked from the rear and took a direct hit from an SA-7 Strella missile. In the mind of many, it was an obvious set up. The crew all perished. It is not clear from the record how many, if any, of the eight passengers survived. The other aircraft was damaged and landed in the valley. After negotiations, they flew out later that day with survivors.

Manu Latloi was killed on April 18, 1974.

He was one of the first Thai students to graduate from the newly established flight mechanic program administered by Hal Augustine.

His first flight upcountry as a fully qualified flight mechanic was in November of 1970 with pilot Ben Van Etten. They were carrying a cargo of canned meat to an outpost near the Mekong where the borders of Laos, China and Burma all come together. The pilot climbed above the clouds and flew using distance, speed and time. When they let down through a hole in the clouds, they did not recognize the area. The pilot went back up and headed toward what he thought was the Mekong. When they descended a second time, they thought they were near Chiang Mai, Thailand. The fuel warning light came on so they landed at what they thought to be a Thai airport. It wasn't. They landed in Burma. They were treated well but were held captive for almost two weeks. It was a heck of a first trip for Manu.

Manu was the last flight mechanic to die in Laos. The crew was in H-45 working out of Long Tieng, LS-20A. They were carrying five Lao passengers, 500 pounds of cargo and 500 pounds of fuel for Tango Pad X. The first officer, a Thai pilot, was flying and overshot the landing pad, rolling over and throwing Manu from the aircraft. He struck his head and died instantly. The pilots and passengers were injured but survived.

June 3, 1974 was Air America's last day in Laos. The last plane out was a C-7A 2389 piloted by Capt. Fred F. Walker and Capt. M. W. Shaver. They crossed the border at 1113Z.

We lost a lot of people in this remote spot of Southeast Asia.

May we never forget who they were or what they sacrificed in the name of freedom.

Chapter IV
The Pilots

By

Stephen I. Nichols

These stories are a few of the more memorable moments
shared with the pilots of Air America

Pilot Bobby Nunez in the cockpit. Steve Nichols far left
Base Manager Clarence Abadie, right facing out
Two unidentified Air America mechanics

Pogo Hunter talking to the Lao people

Pilots in General

I never did figure out how operations paired pilots with flight mechanics, or maybe I have forgotten. Even when I became superintendent and the flight mechanics worked for me, I did not ask. It never really seemed that important. There was no clear pattern. I got to fly a lot with the senior pilots which meant good assignments. Frequently we went to LS-118, the CIA training camp in Northern Laos, a relatively safe area with good living conditions.

At the end of each day, operations posted the flight roster for the next day at various hotels and the Rendezvous Club. Everyone checked the roster which listed the time, plane, pilot, mechanic and mission because it made the difference between a good night's sleep or lying there all night thinking. Sometimes you had to be on the flight line very early which meant the little bus that Air America sent to pick you up was beeping its horn in your driveway at 4:00 a.m. At first, I thought the bus was a nice convenience that the company offered but actually it was designed to get you out of bed and on the flight line at ridiculous hours.

For the most part Air America had all well qualified, great pilots. Some were just greater than others. There were those that you knew you were coming home with and some, maybe not so sure. Some seemed very careful but most were risk takers. They wouldn't have been there if they weren't.

One guy disliked me intensely for some reason. I was only paired with him once. He probably told operations to never assign me to his aircraft again which was a mutual favor.

Some pilots deserve special recognition. Julian "Scratch" Kanach was the best, an opinion shared by most of the flight mechanics. I don't remember him ever bending an aircraft or getting one shot up.

Vern Clarkson saved my life twice in one day. I would have flown anywhere with him or Scratch. Vern was a quiet, unflappable nice guy. He came to Air America from the marines and went back to the marines. The last time I saw him he'd returned to Udorn for a visit. I spotted him in the club in uniform with Full-Bird Colonel insignia on.

There was Steve Stevens and Mick Prulhiere, to name a few, who on separate occasions landed under enemy fire to save another Air America crew. Their stories have been told elsewhere.

There were a couple of pilots who nearly killed me who shall remain nameless.

Some pilots were just flat out crazy. I found that out one night at LS-118A, the site of Tony Poe's living quarters. Tony was a great host with card games and plenty of booze. I always kept in the background watching in amusement, as I did not drink that much, and when I got bored, I retired to one of the shacks for a decent night's rest. This night I retired to a shack with about six bunks with one light bulb hanging from the ceiling. There was a light switch for it somewhere, I think, or maybe it just stayed on all night. Much later, one of the Helio pilots came in and flopped into a bunk. He must not have known where the switch was either because after lying there for a few minutes, he pulled out his hand gun and shot the light bulb out. I was very quiet and hoped I wouldn't snore that night.

Flying with John Fonburg was always fun. John was an oversized ex-marine pilot who never bitched about the aircraft. He just flew it and did his job. He was very thrifty but liked to have a drink and unwind after flying all day. Once at LS-118A, he and Tony Poe spent the night drinking Tony's booze. Tony was always bitching about people drinking his booze but he never seemed to shut anyone off. This one night ended with John hanging over the verandah railing with Tony complaining about the wasted booze.

Another time at LS-118A, I was with pilot Steve Stevens who being Greek liked his hot sauce. After dinner I looked up from whatever I was doing and noticed Steve and Tony each with a big jar of hot bell peppers. They were eating them like they were canned cherries or something. I think each expected the other to quit but neither did. After finishing off the peppers, they drank the juice. All the next day, Steve kept saying how he'd get Tony some real hot sauce and see if he could handle it. In fact, I believe when we returned to Udorn, Steve immediately bought up a bunch of dried red peppers, boiled and re-boiled them into a paste to take back up to Tony. I wasn't on that return trip but it must have been something to see.

In the pilot stories that follow, I have omitted some of the names to preserve their dignity and memory. In all cases, I have the greatest respect and admiration for all of the Air America pilots including those who I did not like and those who did not like me. They displayed courage beyond the call of duty and brought me home almost every time.

Pilots Pogo Hunter and Bobby Nunez

Four Memorable Moments in One Day

We had taken off from a small strip outside of a town called Thakhek, a fleet of four H-34 helicopters with all fairly new pilots. Our mission that day was to pick up refugees and transport them to Thakhek. I was in the co-pilot's seat because I had a trainee flight mechanic downstairs in the cargo area. It was the rainy season and the weather was lousy, overcast with scattered rain showers. The helicopters all made it to the refugee pickup area which was a small clearing in the jungle. Each helicopter dropped in to pick up its load of about 15 people. We were the third helicopter to go in. After loading the people, we made a maximum power take off. At about two or three hundred feet and out of ground effect, the automatic stabilizing equipment (ASE) pitched the nose sharply upward. The pilot punched it off and attempted to back the aircraft down to the clearing. With some luck, we got it back on the ground. So now without the ASE, which makes the aircraft harder to fly, we made a second attempt and got back into the air.

Once all four helicopters were loaded, we headed back toward Thakhek. The weather had turned worse and we were in and out of clouds and heavy rain showers. We went into one cloud as the number three helicopter and came out of it as number four. I couldn't believe it. When we came out of the cloud, two to three hundred feet in front of us was the aircraft that had been behind us. My trainee flight mechanic said he saw him passing under us and didn't say anything because he was quite sure we would miss. Holy shit.

The weather continued to worsen and we kept trying to go around the storms using up precious fuel. The next thing I knew we were separated from the rest of the fleet and the twenty minute fuel warning light flashed on. *Oh shit. This is the part I hate.* My pilot was sweating like someone was pouring a small glass of water on his head. We were over trackless jungle and I didn't see a happy ending.

Out of the blue came the voice of pilot Vern Clarkson over our headsets asking where our aircraft H-14 was. His voice was calm and reassuring.

My pilot responded, "I'm in this cloud and I'm heading for Nakhon Phanom." This was an airbase in Thailand.

Vern quickly but very calmly reminded him that crossing a particular road being built and manned by Chinese troops with anti-aircraft guns would make that tricky. He suggested that we take an ADF steer from him and join up as the customer on board his aircraft knew of a possible place to land. The ADF is an automatic direction finder, a receiver that when dialed to certain preset frequencies has a needle that will point toward the source of the transmitter on the frequency. That's what we did and the equipment worked perfectly.

As we flew down this channel between clouds, I spotted the three other helicopters crossing in front of us. My pilot didn't see them but I did and said so. When we caught up to them, they were landing on a huge rock outcropping in the jungle, the only place to land within miles. They landed leaving us room to put down in the middle. I was very happy to get back on the ground and gave a silent, *thanks, Vern, for saving my life.* If he had not noticed our missing helicopter and called out to us, we would have either run out of fuel or been shot down.

The story did not end here. We were still in the middle of nowhere and needed to get out of there as quickly as possible. After a quick huddle, the pilots decided to leave half the refugees and the two helicopters with low fuel, double up crews and fly out ten minutes apart at different altitudes to avoid collision in the scattered showers and thick clouds.

I took what fuel remained in my aircraft, about five gallons, and put it into Vern's aircraft. My pilot flew as Vern's co-pilot and my flight mechanic trainee and I joined his flight mechanic downstairs in the cargo area. As we took off, maybe fifteen hundred feet in the air on the instruments, damn, if the engine didn't quit. It just quit. Vern issued a mayday and went into autorotation. This isn't good. This was my fourth "Oh Shit" moment in one day.

Just before the engine RPM hit zero, it roared back to life reengaging the rotor head. We flew back to Thakhek with no further problems. *Thanks, Vern, you did it again*, I thought.

When Vern got his helicopter back to Udorn that night, maintenance found that his ASE wire bundle had rubbed and shorted a wire which shut the main fuel valve off. Then it moved and allowed the valve to reopen just before the RPM on the engine hit zero. How lucky was that?

The next day we flew in fuel and recovered the two aircraft and the remaining refugees.

I never saw my flight mechanic trainee again. He never flew again and I did not see him on the ground so I presumed he just left Udorn. It was not uncommon for people to last only a short time. In fact, some people arrived on the train from Bangkok one day and left the next.

I will always be grateful to Vern Clarkson, the pilot who saved my life twice in one day.

The Rain Funnel

"You know, this isn't funny. We're at 8500 feet and still in the clouds."

Pilot Mick Prulhiere and I had been working the Bolovens Plateau area near Pakse. We were done for the day and were about to return to Udorn when the customer asked us to fly about five French rubber plantation people back to Pakse.

This day the weather was questionable at best as it was during the rainy season. We boarded our passengers and took off. We got maybe half way to Pakse when we ran into a wall of really heavy rain. Mick tried to fly through it in three different directions each time turning back.

After the third attempt, he said, "Steve, I don't think we can make it." He then went on the radio and asked for weather input from any nearby aircraft. If we could get above the clouds, we would be okay.

A C-123 in the area responded, "It is all clear at 5200 feet."

"Okay, Steve, I'm going to punch through this," he said with confidence.

We corkscrewed up through the dense rain and clouds to 5500 feet or so. We couldn't see crap. The rain and clouds were so thick that if you looked out the door you could not see the wheel of the helicopter.

Mick went on the air again, "C-123 in the Bolovens Plateau area. We are at 5500 feet and can't see anything. What is your altitude?"

The C -123 responded. "It is clear here at 5200 feet."

We corkscrewed up another 1500 feet. We still couldn't see crap. It was bad and seemingly getting worse.

"C-123, we are at 6700 feet and visibility is zero. Are you sure your altimeter is working?"

"It is fine at 5200 feet," came the response.

We went up to 8500 feet and still nothing. 10,000 would have been about the maximum that we could go with our load. Now Mick was getting ticked and nervous as it would soon be getting dark.

His next call to the C-123 had a certain tone to it. "You know, this isn't funny. We're at 8500 feet and still in the clouds."

The C-123 came back on. "We are not kidding. It is clear at 5200 feet and above."

He sounded sincere to me, but I was looking out at pure white stuff everywhere. I can only imagine what our French passengers were thinking. They had become awfully quiet.

All of a sudden we popped out of the clouds into a clear setting sun.

It turns out that we had been corkscrewing up through a very narrow and tall rain cloud. Had we moved in any direction a little more than we had, we would have been in the clear.

As for me, I had not been too worried. I believe that Mick was either a Navy or Marine Corps trained pilot and they had the best instrument flight training ever. I was never worried too much when I found myself in such a situation with one of the Navy trained pilots. They would always bring you home.

Entrance to Air America compound, Udorn, Thailand
Photo courtesy of Roger Burdwood

The Pilot Got Lost

I was upcountry with pilot Billy Pearson, a fun loving guy, having a relatively good time transporting supplies for the customer around Luang Prabang, L-54, when word came in that Billy was being relieved by another pilot.

Flying upcountry with a particular pilot did not always mean that was the pilot you were flying home with. The union came to Air America pilots at some point so the company tried to adhere to standard airline procedures like after so many hours, a pilot got to rest. This did not apply to flight mechanics. Because Billy and I had been upcountry for several days, a call came in from a fixed wing pilot that his relief was on his way and to meet us at a designated place. You never knew who the relief pilot might be and this day my worst fears were confirmed when the relief pilot got off the fixed wing airplane.

I had not flown with this guy since he almost killed me a month earlier. Billy climbed aboard the fixed wing and departed the area for good food and a hot shower. I felt doomed.

There were two methods of egress into the cockpit of the H-34. The pilot could climb up the steps on the outside of the aircraft, or he could enter through the cargo compartment by stepping onto the flight mechanic's seat and his equipment. While 99.9 percent of the pilots climbed up the ladder on the outside, this one pilot always went through the cargo compartment and stepped on the seat. Now, it was not like we were flying in and out of fancy airports. Many of our landing sites were mud, dirt or laterite, which was red clay. Every time this pilot passed through the cargo hold and stepped onto the flight mechanic's seat, he would leave dirt, mud or clay for the mechanic to brush off. Needless to say, the flight mechanics were none too pleased with this guy. I was particularly annoyed this time as I brushed the dirt from my seat.

Howie, the customer, gave us a load for transport to an area north of Luang Prabang, probably as north as you could get without going into enemy occupied territory. We were off. It was the smoky season, a condition caused by the slash and burn agricultural process practiced in this part of Southeast Asia. For months the air had so much smoke in it that it hindered visibility. We had to fly by calculating distance, airspeed and time. The smoke and endless rolling hills of greenery made the landing site extremely difficult to spot. We flew until we knew we had gone too far. It was clear that we had overshot the landing spot and were in danger of going into hostile territory. We turned back and by sheer luck were able to spot the landing site. We landed, unloaded and took off.

Now things turned from bad to worse. The landscape was trackless. We had no ground reference points, the sun was setting and hitting us directly in the face. There were clouds above us and smoke, incredible smoke, everywhere.

The pilot said, "I'm going up into the clouds and fly with instruments."

I said, "I can see the ground clearly below. I think we should stay down." I probably should have been quiet because he dropped down, way down, barely clearing the trees but still clueless as to where to go.

We started to follow a small river which would lead to the Mekong. Along the side of the river, there were numerous fortifications which seemed to be unmanned or at least I hoped they were.

My pilot went on the air calling for direction from pilots in the area. The response was immediate, as always, from other Air America pilots but to no avail.

Finally I said, "Just follow the river below, it will lead you to the Mekong." Navigation was not my job, but I wanted to live.

"Yeah, right," he agreed and continued to follow the river.

When he finally spotted the Mekong, he shouted, "It's the Mekong. It's the Mekong. It's the Mekong." I could hear the chuckles of the other pilots over my headset.

Then he said to me, "Which way?"

I said, "Down river towards Luang Prabang."

"How do you tell what is down?"

Is this a nightmare or what? I was thinking. "See the boats tied up in the river, see the way they are drifting? Go that way."

We made our way back to Luang Prabang to spend the night. Luang Prabang was the royal capital of Laos where the King resided. It was a respectable town with several streets and a small hotel. The pilot and I shared a room for the night. I probably wouldn't have if I had known that he slept in the buff and walked around buck naked. Let me tell you, I was extremely uncomfortable.

The next morning, Howie gave us a load for the site that Billy and I had been working earlier in the week. We had no problem there so I did not anticipate any problems on this day. Even so, as we approached the site, we kept a close watch on the area. The pilot slowly circled down toward the landing pad, and just as he was making the final approach, all hell broke loose and bullets from intense small arms fire were flying all around us. I dove behind the rice bags as the pilot went to full power yelling, "Intense ground fire," over the radio. I'll give him credit for that. He got us the hell out of there.

We returned, apparently undamaged, to the customer's site. Howie met us as we landed.

Having heard the emergency transmission, he asked, "What the hell happened?"

"We came under attack," the pilot told him.

Howie took a look around the aircraft but saw no damage. It was obvious he was skeptical. But there was no question in my mind. I know when I'm being shot at.

"Go ahead and return to Udorn," Howie said, which, in effect, meant he was firing us. But I didn't care. I was happy to go back to Udorn. I had had enough of this pilot anyway.

An inspection of the aircraft when we returned to Udorn found one bullet hole in a main rotor blade about two feet from the rotor head thus salvaging our credibility.

The mighty Mekong
Photo courtesy of Roger Burdwood

Heroic Rescue

On 17 January 1970, Air America personnel were ferrying cargo and customers between LS-20A and L-22. The day had been uneventful. There were two helicopters, a Huey crewed by pilot Frenchy Smith with flight mechanic Phil Velasquez and one customer type and a second H-34 crewed by pilot Mick Prulhiere, co-pilot Flex Steale and flight mechanic R. A. Ramos. On this particular morning, they took a route thought to be over good guy country.

Because the Huey was faster, it soon moved out ahead of the H-34. As they crossed a plateau, the Huey came under heavy small arms fire, the engine was struck and quit and they had to autorotate down right into the enemy's position. As the helicopter is a big target, not to mention highly flammable, they fled the aircraft to an old bomb crater, returning fire as they scrambled to safety. They were holed up and holding off the enemy and thinking they were not going to get out alive when the H-34 caught up with them and came in for the rescue. The enemy opened fire on the H-34 which also took hits but pulled out in time to avoid a total disaster.

Now the guys on the ground knew they were done for. The enemy was closing in and they were running out of ammunition.

All of a sudden over the sound of gunfire they hear the flapping of the H-34 approaching from behind them. The H-34 lands and flight mechanic Ramos yells, "Come on."

The Huey guys climb out of the ditch and literally run for their lives through the knee high grass towards the waiting helicopter that was some distance away. Gunfire followed them every step of the way.

All the time, Ramos who was fully exposed in the doorway of his H-34 was frantically waving them on, yelling, "Come on. Come on. Come on."

The enemy was so close behind them that Ramos thought they were part of the Huey crew. As the three Huey crew members leapt onto the helicopter, gasping for breath and collapsing on the floor, Ramos kept signaling the enemy soldiers to keep coming until one dropped down on one knee and fired at him. The bullet passed right through his jacket sleeve. Realizing his mistake, he fired back and yelled to the pilot to take off.

As they left the area without taking any more hits, Frenchy, still gasping for breath said, "Mick, why the hell did you come back for us?"

Mick thought about it for a few minutes and then responded, "Who else would I play cards with tonight if you were caught?"

Later that night, I was in the club when Ramos came in proudly showing his jacket with the bullet hole right through the upper arm of the sleeve. It was a really good story to tell but how easily it could have gone the other way.

Phil Goddard

Phil Goddard, a really good pilot, was from Barbados. His family owned half the island or something like that, so no one could figure out why he was in Laos risking his life every day.

I was flying with him one day in an area where H-43 piloted by JJ McCauley with flight mechanic Roger Burdwood had crashed into a hill a few days earlier. Phil decided to fly by and take a look at the wreck. As we got close we noticed that there were two crashed H-34s. *Wow,* I'm thinking, *What the hell happened here?*

Phil and I were discussing it over the headset thinking maybe it was enemy action during a recovery attempt or something like that. We were watching closely for any enemy presence. Phil asked me to get his camera out of his bag in the radio compartment in the back. I went for it while trying to stay connected on the headset. As I stretched out the radio coil to its max, it came disconnected and sprang back hitting the back of Phil's seat. He felt it and thought we'd taken a round. He put the helicopter into a high powered climb. With some difficulty, I climbed back to my seat, reconnected and explained what had just happened. We went on to view the double crash site.

I was on the ground one day when Phil taxied in from a trip upcountry. When the aircraft was parked, the flight mechanic, my friend and roommate, Dick Conrad, jumped out all fired up.

Dick was an interesting roommate. He always managed to meet up with the most beautiful Thai women and move them into our bungalow. Then he would go on a trip upcountry leaving them in my care.

This day he was really ticked and was bitching about almost getting killed. It seemed the customer had asked Phil to make a high speed run over this village to see if the bad guys were there. Note to the reader: helicopters are not high speed aircraft. Phil, known to be a bit of a risk taker, flew over and, yes, the bad guys were there. One round took out the landing light on the landing gear about three feet from Conrad's feet. Another round hit the door track about one foot above his head. He was not happy.

The incident that finally changed Phil's whole attitude about flying occurred upcountry in a Huey with flight mechanic Benny Shafer. After landing at a remote pad, a sniper fired one round striking Phil in the right side of his helmet. The bullet penetrated the helmet, traveled around the back of his head cutting his scalp and exited out the other side of his helmet. The bullet then struck Benny's boom mike which he was holding to his mouth. It shattered the mike and took off the tip of his thumb. They were two very lucky guys.

I never witnessed such a change of character as I saw in Phil after that incident. He changed from a carefree daredevil pilot into a damn serious one. In a year or so, he returned to Barbados.

Scratch Kanach and Ted Cash

Pilot Scratch Kanach, Ted Cash and I were at Nam Lieu, LS-118A, working for Tony Poe. Ted was a new pilot, flying as co-pilot. It was the rainy season. If you did not push the envelope some, you'd always be on the ground. This was one of those days where the pilot had to decide whether to risk it all or not.

The consensus was, "Oh, hell, let's give it a try."

Tony had a small load of miscellaneous whatever that he wanted us to deliver to a site about an hour and a half out each way. We took off and got on top of the weather, passing intermittently in and out of clouds.

After a while from my vantage point down in the cargo department, I noticed Ted's feet shuffling around. I knew he was getting nervous and was about to say something.

Sure enough, Ted said, "Scratch, do you think there might be rocks in these clouds?"

Scratch, in his typical low key manner, responded, "Well, Ted, I don't think so."

About that time we spotted a small hole in the clouds and we went down through it. A few more minutes and we found our site and landed. It was right in the clouds with an elevation of probably 5000 feet.

The people came out of their small huts, grabbed the goods and off we went.

We were back on top of the weather, going in and out of clouds and flying without navigational aids, just compass and time. After about an hour and a half, we dropped down through another hole in the clouds into a valley.

Ted asked, "Scratch, do you know where you are?"

And Scratch replied, "I think so."

I'm thinking, *how could he possibly know?*

Scratch continued, "Well, I think if we can just get over that ridge ahead of us, we'll find 118A."

Sure enough, we flew over the ridge and there it was, 118A.

Sometimes I thought Scratch knew every dead tree, every large rock and every stream in Laos.

The Green Parrots

There were hundreds of green parrots screaming and flying everywhere frantically fleeing the helicopter blades as we just missed the karst mountain by feet.

My pilot and I were scheduled to pick up Hmong army recruits in the Luang Prabang area and transport them to a local training camp. This particular pilot would have a flight mechanic's rating of just above average. In his favor, I will say that during his time with the company, I don't remember him having many serious problems.

We were flying above the weather and looking for a hole to descend down into for the pickup. Visibility was zero. All of a sudden, out of the blue so to speak, while we were dropping down through the clouds, a mountain appeared from nowhere. We thundered downhill at about 70 knots with birds, vines and wet rock 40 feet off to our right. Hundreds of green parrots went nuts, going everywhere. This huge karst outcropping with vines and waterfalls might have been very beautiful at another point in time but not while I was hanging on for dear life.

I yelled, "What the hell are you doing?"

His response was, "My map doesn't show anything above 3800 feet."

Oh, great, I was thinking. Most of the pilots used old French maps which weren't very reliable. Some in fact were mostly white and marked "Relief Data Incomplete."

I think that day was the closest I came to flying into a mountain.

All of the pilots are due a great deal of credit for the time they spent in Laos and lived to tell about it. Flying was very challenging in a country that had a lot of bad weather, no navigational aids, unreliable maps, people shooting at you and limited places to safely land in an emergency.

Chapter V

Helicopter Maintenance
Air America
Udorn, Thailand

Stephen I. Nichols
Superintendent
Aircraft Maintenance/Helicopters
1968 - 1972

Steve Nichols with abandoned Russian helicopter, Vientiane, Laos

Steve Nichols scavenging for parts somewhere in Laos

Burned Porter at LS-20
Photo courtesy of Roger Burdwood

Maintenance Department – Udorn

In William Leary's History of Air America: CIA Air Operations in Laos 1955-1974, on the CIA website, he writes:

"Air America, an airline secretly owned by the CIA, was a vital component in the Agency's operations in Laos. By the summer of 1970, the airline had some two dozen twin-engine transports, another two dozen short-takeoff-and-landing (STOL) aircraft, and some 30 helicopters dedicated to operations in Laos. There were more than 300 pilots, copilots, flight mechanics, and air-freight specialists flying out of Laos and Thailand. During 1970, Air America airdropped or landed 46 million pounds of foodstuffs - mainly rice - in Laos. Helicopter flight time reached more than 4,000 hours a month in the same year. Air America crews transported tens of thousands of troops and refugees, flew emergency medevac missions and rescued downed airmen throughout Laos, inserted and extracted road-watch teams, flew nighttime airdrop missions over the Ho Chi Minh Trail, monitored sensors along infiltration routes, conducted a highly successful photo reconnaissance program, and engaged in numerous clandestine missions using night-vision glasses and state-of-the-art electronic equipment. Without Air America's presence, the CIA's effort in Laos could not have been sustained."

What goes unmentioned is the incredible force behind this effort by the men and women of the various maintenance departments at Udorn and Vientiane.

For five years I was Superintendent Aircraft Maintenance /Helicopters (SAM/H), Udorn. Every morning I was on the flight line at 6 a.m. before the aircraft left for the day to assure that minor issues did not ground any aircraft and fielding other problems that might arise affecting missions.

I feel qualified and comfortable speaking about the superior performance of the Helicopter Maintenance Program for Air America.

Our line maintenance crews and heavy maintenance crews were as good as any, anywhere in the world. We were backed up by our shops people who kept a ready supply of built up quick change engines and main transmissions. Overnight turnaround was routine. Some aircraft would return with battle damage, fuel cells shot up, etc., but it did not matter. We still turned them around.

We had parts and people constantly going upcountry to assist helicopter flight mechanics repair their aircraft and in the case of fixed wing aircraft who did not carry flight mechanics, we would send people out to do minor repairs in the field.

We did complete scheduled overhauls of the Sikorsky UH-34D and Bell 205D and 204B models.

If the aircraft crashed but did not burn, we rebuilt it. If an aircraft went down upcountry due to engine or other component failure we went after it, sometimes in very unfriendly territory. There were times during helicopter recovery when the crew on the ground would have a radio linked to "Fast Movers" out of sight who could be called in quickly if needed.

When our aircraft came in for overhaul, we'd bring them up to date with whatever latest improvement had been made. One was to remove the early "bent leg" landing gear on the H-34 and replace it with the improved wide gear. I remember once we flew one H-34 270 hours in one month.

In my time as Superintendent, we did have a few mishaps. One was the recovery of H-47. Pilot John Ford with flight mechanic Hal Augustine had crashed in a creek during the rainy season and ended up with only part of a rotor blade above water. As was our practice, we set out to salvage the aircraft. We waited until the end of the rainy season when the water had receded. We borrowed a CH-47 Chinook from the U. S. Army to lift out our H-34 and return it to Udorn.

We sent the recovery crew with the lifting fixture used to offload the H-34 from ships. It was attached with the four pit pins that came with it and it was presumed up to the task. However, the aircraft had filled with water and mud and was extra heavy. In route back to Udorn, first one and then the rest of the pins came out and the aircraft was destroyed when it crashed to the ground. This was one helicopter that wasn't repaired. Later we received a very nasty telex from the Air America office in Taipei demanding to know who was responsible for the loss of H-47.

The Chinook returned to Udorn, minus the H-34 and with a huge hole in its roof from the lifting fixture springing back up and coming back down through the roof of the Chinook. Lucky for us, the fixture strap wasn't a few feet longer or it might have gone up into the blades.

I offered to repair the damage at Udorn. We had a sheet metal shop that was superior to anywhere. We could have repaired it in short order and the Army brass would be none the wiser. The Army crew declined.

Martin Best's documentation of the aircraft of Air America on the internet reads, "Over 100 H-34s saw service with Air America. Pilot Clarence Abadie led the first sixteen H-34s from Bangkok to Udorn in late March 1961. Between January 1961 and October 1972, 38 Air America H-34s were reported downed over Laos and three over Thailand. Nine of those losses occurred during the first ten months of service. In addition, 14 UH-34Ds were reconstructed at Udorn, from the remains of H-34s, for delivery to the Indonesian Air Force."

Hotel 15

Sometimes it seemed as if certain helicopters had personalities just like people and pets. Hotel-15 was one such helicopter. It seemed to have a charmed life. It was the first, and I think only, H-34 to achieve 10,000 flying hours and later 15,000 hours plus before the program ended.

While flying, I took H-15 upcountry many times and rarely had a problem with it. If H-15 was on the flight list with me as mechanic and Julian "Scratch" Kanach as pilot, it wouldn't matter where we were going. I knew I would be coming home.

I believe it was H-15 that picked me up following the crash in the Mekong and brought me home. You have to love a machine like that one.

In 1968, pilot Ted Cash and flight mechanic Bob Pigot brought it down on a mountain top 32 miles north of Nam Lieu, LS-118A. The helicopter started sliding down hill until it came to rest against a tree stump some 30 feet below the pad. If it had not been for this single tree stump, the helicopter would have slid down the mountain forever lost. The location and altitude of the crash site made retrieving the helicopter almost impossible and the customer suggested that we abandon the machine atop the mountain. Not H-15. Not me. Not Air America.

I sent a crew up to dismantle the helicopter and bring it home like it did for us so many times before. The crash site was over 5000 feet which meant that H-15 had to be disassembled and carefully lifted off piece by piece.

And she lived to fly another day.

Udorn Maintenance Crew

On 28 May 1969, Air America's H-15 was awarded a plaque for 10,000 flight hours. The pilot was Captain Wayne H. Gentry with flight mechanic Montano L. Centeno.

A second plaque was awarded to Air America by Sikorsky Aircraft on 1 November 1972 when H-15 reached 15,000 flight hours.

H-15 flew out of Udorn until 1974. Her fate is unknown.

Dave

Dave was the contract monitor for the Air Force contract for maintenance of the UH-34Ds of the Lao Royal Air Force. He was personable and good at his job.

One day we received word that one of the Sikorsky H-34s operated by the Lao Royal Air Force had crashed and burned in a hilly area along the Mekong River near Luang Prabang.

After reviewing the maintenance records of the aircraft, Dave asked to go to the crash site to continue his investigation. He had some unanswered questions that he thought a visual inspection might answer.

So Dave, chief flight mechanic Geza Eiler, a helicopter crew and I flew to Luang Prabang and then on to the nearest landing site which was a small village across the Mekong from the crash site.

To get to the actual crash site, we had to cross the river in a 'long tail' boat which was a long narrow boat with a motor with a long drive shaft to the propeller. Then we had to climb up hill for perhaps a mile. The ground was wet and muddy and extremely difficult to navigate.

Dave, who was a big guy and very overweight, was having a lot of difficulty with the climb. In fact the rest of us were in pretty good shape and we were having difficulty with the climb. The Lao people, on the other hand, were laughing at us as they easily navigated the countryside including one elderly woman with a basket on her head who passed us on the ascent.

As Dave struggled, the Lao soldiers, after a while, assisted him by shoving sharp sticks into the muddy hillside to hold his feet in place. Geza and I finally left him behind and climbed up to the crash area without him.

The scene was a dismal sight with the Buddhist Monks from Luang Prabang already in the area cremating the Lao bodies in small fires as was their custom. As tactfully as we could, we bowed and moved to what was left of the helicopter. There was very little there, part of the engine and one engine door. It did appear that the engine had caught fire as flames had scorched the inlet screening areas.

On the way back down, we met Dave about where we had left him, only he was sort of played out. His shirt was hanging out, shoes untied and his face was beet red. I told him what there was to see and he decided to go back to Luang Prabang without going all the way up. *Good decision,* I thought.

From the air, the rolling hills of Laos seemed small and easy to navigate. In reality with the heat and humidity, they presented a real challenge.

Dave didn't show up at the hangar at Udorn for about three days.

We all returned to the bottom of the hill, crossed back over the river and snapped some photos while we waited to be picked up.

Geza Eiler and Lao soldier waiting for transport along the Mekong

Steve Nichols with boat used by villagers for ceremonial
occasions. Village near Luang Prabang, Laos

Chainsaws, Trees and Helicopters

Pilot Lloyd Higgins, co-pilot Harvey Potter, flight mechanic Stash Waite, several Lao soldiers and I set out from Udorn to retrieve a disabled helicopter on a hillside just across the Mekong in Laos, not far from Udorn. The Lao pilot had landed some troops in a small clearing. Things got away from him and the aircraft rolled backwards down into a small stream bed striking the tail rotor in the process.

The aircraft belonged to the Lao Air Force who had their own fleet of approximately ten UH-34Ds and C-47s. Air America did most of their maintenance and we turned aircraft over to them when directed to do so.

As we flew over the site, Lloyd said we could not land due to the large trees in the area. If we landed he said, we would be unable to take off again unless we cut a tree down. So we returned to Udorn.

The next day we set off again armed with two chain saws from Udorn's supply department. We landed safely but I was wondering about our ability to cut this one enormous tree blocking our exit up and out.

Stash and one of the Laos took the chain saws in the direction of the trees while the rest of us worked on winching the helicopter back up the hill so it could be repaired and flown back out.

Very quickly one of the chain saws failed, now we had one chain saw and one very big tree.

But that did not deter Stash who I could hear sawing away while we worked on the helicopter. I was thankful for his determination. The tree was so big that he had to cut a step to stand in so he could get to where the diameter of the tree could be cut with the saw that we had. Much to my relief, Stash prevailed and the tree came down with little fanfare.

After we replaced the tail rotor, pilot Harvey Potter flew the repaired aircraft back to Udorn.

The Fate of Aircraft 803

The word had just come down that 803 had crashed in northern Thailand. The aircraft was piloted by McKenzie, an active duty W-4 Warrant Officer in the Army who was assigned by the Joint United States Military Advisory Group (JUSMAG) to train Lao pilots for the Royal Lao Air Force. He and I did not get along in the beginning. *That dumb Army shit*, I remember thinking time after time. He complained about every aircraft I assigned to him. The last straw was when he said, "It leans left when it hovers." *They all lean left when they hover*, I thought to myself.

In his defense, he was a cautious, conscientious pilot concerned for his welfare and that of the crew and I grew to admire and respect him over the next few years.

At the time, however, I thought we had done everything possible to accommodate him and he could not be pleased.

Finally we decided to let him pick any aircraft and let it be his personal aircraft.

He selected H-67, and from that point on, things went much better. He had his own Army flight mechanic. We did the routine maintenance for the aircraft but otherwise he was on his own. When it came time for scheduled maintenance on H-67, I told him to pick another helicopter.

He picked 803 formerly used in Bangkok by pilot Tom Moher and flight mechanic Rick Strba. It was painted white. Air America rarely used it, preferring the camouflage green for obvious reasons. Originally 803 was used by the International Control Commission, a commission set up in 1962 to maintain neutrality between the opposing forces in Laos. It didn't work out too well because everybody shot at them so eventually they threw in the towel.

McKenzie selected 803 and flew it for about a year before the crash.

I flew to the crash site maybe two days later with pilot John Ford and his flight mechanic. As superintendent for helicopter maintenance, I flew to some air crash sites to help determine the cause of the crash for Air America. The Army representatives from Bangkok followed us to the crash site in their Bell Huey. As I remember, it was a gray rainy day. As we landed, we could see the crash site and bodies still lying on the rice paddy dykes out of the water. The wreckage was barely visible above the water with the tail a few feet away. It is believed that they had jumped from the aircraft before it crashed, as from the look of the wreckage, it would have been impossible to retrieve the bodies from under the water.

No effort had been made to put the bodies in body bags, and the Army had not brought Graves and Registration people with them, so the Army people paid the local people to place them in body bags.

Our pilot John and his mechanic then flew to the province governor's site to get permission to transport the bodies back to Udorn. While they were gone, we waited in the rain until an elderly Thai lady offered us shelter in a field hut which was about seven feet off the ground. Only two of us took refuge in the hut, an American whose reason for being there I do not recall, and me. The others took refuge in the Army helicopter.

The person with me, whom I mentally dubbed the ugly American, stretched out on the floor of the hut and dangled his bare feet out of the door. I quickly told him that waving a bare sole at the Thai people was an insult much like giving one the finger in our culture. I asked him to stop it.

He responded with, "They aren't offended. See, they're laughing."

I was really ticked as he continued to wiggle his toes at the twenty or so Thai in the vicinity. I wanted to deck him but he was already lying down, and as I mentioned, I did not know why he was there or whom he worked for. He did not perform any function that I could see other than insult the Thai farmers.

Our pilot returned shortly with permission to transport the bodies back to Udorn and the local Thai people were nice enough to load the bodies on our helicopter. We left the crash site late afternoon. I was riding in the co-pilot's seat and the young Thai flight mechanic was below. The weather was turning quickly from bad to worse. Due to the lateness of the day and the need to navigate through a low mountainous area ahead, John decided to land at a secret CIA camp to spend the night. When we landed, I was first off and climbed down the side of the aircraft from the co-pilot's seat. I was met by a very hostile guy who asked who the hell I was and why was I there. I wanted to ask him if he thought he was fighting a one man war but thought better of it and referred him to my pilot. He immediately recognized John who assured him I was okay. I was with him and worked for Air America. We spent the night there. The only thing I remember about the place was that the people were damned unfriendly.

The return flight to Udorn took us about two hours and I was grateful for the co-pilot's seat. Needless to say by the time we taxied up to our ramp spot at Udorn, the cargo compartment was not a pleasant place to be.

The cause of the crash was easily determined. As soon as I saw the crash site with the tail section intact but separated from the rest of the wreckage, I knew that one of the rotor blades had most likely dropped down and cut the tail off. On further investigation when the wrecked helicopter was back at Udorn, we found that one main rotor blade horn locking pin had backed out in flight due to a small lock plate not being in place on the rotor head assembly. This caused the rotor blade to drop down and cut the tail off.

To understand how this happened, you have to understand a little helicopter history. This is how I remember the chain of events. The H-34s were produced by Sikorsky Aircraft beginning in the 1950s for the Navy for antisubmarine warfare work. Shortly after the start of production, a US

Army H-34 crashed in Germany and a design flaw was discovered where the main rotor blade horn locking pin could unscrew itself and back out during flight even though the hand knob was safety wired.

Sikorsky corrected the problem and all rotor head assemblies contained a small lock plate which kept the locking pin in place. Rotor head assemblies are replaced on H-34s on a regular schedule, based on hours flown.

In 1962, the Army started replacing their H-19s with H-34s which could carry 18 passengers or 8 medical litters. The Army did not want the assembly with the lock plate but preferred to install a permanent bolt when they installed the rotor head assembly. So their overhaul instructions had neither the lock plate nor the permanent bolt.

During my tenure with Air America, we had helicopters flying up to 5,000 total hours a month which included our H-34 fleet, the Bell Huey fleet and the Royal Lao Air Force H-34 fleet. Along with the heavy flight schedule there was a huge demand for parts. Hence we ordered parts from any and all available sources. Unfortunately, we received the Army rotor head assemblies which were certified ready and one made its way onto 803 at some point.

Upon this discovery of the unmodified army rotor head assemblies, we checked our supply chain and found that three or four other helicopters had the Army rotor head assemblies. All three were currently upcountry. We immediately manufactured lock plates in our machine shop and flew them upcountry with a mechanic to install them in each helicopter.

This seemingly innocuous decision by the Army to do things differently cost two American soldiers their lives, one with twenty eight years of service. McKenzie, I believe, told me he had nine children.

Parts of 803 brought back to Udorn
for accident investigation

MRH Blade Cuff Locking Pin used for folding MRBs.
When tightened and safety wired the outer barrel could
rotate pulling the pin out. Small lock plate was
retrofitted to prevent this.

H-43 Recovery

As I have said before some helicopters seem to have good personalities and some are just plain doomed. Portions of the following accident history come from an article on the University of Texas at Dallas web site on the history of Sikorsky UH-34D helicopters written by Dr. Joe F. Leeker.

H-43 was a brand new helicopter direct from the factory, Sikorsky Aircraft, in April 1966.

In one of its first flights out, there was a fire on board and in a flight two weeks later, it took two bullets in a rotor blade in the Luang Prabang area. Both incidents were with flight mechanic Roger Burdwood onboard.

In September of 1966, the aircraft crashed with pilot JJ McCauley and flight mechanic Roger Burdwood near a ridge in the Luang Prabang area, sustaining major damage. It was repaired at Udorn.

Chinook bringing H-43 back to Udorn
September 1966

On 23 April 1967, the aircraft incurred substantial damage after an engine failure in a Muong Soui area village while flying from Long Tieng, LS-20A, to Muong Soui.

H-43 crash scene photos courtesy of Rick Strba

Jim Hyder led a recovery team from Udorn consisting of Rick Strba, Don Whiting and a flight mechanic whose last name was Ward. They flew up to LS-108, Ban Nam Keng/III, and drove to the crash site in a small pickup truck provided by the customer.

They were able to remove the cockpit seats and the cabin seats and clean out the maintenance cabinet. At that point, Jim decided that there wasn't anything more to be done until a road was built into the crash site. The recovery team returned to the airstrip for the return trip to Udorn.

The aircraft was later returned to Udorn and rebuilt for continued service with Air America.

On August 8, 1967, H-43 crashed into a mountain cliff in bad weather in route to Ban Thateng, PS-28, near Pakse, Laos, killing the pilot John J. Cooney and flight mechanic Earle E. Bruce. The aircraft was completely destroyed by fire.

This aircraft lasted approximately one year and four months. I would estimate the average life span for an Air America H-34 in Laos, during the time period I was there, was a short lived 3,500 to 4,500 flying hours.

Light Aircraft Transport Rig

UH-34Ds with rig for transporting disassembled light aircraft such as Porters and Helios. Initially when sent out to recover downed small aircraft, we had to transport them the best we could using anything we could. This sometimes resulted in considerably more damage to the aircraft. Recognizing the need for a better way, we designed and fabricated the recovery rig shown above.

Sikorsky 58 Turbine (S-58T)

Everyone involved with the UH-34D knew that it should be converted to a turbine. That is to remove the heavy old 1820 reciprocating engine and replace it with a gas turbine power plant. The British did it with the Rolls Royce Gnome (GE T-58) in the Westland Wessex sometime in the late 1950s. And Sikorsky had turbinized the H-19 with a boat hull for the Coast Guard in the early 1960s.

As the story goes, in 1970, George Doole, the head of Pacific Corporation, the company that operated Air America and several other clandestine airlines, and Frank Carson of Carson Helicopters came to an agreement with Sikorsky Aircraft Corporation where Sikorsky would develop kits to convert the UH-34D to a turbine engine powered helicopter if Pacific Corporation and Carson Helicopters would purchase a minimum of twelve conversion kits. Doole and Carson apparently agreed to take six each.

Air America Captain Bob Davis was selected as the S-58T program pilot/engineer and I was the S-58T program maintenance superintendent.

When the prototype was developed and ready to fly, Bob and I met George Doole at the Sikorsky plant in Connecticut to watch the first flight. We got to see it run but for some reason they chose not to fly it.

As we walked back into the plant for lunch, George Doole came up beside me and asked, "Nichols, if we take delivery of the six kits, how long will it take to have them in the air?"

"If we have the aircraft frames, we'll have the first one in the air in thirty days and one every fifteen days thereafter."

He didn't comment. I don't think he thought it possible. Even he did not know what an exceptional crew he had in Air America maintenance at Udorn. In fact, we delivered the first Twin-Pac in thirty days and the rest every fifteen, except for the last one which was done in twelve days.

We used air frames flown in from the Pacific Missile Range in Hawaii by an Air Force C-124.

Removing the big Curtis-Wright 1820 engine and replacing it with the Pratt and Whitney PT6 Twin-Pac unit made one hell of a good aircraft in the S-58T. With twin engines, it was more reliable with far better altitude performance and with more power.

There were some teething issues with the program in the early days of operation. I would leave the Air America compound late evening and no sooner had I arrived home when I got called back for a Twin-Pac coming in with a false fire warning light on or an occasional compressor stall. It made for long days and little sleep for months.

Overall, they were great aircraft and everyone wanted to fly them. The twin engine aspect in a war zone made the fact that it could fly on one engine a very attractive feature. Many more were converted around the world and are still in use today.

Before

During

After

XW-PHA

First Flight
March 17, 1971
Udorn, Thailand

Twin-Pac, Sikorsky S-58T, Prototype
1970

A few years later, circa 1976, we used the Twin-Pacs for Carson Helicopters in Jeddah, Saudi Arabia. Frank Carson bid on a contract to unload 600,000 tons of bagged cement in one year. Other helicopter companies bid but wanted guarantees like start up costs, etc. Frank bid without guarantees and won the bid.

His plan was for just two drop zones and to unload two ships at a time that were no more than 1.5 miles off shore. Even with late hindrances, Carson did the job, over 600,000 tons, within the year. The empty bags alone weighed 16000 tons and the Twin-Pacs flew over 15,000 hours.

I was maintenance chief during most of the contract. Most of the pilots were former Air America and most of the mechanics were former Thai and Filipino Air America employees. When the operation ended, I was able to find jobs for the last four mechanics with Bin Laden Aviation at the Jeddah airport. They worked there for the next twenty years or so. Picture that.

Fleet of Twin-Pacs
Carson Helicopters
Jeddah, Saudi Arabia

Twin-Pac dropping a 4400 lb load of cement bags from ships
one and a half miles off shore. Jeddah, Saudi Arabia, 1977
There were eight aircraft in two race track patterns. Each
helicopter set down a load every one and a half minutes.

Chapter VI
In Conclusion

Mad River Farm
Ledyard, Connecticut

In the End

On June 3rd of 1974, the last Air America aircraft crossed the border into Thailand.

For ten years, we managed to hold Laos and presented a buffer between North Vietnam and Thailand. During this time, North Vietnam army resources were committed to Laos that could have been used against our troops in South Vietnam. Additionally, during this same time period, the Thai army morphed into a fairly good force.

In the end, the US Government elected to pull out of Laos leaving the people who had worked with us for ten years at the mercy of the communists. They were shown no mercy and had to flee the country in great numbers. Many ended up in relocation camps, many were just slaughtered and the more fortunate were able to immigrate to the United States. In Vietnam, hundreds of women and children drowned fleeing the country in small boats. None of this ever seemed to bother the likes of Jane Fonda or John Kerry.

The CIA's clandestine effort to support the Lao people against the communists failed miserably as its efforts in other countries had in the past and continues in the present. In fact the CIA does not have a very good track record of success for this type of operation.

Why does the United States, the strongest nation in the world with the latest technology, weapons and equipment and the best fighting forces in the world, run away when the going gets tough? Just imagine the aftermath of leaving Afghanistan when the Taliban return with a vengeance.

The answer lies with the leadership of this country and the infiltration of socialist and communist values into our society. The constant brainwashing of the American people by the left wing news media including such icons as Walter Cronkite and the influence of liberal colleges on our youth become insurmountable and we find ourselves where we are today, 2013.

Politicians cannot and should not run wars from the boardroom. Lyndon Johnson comes to mind. You cannot give the enemy sanctuaries. The rules of engagement should not favor the enemy. We spend billions on a War College and think tanks and apparently most is wasted.

We did not lose the Vietnam War. We won every battle. We negotiated a cease fire which we honored and our enemy did not. *That was a surprise.* In my opinion, the men and women who died in Southeast Asia were sold out by a weak Joint Chiefs of Staff and a weaker President Lyndon Johnson.

Needless to say, I am disappointed in my country for its failure to support the people who made the ultimate sacrifice in Laos and Vietnam. I am further disappointed in the direction we seem to be taking in world leadership today and I am deeply concerned about the authoritarianism practices of our current President. When your Government loses an ambassador and three other Americans in a terrorist attack on our consulate in Libya and no one is held accountable, you have the beginning of a serious problem.

My time with Air America remains one of the best experiences in my life as it was for most of the guys who joined me in this effort to make our stories known.

Air America left an imprint on Southeast Asia having trained thousands of Filipino, Thai, Lao and Vietnamese in a variety of trades and career fields that carried them forward for generations. Our role in Laos was never as aggressor but as a responsible employer providing logistical support and humanitarian aid to the people of Laos. The company also provided an opportunity for a lot of young people such as my friends and I to develop skills and character that lasted a lifetime.

After seven years with the company, I returned home to Connecticut and bought the farm I so very much wanted. However, I was not a very good farmer. I was a better aircraft mechanic and later an antique dealer. I operated Hope Valley Antiques with my sister, Sandra Avery, for over twenty years.

I owe a great deal to Air America, Jack Forney, John Aspinwall, my friends and all the pilots who brought me safely home, time after time.

My daughter, Amanda Pauline Nichols, and I

Fast Forward
Year 2000 and Beyond

Tom Cournoyer and car

Bill Long and
Frank DeVito

Steve Stevens and Matt Luca
2000 Air America Reunion

Frank DeVito
And Dave McDonald

Joe Lopes, Steve Nichols, Joe Cicippio. Cicippio worked with Steve in Saudi Arabia. In 1986 while working in Lebanon, He was kidnapped and held prisoner, chained to a wall, for five years by Hamas. He was released in December 1991.

Ted Moore and friends

Steve Nichols and Paul Scannell
H-34
Air Museum at Bradley Airport
Hartford, CT

331

List of Works Cited

Anthony, Victor B. and Richard R. Sexton. The War in Northern Laos, Center For Air Force History (1993). http://www.gwu.edu /~nsarchiv/nsaebb248/war-in-northern-laos.pdf

Best, Martin. Air America, Inc. http://www.vietnam.ttu.edu/airamerica/ best/airamerica

Cates, Allen. "Honor Denied, The Truth about Air America and the CIA." Bloomington: iUniverse, Inc. (2011): 148-49

Davis, Charles O. "Across the Mekong, The True Story of an Air America Pilot." Charlottesville: Hildesigns Press (1996): 124-128

Leary, William M. and E. Merton Coulter. Air America: Played a Crucial Part of the Emergency Helicopter Evacuation of Saigon (2005). http://www.historynet.com/air-america-played-a-crucial-part-of-emergency-helicopter-evacuation-of-saigon.htm

Leary, William M. CIA Air Operations in Laos, 1955-1974. http://www.cia.gov/library/center-for-the-study-of-intelligence/csi-publications/csi-studies/studies/winter99-00/art7.htm

Leeker, Joe F. The Aircraft of Air America, 5th edition of 4 March 2013. http://www.utdallas.edu/library/specialcollections/has/cataam/ leeker/aircraft

Lewin, Howard S. "Sunsets, Bulldozers and Elephants: Twelve Years in Laos, The Stories I Never Told." Hawthorne: Lewin (2004).